PER ARDUA

PER ARDUA

Training an RAF Phantom Crew

PHILIP KEEBLE
AND
DAVID GLEDHILL

FONTHILL

Fonthill Media Language Policy

Fonthill Media publishes in the international English language market. One language edition is published worldwide. As there are minor differences in spelling and presentation, especially with regard to American English and British English, a policy is necessary to define which form of English to use. The Fonthill Policy is to use the form of English native to the author. Philip Keeble and David Gledhill were born and educated in the United Kingdom; therefore, British English has been adopted in this publication.

Fonthill Media Limited
Fonthill Media LLC
www.fonthillmedia.com
office@fonthillmedia.com

First published in the United Kingdom and the United States of America 2019

British Library Cataloguing in Publication Data:
A catalogue record for this book is available from the British Library

Typeset in 10.5pt on 13pt Sabon
Printed and bound in England

This book is dedicated to two good friends—Chris Lackman and Jack Thompson—of No. 228 Operational Conversion Unit who were lost when their Phantom crashed at an air display at Abingdon in 1988. They are pictured in the colour section of this book, in the environment they loved. May they rest in peace.

Foreword by Air Marshal Cliff Spink, CB, CBE, FCMI, FRAeS, RAF (Rtd)

David Gledhill and Phillip Keeble have written this book from the important perspective of taking on the many challenges of getting into the cockpit of arguably one of the most effective fighter aircraft of the Cold War era—the Phantom. They take the reader through a journey that many have previously attempted, but of the hundreds that started this journey, few achieved their ultimate goal. They tell the story with candour, modesty, and humour because as the age-old adage of the Royal Air Force goes, 'If you can't take a joke, you shouldn't have joined'.

Of the many hurdles that exist at each stage of training, it is easy to forget that the first vital hurdle to clear is to be accepted by the Royal Air Force. The RAF was, and continues to be, a meritocracy, with the fundamental criteria not of where you have come from, but whether you have the qualities to succeed in one of the most mentally and physically demanding occupations bar none. Dave and 'Keebs' exemplify two young men who had the dream and the drive to join this elite service, and they succeeded; however, as they are the first to admit, this was only the prelude to many months of intensive and demanding training.

That training was in the main very good, excellent in parts, but they identify areas of that training that were not the best. Indeed, they implicitly describe a training system that was in some ways trying to catch up with the demands of the aircraft on the front line. At that time, there were a multiplicity of new and fast jet types supplanting the heavy bomber types—Buccaneer, Harrier, Jaguar, and, of course, the mighty Phantom. All were placing new demands on a training system that was evolving to meet these demands, but in doing so induced an additional burden on people manfully trying to succeed in their training. Yet succeed they did, and, eventually, they arrived at the front line on the F4 Phantom.

I flew the Phantom on and off for around ten years and crossed paths with both Dave and Keebs on many occasions. They typified the young professionals with whom I was very proud to serve and later command. The Phantom was enormously capable and served in the RAF as a fighter, fighter bomber (both strike and ground attack), and fighter reconnaissance. It was a demanding aeroplane and they have admirably captured the pressures of being at the front line—both from a technical perspective and the fast pace of life that existed on a fighter squadron.

This is not only a very entertaining read, but it is also an important historical record of the life and times of fighter aircrew in the Royal Air Force at the latter stages of the Cold War. David and Phillip have brought those times into sharp focus, and I commend the book to you.

Cliff Spink
Keyston
March 2018

Cliff started his flying career on the Jet Provost at Cranwell followed by advanced flying training on the Gnat. A period of tactics/weapons training on the Hunter preceded his operational conversion Training on the Lightning at RAF Coltishall. He then served with 111(F) Squadron at RAF Wattisham flying the Mk 3/5 Lightnings (weekends were spent as CFI of the local gliding club). Following a weapons instructor's course, he was reposted to 'Treble One' before moving to 56(F) Sqn in Cyprus on the Mk 6 Lightning. It was during this period that the Turks invaded the island and 56 Sqn were heavily involved in the subsequent air operations. The squadron returned to Wattisham in 1975, and Cliff finally left the Lightning Force the following year, having amassed 1,300 hours on the 'most exhilarating rocket ship any young man could wish to fly'.

A ground tour followed and during this period (playing truant from his desk) he reacquainted himself with the Chipmunk to stay sane. In 1979 a refresher on JP5 followed by some Hunter FGA 9 weapons training preceded his introduction to the Phantom FGR2 at Coningsby. After a short course, it was back to 111(F) Sqn, now flying a mix of FGR2/FG1 Phantoms at RAF Leuchars. Cliff was to be associated on and off with the F-4 for the next ten years; this included two and a half years as the squadron commander of 74(F) Sqn, 'The Tigers', flying the F-4J (UK) and a year in the Falklands as station commander of Mount Pleasant Airfield. Aside from flying the F-4M in the South Atlantic, he also flew the Hercules and the Sea King helicopter. Returning to the UK, he converted to the Tornado F3 before taking command of RAF Coningsby. A couple of weeks later, he went to Saudi Arabia as the Tornado detachment commander at Dhahran for the duration of the Gulf War. Back at Coningsby in April 1991, he had his first trip in a BBMF Hurricane and, in the next two years, he also flew the Spitfire II, V, and XIX in addition to the Tornado. The end of 1992 was to see a drop in Cliff's front line fighter flying, although he stayed qualified on Tornado, Hawk, and Nimrod until he finished as a group commander in 1998.

Importantly, however, Cliff continued to fly the Warbirds following his introduction to them on the BBMF. The majority of this flying has been done at

Duxford and he regards himself as one of the 'luckiest and most privileged pilots' to have flown a variety of famous and historic aircraft. These include Spitfire II, V, IX, XI, XIV, XVI, and XIX; Hurricane II and X; Bf 109G; Buchon; Mustang; Sea Fury; Corsair; Thunderbolt; Kittyhawk; Wildcat; Polikarpov I-153; T-28 Trojan; Vampire; T-33 Silver Star; F-86A Sabre; and Hunter.

Phil and Dave would like to express their gratitude to Air Marshall Cliff Spink for his apposite foreword to their book and are most grateful for his generous words.

Authors' Notes

Philip Keeble

There have been numerous occasions where I have sat in the cockpit of a fast jet and thought to myself, 'How on earth did I get here?' Many such instances spring to mind but perhaps the foremost instances include landing in a F-4 Phantom after my first live QRA scramble up in Scotland; secondly, in Cyprus after landing from a four *versus* four dissimilar air combat sortie where we fought the US Navy; and thirdly, after landing in Hong Kong from a particularly hairy trip up from Singapore via the fringes of the Vietnam War in a Canberra PR9. All of those sorties, plus many more, gave me reason to ponder, 'Just how on earth did I get here?' Being such an excellent question and one that I have never sat down and answered before, I will do so now.

Just who was I and what was so special about me that I flew as an RAF fast jet fighter pilot? The answer was fairly simple—I was in the right place at the right time and with the right attributes and qualifications. I was the typical Cold War cannon fodder of the 1960s, average at school, average in pilot training, and average as a fighter pilot (well, to begin with anyway); yet, whatever I was, I had made it on to the front line of the Cold War as a pilot and I was thrilled. To see how I got there I need to take you via the progression and development of an officer and a pilot, from joining the RAF and eventually on to a front-line fighter squadron; my erstwhile colleague and long-time friend, Dave Gledhill, will do the same for navigator training. I must, of course, add a disclaimer and that is that all that is contained in these chapters is primarily historical and that the selection and training processes of today's RAF have changed enormously over the years but that is not the point of the book. This is not so much a 'how to do it' book but 'how was it done', specifically how did the RAF select and train young people to become Cold War operational Phantom crews?

Dave and I flew together quite a number of times over the years on both F-4 Phantoms and Tornado F3s, and I know from experience that there is not a better person to tell the navigator's side of the story. For the pilot's perspective, I shall take my own experience as the model and explain how I got to the front line in the hope that others might be inspired to do the same in the future. For those of you who have no ambitions to be a combat crew member, or even any sort of operational pilot, then I just hope that you enjoy the book and experience the ride.

I flew the Phantom from 1981 to 1987, serving on Nos 43(F) Squadron, 64(R) Squadron/228 OCU, and 23(F) Squadron in the Falklands; I logged 1,321 flying hours on both the FG1 and the FGR2.

David Gledhill

People often ask whether I was merely a frustrated pilot. Even though I had qualified as a pilot before I joined the RAF and felt obvious disappointment at not being offered training as a pilot during my selection procedure at Biggin Hill, I rapidly adapted. The RAF of the early 1970s was contracting in size and training standards were not just high, they were brutal. Anyone who has watched the BBC TV series *Fighter Pilot* will remember that it showed only one pilot out of a prospective course of twelve reach operational status on a squadron. What many do not know is that the pilot who was eventually filmed flying his Buccaneer operationally was 'parachuted' into the course as there had been 100 per cent attrition. Times were harsh and standards were high.

With the benefit of hindsight, I was a much better navigator in a fast jet than I would have been as a pilot. I suspect given my inexperience and naivety as a young man, I may have found my way to a transport squadron as a co-pilot rather than into the single-seat cockpit of a Jaguar had I been offered pilot training.

I would be less than honest if I said I enjoyed navigator training. The academic training was ill-focused for the role I went on to adopt, and the mercifully few events I failed *en route* were less than relevant to my future employment. Even so, training was vital as flying any aeroplane is a complex business and unprofessionalism is punished. Even so, it was hard. The staggering expense of training an operational crew with flying hours, even then, costing over £10,000 per hour in a Phantom, meant that the margins for failure were narrow. Two failures at the same event meant almost guaranteed removal from the course so the pressure was relentless. It did not stop on the squadron and only with the award of the coveted 'Op. Badge' did I begin to believe that I had achieved my ambition.

In terms of navigator training, this book is a snapshot. While my own training left me ill-equipped to fly a Phantom, much work went in over the following years to adapt the syllabus, better to prepare an air defence navigator. New training aids were brought into service along with computer training to introduce interception theory earlier. A flying phase on the Hawk meant the leap from basic training to the operational conversion unit was mitigated. Navigators by the end of the Cold War had a much more focused work-up.

The topic of photographic quality is a constant discussion point and we have included many shots that may not meet the pristine standards of today's digital equipment but, hopefully, reflect life during the Cold War.

It has been a delight co-authoring this book with Philip Keeble, or 'Keebs' as we knew him on the squadron. While our styles are very different, I hope the combination works.

We have used the terms 'man' and 'his' throughout the book. Times have changed but during the Cold War, women were precluded from combat duties and flying the Phantom was exclusively a masculine activity. I hope that this is not misconstrued as chauvinism.

I can only echo Keebs' thoughts. I hope you enjoy the ride.

I flew the Phantom from 1976 to 1985, serving on 56 (F) Squadron, 92 (East India) Squadron, and 64 (R) Squadron/228 OCU; I logged 1,960 flying hours on type mostly on the FGR2. I also flew a few sorties in the FG1 and F-4F variants.

Our thanks go to the following contributors for pictures used in this book: Jerry Ward, Charlotte Pateman and the Oliver family, Terry Senior, Linton Chilcott, Andy Lister-Tomlinson, Al Sawyer, Stuart Forth, Jeff Jefford, Dave Shaw, Kevin McGee, Paul Heasman, and Geoff Lee. Two talented photographers offered potential images for the cover and each produced a very similar image that heads the cover. To ensure that we have given appropriate recognition, we would like to thank both Keith Campbell, of Capture a Second, and Dave Hodgkiss for their superb contributions.

Contents

Glossary

AD:	air defence.
ADIZ:	air defence interception zone—the restricted airspace between East and West Germany.
ADF:	automatic direction finding.
AEW:	airborne early warning.
AFTS:	Advanced Flying Training School.
AOC:	air officer commanding.
APC:	armament practice camp.
AR5:	aircrew respirator mark 5. The aircrew flying equipment that gave protection against nuclear, biological and chemical threats.
AWACS:	airborne warning and control system.
Backseater:	navigator (RAF); WSO/'Wizzo'/RIO (USAF/USN).
Bingo:	fuel minimal, return to base.
Buster:	maximum dry power (See 'gate').
CAP:	combat air patrol.
CO:	commanding officer.
CR:	combat ready.
CSRO:	combat survival and rescue officer.
DCO:	duty carried out.
Div:	diversion.
ECM:	electronic countermeasures.
EW:	electronic warfare.
EWO:	electronic warfare officer.
Endex:	end of exercise.
FC:	fighter controller.
FOB:	forward operating base.

FOD:	foreign object damage—damage to a jet engine caused by debris.
FGA:	fighter ground attack.
Fox 1:	firing a semi-active radar-guided missile.
Fox 2:	firing an infrared heat-guided missile.
Fox 3:	firing a gun (RAF); later, 'guns, guns, guns'; later adapted to mean firing an active radar-guided missile.
FRC:	flight reference cards, aircraft checks and emergencies.
FTS:	Flying Training School.
Gate:	select maximum reheat.
GCA:	ground-controlled approach.
GCI:	ground control interception (or an AD radar unit).
HAS:	hardened aircraft shelter.
HDU:	hose drum unit, the refuelling unit on an air-to-air tanker.
HOTAS:	hands-on-throttle-and-stick controls.
IOT:	initial officer training.
Int:	intelligence.
IFF:	identification friend or foe.
IFR:	instrument flight rules.
ILS:	instrument landing system.
INAS:	inertial navigation attack system.
IGB:	inner German border.
IRE:	instrument rating examiner.
JENGO:	junior engineering officer.
Judy:	to take control of an intercept.
LCR:	limited combat ready.
Liner:	select cruise power normally to come subsonic.
Maxeval:	a Strike Command-generated exercise leading to TACEVAL.
Mineval:	a station-generated exercise.
MPC:	missile practice camp.
NATO:	North Atlantic Treaty Organisation.
Navaids:	navigation aids.
Navex:	navigation exercise.
NDB:	non-directional beacon.
OC:	officer commanding.
OCU:	operational conversion unit.
QFE:	brevity code; when set on the altimeter gave height above the runway.
QFI:	qualified flying instructor.
QNH:	brevity code for airfield or regional pressure.
QRA:	quick readiness alert, sometimes abbreviated to 'Q'.
QWI:	qualified weapons instructor, often annotated with 'P' for pilot (QWIP) or 'N' for navigator (QWIN).
PAR:	precision approach radar.
PD:	pulse doppler.

PI:	pilot instructor
PR:	photo reconnaissance.
PT:	physical training.
Radalt:	radar altimeter.
RSO:	range safety officer.
Recce:	reconnaissance.
RoE:	rules of engagement.
SENGO:	senior engineering officer.
SNCO:	senior non-commissioned officer.
SNEB:	rocket pod.
Spiked:	locked on to by an enemy radar.
Stack:	time to go home (on ground).
Staish:	slang for station commander.
STCAAME:	Strike Command Air-to-Air Missile Establishment.
TACAN:	tactical air navigation beacon.
TACEVAL:	tactical evaluation (exercise).
Tally:	short for 'tally ho'; enemy sighted.
TLAR:	'that looks about right', a feeling in the water.
TWU:	tactical weapons unit.
UKADGE:	UK air defence ground environment.
VFR:	visual flight rules.
Visreps:	in-flight visual report.
VOR/DME VHF:	omni-directional radio range, a radio beacon. The VOR gave bearing information and the co-located DME gave distance or range.
WSO:	weapon system operator; the US term, and later RAF term, for a navigator.

1

Life Before the Royal Air Force

Philip Keeble

I consider myself very fortunate to have been born after the Second World War, when Europe enjoyed a period of relative peace. I say 'peace' somewhat tongue in cheek because apart from the Korean War (1950–1953), the twelve-year Malayan Emergency (1948–1960), the Indo-China War (1946–1954), the Greek Civil War (1946–1949), the innumerable Indo-Pakistani wars and Arab-Israeli wars, the Mau Mau Uprisings in Kenya (1952–1960), the Algerian War (1954–1962), the Suez Crisis (1956–1957), the Hungarian Revolution (1956), and the Vietnam War (1955–1975)—yes, despite all that tumult—the world was theoretically at peace. I forgot to add the Congo Crisis (1960–1965), the Cambodian Civil War (1967–1975), the Rhodesian Bush War (1964–1979), and about ninety-six other wars, insurrections, revolts, rebellions, confrontations, and uprisings but you take my point—there was not actually another global world war; in actual fact, there was, but it was not fought directly between the world superpowers of America and Russia but peripherally around the world, as the above catalogue of examples demonstrates. This was the Cold War; as the struggle for supreme power was pursued, many people died during its passage of history but nowhere near as many as who would have died had USA/NATO and the USSR/Soviet Bloc resorted to using nuclear weapons.

As a teenager, all this kerfuffle passed me blissfully by, that is, until the Cuban Missile Crisis of October 1962 when I began to take notice of world events in the news that we on planet Earth may not make it through until Christmas. That is the moment when I decided that the Royal Air Force really needed me. However, my desire to fly goes back even further than that, so I had better start there.

My father had flown on operational missions during the Second World War, flying Vickers Wellingtons on a Special Signals squadron in Egypt. While he did not say a lot about his experiences, I had his pilot's logbook and when pressed, he would answer some of my questions. I was captivated by the idea of flying and filling in a logbook of my very own.

For trips out in the summer in the late 1950s, we would pack up a picnic and head for the beaches of Hayling Island, on the south coast of England where the RAF Hawker Hunter squadrons would detach to RAF Thorney Island to practise their formation aerobatic displays. Watching the squadrons, such as 43 and 111, do their formation loops in 'Diamond Nine', I was further gripped. This was my future.

As a reward for passing my Eleven Plus exam, I was given a thirty-minute passenger flight in a de Havilland Dragon Rapide biplane from Eastleigh Airport, Southampton. It was my first time airborne and I was now truly obsessed, the future was set, and aviation was not going to let me go until I had 6,000 hours flying under my belt—5,679.30 officially in my logbook and 300, or so, not recorded.

At school, I was a member of the Combined Cadet Force and at the weekends and in the holidays, I managed to get to Hamble airfield near Southampton as often as I could to fly with our cadet unit in the AEF de Havilland Chipmunks. I still remember flying the 'Chippies' around the Solent as if it was yesterday. I recall the first time the instructor let me fly the aircraft. How could you forget a monumental event such as that? I vividly recollect the first aerobatics we did, with the sky and the ground swapping their positions around us. Wonderful.

Philip Keeble at his first combined cadet force camp at RAF Gaydon in 1960.

I had broken free from the shackles of gravity; I was just a lad following in the footsteps of my childhood heroes, people like my father and the famous test pilots of the day—men such as Neville Duke and Peter Twist. Theirs were the photographs, posters, and cigarette cards that lads had in their collections, and as a cadet, I could 'slip the bonds of surly earth' and get up into the blue skies and white clouds with the best of them. We were part of the fraternity of aviators, and I am sorry but I do not count an Airbus flight to Spain as being in that notable category.

So, I have established that I loved flying and wanted to join the RAF after school. The first step was getting my educational qualifications. In those days, five good GCE 'O' Levels were required for a direct entry commission with an additional two 'A' Levels for a scholarship to the RAF College at Cranwell. It looked as if I would achieve the first educational hurdle and so I applied for a scholarship to see me through sixth form. I was invited to attend the Officer and Aircrew Selection Board at RAF Biggin Hill, Kent, a daunting experience and process for a fifteen-year-old.

The selection method was rigorous to say the least. There were interviews, exams, and aptitude tests in maths, English, and physical mechanics. Then came more interviews and medical examinations. A ten-minute presentation on a hobby or interest preceded the mission-solving exercises and then for those successful candidates followed the leadership phase; this began with three-dimensional task-solving problems, for example, we would be asked to construct a complex bridge over a chasm using six short planks of wood, and a length of rope, or perhaps climb a high wall using oil barrels and another large length of rope. There were six individuals in each team, each member had a chance of being the leader on one exercise and part of the team for the others. It was a test not only to see how you solved a problem and how you led a team, but just as importantly how you worked with others.

'All done chaps, off you go back home and we will let you know by post if you are what we want, or not'. We dispersed to the four corners of the UK waiting for the postman to call, and he did quite soon. For me, it was bad news as I had not been seen as suitable for the RAF; yet the letter went on, 'Please try again in two years' time, if you still want'. What they did not add was, 'You'll be lucky son', or that is how it seemed to me at the time.

Right, it was back to school and work on my 'O' Levels. I achieved two very good ones and three average ones plus two fails. It was just enough to allow me to progress into the sixth form. For reasons that I will not go into, as I hate to blame others, I did not make it to the end of my education, so it was out into the big bad world to earn a living.

My first job was as a junior laboratory chemist with the Southern Gas Board at Poole Gas Works. I was not 'captivated' with the gasworks, I was not 'gripped' by the laboratory, and I was not 'obsessed' with being a chemist. In fact, I disliked it and thus soon left to do something more stimulating.

I considered the Royal Navy Submariner's Branch but my dad was dead against that. 'Do something outdoors,' he said and I did. I applied to join the police force. This was not quite as random as it may seem because my uncle, my great grandfather, and a number of my cousins' husbands were all coppers and they seem to have done pretty well. I joined the Hampshire and Isle of Wight Police Force as a cadet and found that I was a fairly squarish peg in a fairly squarish hole. I especially enjoyed being out with the traffic boys one day a week as an observer in the patrol cars, I liked the outdoor duties when shadowing a proper bobby on the beat in Aldershot and Lymington, and I thoroughly enjoyed working in the radio control room at Police HQ in Winchester, which had its moments of excitement—but I still hankered to be a pilot.

One day, I was at Eastleigh College on day-release education, and while in town, I happened to pass the Southampton RAF recruiting office. I wandered in.

'Yes?' said the sergeant sitting behind the desk.

'Please, sir, I would like to be a pilot, or failing that an RAF Policeman with a big dog'.

'Have you got five 'O' Levels including maths, English, and three sciences?' he asked.

'Yes, I have'.

'Fill this form in and we will be in touch'. The rest, as they say, is history.

I went back to RAF Biggin Hill selection for a second time and much better prepared than previously as I now had some life experiences and useful skills. It went much better and when the second letter arrived on my doorstep, this time it was good news. The RAF accepted me. Sensible chaps—think what they might have missed. I was lucky, being in the right place at the right time, during the 1960s, the Armed Forces were hoovering up hundreds of young men from 'Civvy Street' and putting them into uniform as quickly as they could. Everyone thought that a third world war could, or would, start at any time soon.

I went back to the police headquarters and handed in my notice where they immediately took me out of uniform and assigned me to CID. This was an interesting move because I suddenly found myself in a part of police work that seemed to fit my nature: rational yet active, informal yet disciplined, long hours without being tedious. This could be just perfect if I were to stay but it was too late; my notice was in and I was off to be a fighter pilot. My service in the RAF, working to achieve my boyhood dream of flying fighters, had begun; the only problem was that it would take me a further fourteen years to achieve that particular goal. Was it worth the wait? Oh, yes it was indeed.

This book is not an autobiography, but it illustrates the process and preparation that all applicants should undertake before arriving at their selection course, the following points will benefit anyone thinking of applying. They did then and they do now.

You will need to complete the following:

Achieve the educational qualifications. Check the latest requirements.
Undergo practice questions and answers sessions.
Have social skills to offer such as volunteering and community work.
Have seen something of the outside world through travelling.

Swot up on the latest RAF topics and some of the RAF's history.
Read and understand the world at large, internationally and locally.
Decide on a selection of subjects/hobbies to discuss.
Prepare and practise giving a short talk.
Be physically and mentally fit.
Give good reasons as to why you want to join the RAF and, why you would be a
benefit to them.
Above all, stay calm, be honest, be natural and be yourself.

If you fail at the first attempt, go away and come back better prepared next time.
If you are selected and finally join up, just do your best for that is all you can offer
and hope that the RAF sees you for the person you really are.

Before you disappear off into the wide blue yonder as an operational pilot, crew
member, engineer, administrator, or even as a policeman with a big dog, then let
me offer a little extra advice in case you might wish to write a book of your own
one day: take plenty of photos of yourself, your mates, your environment, and
especially your aircraft, not forgetting to keep a record of what is what. Keep a
detailed journal, alongside any RAF logbooks to fill in the gaps with anecdotes
and your feelings at the time. Keep a scrapbook of newspaper cuttings, letters, and
certificates. I did not do any of those things and it has been hard work collecting
and collating all the pertinent information for this particular book.

I have one other piece of advice for any future aircrew and that is to avoid
thunderstorms like the plague.

David Gledhill

Being an RAF officer was not a job; it was a way of life and to join as aircrew
meant committing twenty years of my life in the service of my country. I knew
that this might mean actually giving my life even though the chances of dying in
combat were low during the Cold War but the chances of perishing in an aircraft
in training were higher than the recent losses in combat. Does that mean anything
to a seventeen-year-old youth? Absolutely not. At that age, we are all invincible
and consequences are secondary to dreams.

Before I walked through the gates at RAF Henlow on my final day as a civilian,
I had worked relentlessly towards the first goal. As a child, I had been a passionate
air enthusiast and my father barely suppressed his frustration at the latest request
to visit obscure airfields around the countryside. I watched the Red Arrows in
their red Gnats at the 'At Home Day' at RAF Finningley and dreamed like any
youngster. The first real step in my future career was to join the Air Training
Corps at the age of thirteen. At that time, the officers were mostly ex-RAF and had
served during the war as aircrew. It was, after all, only twenty-three years since the
war had ended. Charles Lee had served as a fighter pilot and Jack Cockerham as
a navigator. Both told tales that had me hooked from the outset.

The unit, No. 208 (North Leeds) Squadron, was based in an old territorial army facility. Although the headquarters building was a relatively modern wooden-built structure, the driveway outside led down to an old hangar where the hardstanding was ringed with Nissen huts. The hangar was the home of the squadron hovercraft, a homebuilt contraption that was one of my early experiences of leaving Mother Earth, albeit on a cushion of air. Being a cadet taught self-discipline, although drill and ceremonial was a new concept. Having to adopt the 'short back and sides' was a heavy price to pay for a youngster in the progressive late '60s and early '70s, and wearing a uniform through the suburban streets on 'parade nights' attracted attention from local yobs that often led to more than verbal taunting.

My record of service, known fondly as the Form 3822, shows my enrolment on 24 January 1969. The grounding was priceless. Lectures in subjects that would become fundamental to my life began in earnest. The theory of flight, aerodynamics, airmanship, instruments (the term avionics had not yet been coined), and meteorology became weekly fare. I was lucky enough to emerge with an 'O' Level in air navigation schooled by a wartime navigator skilled in traditional navigation techniques and eager to pass on his knowledge. These academics were supplemented by other activities. Shooting and handling guns were fundamental. Handling the Browning .303 rifle was alien but fascinating and the fact that we had a shooting range at nearby RAF Church Fenton meant regular practice. Exams led to promotion from first class cadet through staff cadet, eventually to squadron warrant officer. My military grounding had begun.

Later, as I became more experienced, the chance to take part in the Duke of Edinburgh's Award scheme culminated in a gold award and a trip to Buckingham Palace. My enthusiast's skills came to good use when I became captain of the squadron aircraft recognition team, a skill which was to be particularly useful in later years as an air defence navigator. Geeky was a term not yet coined.

Annual camps were the highlight of the year from my first eye-opening experience at RAF Colerne, then a C130 maintenance base, through Old Sarum leading to being selected for an overseas camp at RAF Laarbruch in Germany, at that time an operational Buccaneer and Canberra station. It was my first taste of the front line.

I was hugely fortunate to be selected to take part in the International Air Cadet Exchange programme visiting the eastern seaboard of Canada and met many fellow cadets who would go on to join the RAF. It was grounding in life, not just the military.

The first thrill of flying was to be in the form of air experience flights. The mount for the units at that time was the venerable de Havilland Chipmunk T.10, flown mostly by former wartime pilots with only a smattering of more recent pilots. No. 9 AEF, based at RAF Church Fenton, then the home of the Elementary Flying Training squadrons (EFTS), provided a local venue for this keynote event. My first visit, during which I was simply desperate to get airborne, proved frustrating. A thick fog blanketed the airfield and, although the Chipmunks had been pulled out on to the apron, they flitted in and out of the murk at monotonous

David Gledhill at his first air training corps camp at RAF Colerne in 1969.

intervals. Hopeful glances through the window trying to spot a discernible lifting of the low stratus were in vain. It was what I was soon to recognise as a 'Black Flag' day and the legendary '10 Zulu Clearance' was never likely. My first flight came on 22 July 1969 in WG460 and lasted a mere thirty minutes. It was a thrill that never got old. My record shows a regular diet of rides through to November 1972, by which time I had qualified for my own pilot's licence.

There were regular opportunities to fly as a passenger and the more notable types included a Beaver, Schweitzer glider, CC-137, Convair CC-109, and C-130 transports.

My first chance to fly solo was not to be in a powered aircraft but in a glider. My first flight was in a Slingsby T.21, WB978, fondly known as the 'barge'—a truly apt description. Operated by No. 642 Gliding School at RAF Linton-On-Ouse, places on the precious courses were allocated by the ATC Wing headquarters. My first winched launch lasted a mere six minutes and was over almost before it began. My overriding memory is of utter peace as the pilot released the tow cable and the rush of air was replaced by the utter stillness of free flight. Some twenty-three more flights followed over a two-week period before Pilot Officer Edwards cleared me to shed the 'surly bonds' alone. Three further launches in the tandem seat T-31, WT905, followed that same day but the rear cockpit was empty. My perception of life had changed forever. I volunteered as a staff cadet,

The view from the rear seat of the Chipmunk. This shot was from the rear seat of the BBMF Chipmunk WB833 with a Spitfire pilot flying a continuation sortie.

hitchhiking from Leeds to Linton-on-Ouse on a Friday evening returning on Sunday evening to begin a new school week. My confinement to the circuit ended and I experienced the thrill of chasing thermals as the sortie durations crept up. Stalling, thermalling, and spot landings became the norm rather than simple circuits. The bug had bitten.

The true thrill of solo flying was to be realised when I applied for a flying scholarship. The scheme awarded lucky recipients with thirty-five hours of flying instruction at a civilian flying school. At that time, private pilots required forty hours to be awarded a private pilot's licence, leaving the recipients with a shortfall. I suspect this was a deliberate ploy to ensure that winners of the award had the tenacity to continue their training after the end of the course. Those who failed to do so might not have had the will to fight through the RAF training machine.

The first stage was to visit the Officer and Aircrew Selection Centre at the historic former RAF station at Biggin Hill. Having taken the aptitude tests, more of which later, I returned home to endure a tense wait until I received the momentous letter. 'The RAF is delighted to inform you that you have been selected to complete a flying scholarship. Please sign here within the next week to accept the offer'. It took ten seconds to return the signed acceptance in the pre-paid, 'On Her Majesty's Service' envelope.

From selection to starting the course was a short few months, and on a momentous Sunday evening, I drove into the car park at Doncaster Flying Club, was allocated my room, and met my fellow *ab initio* pilots. My student pilot's licence, issued on 22 May 1972, stated grandly that 'The holder of this licence is entitled to fly as pilot-in-command for the purpose of becoming qualified for the grant or renewal of a pilot's licence'. A few days earlier, I had qualified to drive a car and now I was being entrusted with a flying machine. Things were becoming serious.

The ground school was remarkably short but given that the course was only four weeks long, not surprisingly so. A few brief lectures on the Rollason D62b Condor, which was the aircraft operated by the club for flying training, was supplemented at various times with academic lectures, most of which I had become familiar with as a cadet. I was allocated to a grumpy Australian flying instructor who was using his time to build hours towards his air transport pilot's licence. I suspect students were a necessary evil hindering his progress and he sat firmly in the 'stick' camp of instructional technique. There was precious little coaxing and much berating in what was still an alien skill for a seventeen-year old.

My first trip in G-AWSR on 11 July 1972 was a blur. The Condor was a home-built design aimed at offering affordable flying to the masses. It took its design more from a Hurricane than a Cherokee, albeit it was significantly less powerful than its illustrious predecessor. Every Condor bore an identical yellow colour scheme with a bright blue flash along the fuselage and had its roots as a homebuilt aircraft. The fuselage was a light wooden construction with wooden wings covered in doped fabric. Its Rolls-Royce 100-hp Continental engine powered it along at a gentlemanly cruising speed of 90 knots and, with full flap, it crossed the approach end threshold at 55 knots. The interior was basic in the extreme with a rudimentary flight instrument panel and a centre-mounted throttle. Twin stick-type control columns allowed it to be flown from either seat. Access was gained through an opening Perspex panel in the side of the canopy making entry and exit somewhat ungainly. The fuel gauge was, literally, a cork on a stick and mounted on the front coaming outside the cockpit. I was somewhat jealous of some of my peers who had been allocated courses on modern Cessna and Pipers, but it was to be a blessing in future years to have begun on such a basic type, particularly a 'tail dragger'.

My early logbook entries showed rapid-fire exercises covering the basics of effects of controls, through climbing and descending to stalling and procedures in the circuit. At this stage, the concept of coping with an in-flight emergency was introduced to ensure that once airborne alone, I could handle any systems failure and recover the aircraft safely. With the final dual ride being exercise thirteen, and including engine failures after take-off, I approached the fateful milestone of 'first solo' with a degree of nervous anticipation. With two sorties that day already under the belt, after a rather bumpy three-point landing, we rolled off the grass runway and pulled to a halt to complete—or so I thought—the after-landing checks. My instructor had other ideas and after a glance at his watch, showing it was approaching the time at which the airfield closed for the day, he came to a decision. His last words before he left me to my own devices was, 'That wasn't very good. Do you think if I climbed out you could do any better?' With that, the tiny Perspex flap of a door opened and he departed. I think he muttered something about enjoying it as he struggled through the prop wash. I was about to commit solo aviation once more.

On reflection, I guess I had done reasonably well. It had taken only seven sorties and six hours and fifty minutes in the air before I had taken to the skies alone. I felt reasonably comfortable with my efforts. Flying solo was a significant milestone, but it was only the start of my aviation training. More sorties followed, with the emphasis shifting away from the pure flying skills and towards the broader aspects of operating an aircraft. One key issue with any single-engined aircraft is what to do when the engine stops, or forced landings as they are more euphemistically known. Initially, the instructor pulls the throttle back to idle and the world goes quiet. Fly the aircraft first, establish the small craft in a steady descent at a suitable speed, and put out a 'MAYDAY' call. This call was ill-advised for a practice engine failure as the lesser call of 'Practice PAN' was more appropriate. Look around for a suitable landing site into the wind and set up the engine-out pattern. Decide what type of surface you had selected and then configure the aircraft for landing, hopefully arriving upright and without connecting with a wall or a hedge. Happily, never having been in that situation for real, I would imagine the adrenaline shot would be spectacular. Spinning techniques were one of those skills that are seldom taught nowadays, training being limited to avoiding such situations. Back in the day, full-blown spins were an integral element of the syllabus. Making a light aircraft spin requires either conscious effort or mishandling of epic proportions. With a service ceiling of 12,000 feet, it took some time to reach a safe altitude to complete the exercise and recover while still above the base height of 5,000 feet. After the pre-spinning checks, the nose was lifted in a gentle fashion until the stall warning made the aircraft's displeasure known and was followed by a rapid input of aileron in one direction and full rudder. The rapid gyrating spirals which followed were truly mind-blowing but, fortuitously, the Condor had benign handling characteristics and responded quickly to the spin recovery drills. Even so, resisting the urge and allowing the spin to continue for three turns was a lesson in forbearance. The adrenaline rush is spectacular but the urgency of the recovery can never be underestimated. Again, it was a skill I was never asked to use for real, although the Phantom spin recovery drill became burned into my psyche through successive air combat briefings.

Radio and visual navigation techniques followed, which began the lead into the concluding events of the syllabus, namely the navigation exercises. Thankfully, flown dual in the first instance, I was taught the art of following a line on a map travelling at the sedentary pace of 1.5 miles per minute. The first event was to depart the circuit at Doncaster and head for the first destination of Nottingham Tollerton airfield. Equipped, unusually, with a VHF radio, I began my introduction to talking to air traffic controllers, which proved to be a novelty as most of the Condors on the fleet were not fitted with radios. After a short stay at Nottingham, the return journey was via Netherthorpe, a small airfield near Worksop. A landaway at Sherburn gave the final familiarisation before the qualifying cross-country flight. The final handling test checked that all the lessons had been learned and stored in the memory banks. Although not intended to teach instrument flying skills, the penultimate exercise gave an overview of the techniques required should a newly qualified seventeen-year-old private pilot inadvertently enter cloud. Suffice to say that, at that time, such carelessness may have constituted a minor emergency.

The culmination of the course was a solo navigation exercise around the East Midlands at the controls of the mighty Condor following a similar route to that one I had already practised. Again, the first destination for the landaway was to be Nottingham but the return trip to the second landing at Sherburn was to be via Brough in Yorkshire. I would love to say that I demonstrated my new navigation skills flawlessly but that would be less than honest. Nottingham Tollerton lies to the south of the city, not far south of the river Trent. A stiff crosswind meant that I had drifted somewhat east of the track as I had headed south and, while the massive conurbation was reasonably easy to spot, my attempts to locate the airfield with my untrained eyes proved elusive. A few orbits later, I realised that my new friend the VHF radio could come to my assistance and a quick call to a friendly air trafficker gave a vector to the field. It would have been far better if the gentleman had not then appended the true facts to the 'chit' proving that my arrival had been less than efficient; however, discretion proved to be more palatable than valour.

Firing up the trusty Condor once more, I would like to say that my efforts on the way back were better. I was beginning to think that air navigation might not be one of my strengths despite my 'O Level' qualification. Determined not to be caught by the stiff crosswind again, I laid off a few extra degrees to compensate. This would have been fine had I steered the correct track, but another self-induced error meant that quite quickly, nothing on the ground matched the features I was expecting. Fortunately, I was heading into the wilds of Lincolnshire rather than the congested airspace of the Midlands but even so, I drifted well left of track. It was only the chance encounter with a Hastings as it climbed out from Lindholme airfield that alerted me to my predicament. Yet then again, what is 8 miles off track between friends? After a swift replan of my route, the Humber Estuary proved much easier to find and the remainder of the sortie ran on rails. When the chimneys in the circuit at Doncaster rose into view in exactly the correct place at the right time, I was positively elated if not secretly relieved.

I was awarded my Civil Aviation Authority private pilot's license (aeroplanes) on 6 August 1972 at the tender age of seventeen by Chief Flying Instructor John Watson, another ex-RAF fighter pilot and a true gentleman. John was tragically killed in a flying accident at Doncaster Aero Club some years later, when the student with whom he was flying stalled on approach. It was a salutary lesson that flying had consequences.

My Form 3822 carried a discharge certificate from the Air Training Corps on the final page. Dated 26 October 1973, it stated simply 'Joining the Royal Air Force'.

The pilot aptitude rig similar to the one in use at the Officer and Aircrew Selection Centre in the 1970s.

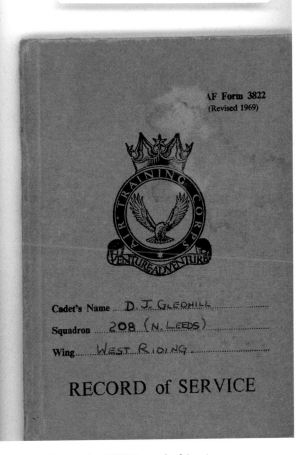

David Gledhill's original flying licences. RAF Form 3,822 was the ATC Record of Service.

Arriving at the Officer and Aircrew Selection Centre, RAF Biggin Hill, located at the historic Battle of Britain fighter station for my second visit for my formal aircrew selection tests, I felt a little more relaxed. Confident that I understood the process a little better, I had thought hard about where I felt I had failed to respond as well as I might on my first visit. Although I had been successful, I knew I could do better. Still too young to drink a pint of ale legally, I thought it might be prudent not to press the issue and to have a clear head for the tests the following day.

The selection process followed the same format as before. The first day was taken up with aptitude tests carefully designed to test each skill required both in the cockpit and on the ground. Some were obviously focused on hand-eye coordination to decide if my piloting skills warranted a place at a flying training school. Given the complexity of modern, computer-controlled flight simulators, a present-day candidate would be amused at the technology. Seated in a chair and staring at a monochrome television tube, a rudimentary stick and throttle offered the means to keep a lively dot in the centre circle. As it was, I was quietly confident that I kept it well under control. Mental arithmetic tests against the clock involving a plethora of aviation-related challenges might be relevant to both pilot or navigator roles as I was to find out later in my training. Other tests to measure mental agility and physical coordination were less obvious. I came away feeling confident.

The next day involved team challenges and leadership tests. Each candidate was given the chance to lead a team and to solve a relatively complex problem. What I did not know at that time was that the assessor was probably just as interested in my response as a subordinate as my skills in marshalling my team. Both attributes would be vital as an RAF officer. Some tests were simple and involved appropriate inanimate objects. Others introduced the venerable pine pole, which was to be a feature of RAF leadership tests as I progressed. The details have long faded but, again, I felt reasonably content at my performance.

The final morning was the interview where a panel of three grilled each candidate to determine whether they would be accepted into the fold. The topics were wide and varied but I could not sense a trend, despite having endured the grilling once before. I recall the fact that I should have paid more attention to the technicalities of the Lee Enfield rifle, but that honesty rather than bluster was the best policy. By late morning, my fate was sealed and, as I left the historic gates for the final time, I felt reasonably confident that I had given it my best shot.

When the letter finally arrived offering me a permanent commission in the general duties branch of the Royal Air Force, I read the words with mixed feelings. It would mean shelving my hitherto dogmatic intent to qualify as a military pilot as I had been given an alternative option. I was to train as a navigator.

"AIRTOUR" FLIGHT LOG

PILOT... GLEDHILL .... DATE...... AUGUST '72 ...... A/C... CONDOR GA

FROM... DONCASTER ...... TO... DONCASTER ...... DIST...... 128 MILES

ETD................. ETA................. FUEL O/B...... 15 GALS .... RANGE.................

CLEARANCE

ALTERNATE

STAGE	T.A.S.	Height	WIND	Track	Co(T)	Co(M)	G.S.	Dist.	Time
SPROT – NOTT	75	2500	260 / 35	174	202	210	64	36	34
NOTT – BROUGH	75	2000		022	358	006	88	51	35
BROUGH – SHERB	75	2000		231	270	278	41	24	35
SHERB – SPROT	75	1000		176	204	212	63	17	16
POINT OF NO RETURN						TOTALS		128	120

TIME	10 10 START ENGINE OBSERVATIONS	ETA	HDG	DT	FUEL
20	S/H SPROT		210	√	√
28	¼ WAY	28			
33	½ WAY	33		√	
48	¾ WAY	46	200		
05	ARR NOTT SHUT DOWN 09	54		√	
42	S/H NOTT START ENGINE 38		006		
52	¼ WAY	50			
01	½ WAY	02			
11	¾ WAY	11			
23	S/H BROUGH 4 W 10° OFF S	22	278		
39	½ WAY	46	300		
49	ARR SHERB STOP ENGINE 00	49			
06	S/H SHERB S/E 00		212		
14	½ WAY	14	180		
22	SPROT	22			

David Gledhill's original flying log for his qualifying cross-country flight in 1972. The RAF method was significantly different using log on chart techniques.

A recruitment poster for pilots in the 1970s. (*UK MOD Crown Copyright*)

YOUNG MEN REQUIRED FOR SUPERSONIC BATTLE OF WITS.

As navigators.

In RAF Phantoms. Fast jets which seek out unidentified intruders in our airspace, and intercept them. And if they're not so innocent, escort them away.

We are looking for young men capable of rising to such challenges as these – who want one of the most exciting and rewarding careers possible – as navigators in the Royal Air Force.

Using the highly advanced navigational and radar equipment you've mastered in training, you'll be responsible for directing your aircraft to its target with pin-point accuracy. And then, in time of war, for releasing the correct weapon against it.

That's just part of the job.

As a navigator, you'll also be responsible for electronic counter-measures to outwit enemy fighters, missiles, guns. And for the safe navigation of your aircraft at all times.

You will need to be alert to all aspects of flying, and to have a comprehensive understanding of your aircraft and its capabilities in all conditions.

Just what kind of person are we looking for, then?

We're after quick thinkers and decision makers. Men who can stay cool, calm and collected under pressure. Men who enjoy working as part of a closely knit team. Well educated. With at least five or more GCE 'O' levels at Grade C or above (or equivalent) including English Language and Maths. 'A' levels or a degree? So much the better.

If you're one of these people, if you fit the bill, we'll do the rest.

You'll be airborne around two months after completion of your initial officer training. About 18 months later, as a fully fledged navigator on a salary of at least £5,512, you'll probably be streamed into one of four different roles.

As we've described, you could be in a Phantom flying interception missions.

You could be a tactical navigator in a Nimrod, on reconnaissance or submarine hunting missions over the Atlantic.

You could be in a Hercules, navigating the aircraft in its tactical transport role, anywhere in the world. Or you could be in a Buccaneer,

one of the long-range strike aircraft of the Royal Air Force.

Right now, gratuity-earning Short Service Commissions are available (for twelve years with an option to leave after eight) as well as permanent pensionable commissions.

Promotion prospects are excellent, with good opportunities to reach high rank. You can also be sponsored while you study at University or Polytechnic through our University Cadetship Scheme. It's worth £2,161* per annum.

For further details either fill in and return the coupon on right or call at your nearest RAF Careers Information Office – address in the phone book.   *Under review

To: Group Captain T. R. Morgan RAF, Officer Careers (96IAZ/4), London Road, Stanmore, Middlesex HA7 4PZ.
Please send me further information about:

RAF NAVIGATOR OFFICER CAREERS ☐   UNIVERSITY CADETSHIPS ☐

Name_____

Date of birth_____
(Age limit 17-23½ years)

Address_____

Please enclose a separate note listing your present/intended qualifications. Formal application must be made in the UK.

RAF officer
NAVIGATOR

A recruitment poster for navigators in the 1970s. (*UK MOD Crown Copyright [1976]*)

2

Initial Officer Training: RAF South Cerney (1965–6)

Philip Keeble

After my letter inviting me to join up arrived, there was not a happier person on the planet. It informed me where and when to arrive at my first RAF station for initial officer training (IOT); contained within was a travel warrant and instructions describing what clothes I would require and that I should have a short haircut before arrival. The clothes list for a trainee officer would be laughable today; it included one plain dark suit, one checked tweed sports jacket, one trilby hat, a pair of smart leather shoes; it was all to be packed in one medium-sized suitcase. Luckily, I had most of that stuff already although my snappy Italian suit would have to go back in the wardrobe until I managed to get home again. Off I set, an innocent abroad.

On this occasion, I did not use the train but was given a lift by my parents to RAF South Cerney in Gloucestershire, where they deposited me at the main gate. We said our goodbyes and off they set on the return journey. Dad was so deliriously happy that he crashed the car on the way home; was it because of the tears in his eyes? Anyway, I was oblivious to all this as communications were not permitted for the first few weeks. I checked in at the guardroom, had my name ticked off on a sheet, and was told to report to our barrack block alongside the parade square. It was a large brick-built edifice put up during the war. There were hundreds of them built in the same style on dozens and dozens of RAF stations around Britain. A central lobby was divided into two wings, each with dormitories downstairs and up. Each block held about sixty beds and included the ablutions and drying rooms. The place was immaculate; the floors were wooden and reflected like a mirror, as they gleamed in the light. The cleaners obviously did a great job keeping it up to scratch.

A bed was allocated: 'single bed, cast iron, horsehair mattress, airman for the use of'. Along with the bed came a bedside locker with a mirror and a wardrobe; that was it. It was to be my home for the next ten weeks. There was no tea making equipment, no TV and no pictures on the wall, there were not even any carpets. Nothing else was allowed. It was stark. For those who had been to boarding school, or had been in the school cadets, it was not anything unexpected but for some it came as a huge culture shock.

'Right, gentlemen,' came a loud voice. 'Pay attention. I am Sergeant Vader and I shall be responsible for your welfare while you are here. I will call you "Sir" and you will call me "Sir" but only you will mean it. First things first, put your suitcase away in your lockers and follow me for a proper military haircut. Try and march even though you haven't been taught yet. Then we shall get you kitted out and looking like proper little servicemen'.

The haircuts were a brutal short back and sides. The No. 2 uniforms were made from rough wool and were very hairy and scratchy. The collars to the shirts were separate and held on by collar studs. The boots were clumpy and were a dull, dimpled, stiff leather but we were assured that 'they would soon look very different and soon shine like black diamonds'. I knew what was coming, and so it transpired. We were issued with a kit of bootblack (polish), two boot brushes, a spoon, plus a candle— in addition, a webbing belt and puttees, a tin of brass polish, a button stick, cleaning cloths, a tin of Blanco, and a brush—how very thoughtful of the RAF to provide this for our batman. All this haircutting and the issue of uniforms from stores took a while and, before long, it was time for tea in the NAAFI canteen: meat and two veg. followed by stodgy pudding. Yum, it was just like being back in the police force.

'Gentlemen, there will be three square meals a day. That is what you will consume. No beer. However, sticky buns and milk you can purchase at your own expense. For all this luxury you will be paid the grand sum £1 2s 6d a day before stoppages. Any questions? No? Good, let's keep it that way. After tea, you will be shown how to press your uniforms, how to keep your bed space tidy, how to fold and put away your clothes and, most importantly, how to bull your boots. After that, you will clean your rooms and the toilets and make your beds. Lights out will be at 2200 and reveille will be at 0600. At 0600 you will arise promptly, get shaved, washed and dressed in your uniforms and then clean this block from top to bottom. Breakfast will be at 0630 and I will be waiting to inspect your efforts at 0700. Any questions? No? Good.' I should have asked 'What do the cleaners and the batmen do?' Yet I already knew the answer.

So, it began: five long weeks of phase one officer cadet training, or 'square-bashing' as it was known. We would find out the next day why it was called that. By the way, what were the spoon and the candle for, you ask? Well, you heated up the back of the spoon in the candle flame and then with the red-hot spoon, a dollop of black polish, and a good measure of spit, you proceeded to iron out all those lovely manufactured dimples on your issue boots to make them as smooth as a mirror. What went on over those next thirty days has stuck in my memory indelibly, despite psychotherapy. Sergeant Vader did his daily inspections, but our uniforms were never as sharp as they should have been, our room was never as tidy and as sparkling as it should have been, and our boots were never quite polished to a shine as good as they should have been. I think you get the picture.

In addition to all this fun, our beds had to be made into a 'bed pack'. This was a sort of blanket-sheet-blanket sandwich where everything was wrapped and bound tight in the blanket with the pillow (singular) on top. It was all assembled to an exact size and shape. A penny should be able to bounce off the bed pack, and there was no room for error. Our lockers were laid out and displayed to a standard pattern: towel, shaving kit, polishing kit and so on. The wooden floors were unbelievably shiny and as we found out that there were no cleaners coming in every morning, it was all down to ourselves. We had a gallon tin of floor wax and a cast iron floor bumper with a felt duster underneath that was worked backwards and forwards like some sort of eternal punishment out of a Greek fable. We never walked on it with our boots except for inspection. The rest of the time we only wore socks as, sadly, no furry slippers had been issued.

A form of cricket was played on these floors using an improvised bat and a rolled-up sock for the ball; you can guess what happened when a bowler tried to stop after making a delivery. It would be four months on sick leave waiting for one's knees to mend, as happened to a mate. It was a dangerous life in the armed forces but it seemed like good sport at the time.

Every day, after the cleaning was done, we were 'requested' to join our sergeant outside for a little walk in the fresh air. By that, he meant an hour's drill on the adjacent parade square. Once 'freshened up', we would be sent for lectures on a wide variety of subjects. These included maths, navigation, English, general service training, politics, Air Force law, and so on. It was in this latter subject that I actually excelled—the only one to be exact. Our Canadian exchange instructor made the fatal mistake of asking the class if anyone knew what 'arrest' was? I put my hand up.

'Yes cadet, what is it?'

'Arrest is the taking or restraining of a person from his or her liberty in order that he or she may be forthcoming in answering an alleged, or suspected, crime or offence, Sir'. Silence followed.

'Cadet you are excused today's lesson, you may go and get yourself a cup of tea'. Woohoo—one up to the little guys.

In addition to all this learning, we were persuaded to improve our physical fitness in a variety of cruel ways. Firstly, it was P.T. in the gym. There were bunny hops, star jumps, and press-ups to warm up with, but then the real workout started: running around the airfield perimeter track either solo with a medicine ball, or as a four-man unit with a full-sized telegraph pole. We then returned to the gym for a 'warm down' over vaulting horses and up vertical ropes. Later that day came the assault course. 'Fiendish and malicious' best describes this torture but, funnily enough, I quite enjoyed risking my neck. Sport was included but not golf, croquet, or tennis. On a Wednesday afternoon and Saturday morning, it proved to be cross-country running, with football and rugby thrown in later to promote teamwork. It was twelve hours of physical and mental trauma every day except Saturday afternoon and Sunday.

Joining the course in the winter month of November proved not to be such a good idea as it was bitterly cold; a heavy frost greeted us most mornings and our drill sergeant's 7 a.m. welcome was not much warmer either. If it was raining, we were allowed to exercise in an empty hangar; that was not to protect us, but our rifles. The inevitable followed. We got fit—very fit and very quickly, except for those who pulled muscles or broken bones; they were re-coursed to try again later. Each day was like *Groundhog Day*: Get up, shave, dress, polish, have breakfast, drill, P.T., assault course, more lessons, sport, more drill, more polishing, and so on. It continued in this way until we were knocked into shape and ready to move on to the next phase. Sadly, I was not going to move on at this stage as, unfortunately, I failed my navigation exam and was re-coursed along with a handful of others to try again, despite the fact that I did not want to be a navigator.

I would repeat the whole thing right from the beginning again, which was not nice at the time but at least I restarted the phase with shiny boots. However, by the end of that, I was not just super fit, but perhaps even über fit and that stood me in good stead for the next stage: phase 2, leadership training.

Having inspected our minds and punished our bodies, it was now time to have a look at our true mettle—namely, what sort of leaders we would make. Needless to say, the pressure of keeping ourselves and our environs pristine did not let up, but the classroom lectures did for a while. Now we were in the great outdoors learning how to build engineering structures from wooden poles and hanks of rope. Once the basic principles of tying knots and frames were mastered, it was down to the Cerney gravel pits with the ever-present 40-gallon oil drums, yards of rope, and numerous pine poles to build replicas of the *Titanic* (culminating in a similar fate). Notwithstanding the physicality, I loved all this action; I was in my element. We now knew how to span wide gorges and float across vast waters, so exercises were added in which all our skills came into force together as we pitted ourselves against other teams of recruits. Alongside all this Action Man stuff, we learned how to live in the great outdoors; how to hide, survive, navigate, and eat; and how to do a useful bit of first aid.

In between all this activity, the Christmas holidays intruded giving us a bit of a breather for a week. We returned to South Cerney before the New Year to get ready for adventure training in the Black Mountains of Wales. A tented camp was set up in the foothills and we were set various challenges such as spanning real life gorges many thousands of miles deep using 'A' frames and a bosun's chair, all built out of our ubiquitous poles and rope. By now, we had pulleys, blocks, and shackles to contend with, but what we did not have was any remote resemblance to health and safety regulations. There were no hard hats, no safety lines, and no harnesses; we had nothing but our skills, brute force, ingenuity and, of course, the desire to stay alive. Apart from the odd bit of first aid, no one got hurt in the making of this story. Other events such as going for a 'brisk stroll' in the mountains were planned, which sounds nice, but we had a 20-foot telegraph pole and a 50-yard hank of thick ship's rope to carry between the four of us in the team. Appreciating the beautiful snow-covered views was not on our itinerary. By the time we wended our way to the rendezvous that, naturally, sat atop a one-quarter scale Mount Everest, we were given a choice: we could either go back the way we had come, which was about 12 miles in a roundabout way, or go back via the lanes, which was about 4 miles in a straight line. It was obvious that there must be a catch, and there was. The latter option had the caveat that we would run all the way without stopping if we chose the lanes, which, being downhill and with the inertia of 100 lb of a wooden pole, gave our feet wings.

When we arrived at our camp at the bottom, we encountered a lane that crossed over a swollen, icy stream. 'OK, you look hot, so it's time to cool off. Into the water, under the bridge and out the other side. Go,' ordered the instructor. That was certainly one way to cool off and probably an excellent way to either have a heart attack through thermal shock or catch pneumonia. Luckily, neither occurred, preventing both a coroner's enquiry and a subsequent court-martial.

This all sounds very physical and was not what we joined up to do; also, I did not understand what this had to do with learning to fly or, come to that, being an RAF officer, but there was a reason for these tests. We had to be able to think straight when cold, tired, wet, and under duress, and the evaluations would weed out those who were physically and mentally unsuitable. Even so, while we were being stretched to our limits, there were moments of pure fun, like visiting the ranges for weapons training and learning how to fire, strip, and clean a variety of weapons; I knew some from my cadet days, like the trusty old .303 Lee Enfield Rifle, but some were new, such as the Sterling 9-mm sub-machine gun and my personal favourite, the .38 Smith and Wesson revolver. Now, this was more like it. It was proper military stuff, not slogging about like soldiers getting blisters and chilblains. As the army often said of us, 'Sleeping under the stars for the RAF was about understanding how many stars the hotel was awarded!' That was cruel but fair. More than once, I thought it strange that we had not yet been taught very much of how to be officer aircrew. Apart from a bit of navigation, it was how to march, yomp, climb mountains, build bridges, fire weapons, and tackle assault courses; it all seemed a little distant from my future role. I could see us being sent off to some remote part of the British Empire to fight for Queen and Country before we ever even saw an aircraft. What I did not realise was that in most of the places over which the RAF flew in those days, these skills might come in handy one day. They did, but luckily only for my yet-to-come RAF survival courses.

All good things must come to an end; five weeks later, phase two culminated in a weekend pass when I was allowed to travel home before setting out on the final phase of our course, which would turn us from cadets into officers. The biggest difference between phase three, and those of phases one and two that had come before was moving from the barrack block into a complex of wartime wooden huts at the other end of the airfield. The huts were a lot more comfortable with their own kitchens and a bar; here, we shared two to a room—rooms with curtains no less. It was run on the lines of an officers' mess and in addition to all the customary running around and keeping fit exercises, we were introduced to finer points of mess life, even to the extent of having a practice cocktail party, or as it is called these days, 'networking'. The trickiest part was finding a young lady to invite and that took as much initiative as some of the harder training exercises. With hindsight, it was probably part of the course. If there was one of these events every five weeks, as each course came to an end, then I suspect that most of the local girls would have been familiar faces to the directing staff.

Was I still enjoying myself after all this time? Actually, I was, but instead of coming in the last four on the cross-country runs, I was now coming in the top four. Being fit made an awful lot of difference to just existing. I had discovered muscles that the police force had failed to find. My boots were now bulled to a high gloss that kept the sergeant off my back and my creases were razor sharp. There was only one fly in the ointment and that was my maths; I had failed to reach the required standard yet once more—and so on the day when I should have received my Queen's commission on my passing out parade, I was in Support Flight awaiting my fate.

Luckily, a further re-course was recommended, which did not turn out too badly at all. Those of us who were in the same boat were moved to a very quiet side wing of the huts; we were required only to attend remedial maths lessons twice a day—once at 10 a.m. and once at 2 p.m. That was it. It was sheer bliss for four weeks with a lie-in in the morning and getting away early in the afternoon for cream teas in Cirencester at the Mad Hatter Tea Rooms. It was very gentile as the ladies from Lloyds Bank, which closed at 3 p.m., joined us for tea. We were only after one thing, and that was not their counting and maths skills. In the evenings, we adjourned to one of the local Cotswold hostelries, of which there were many; the only trouble was a lack of suitable transport as most of us did not have 'wheels' and, strangely, those who did seemed to adopt three firm friends. Some of their cars were knackered and needed a push/bump start to get going, and thus our friendships were a kind of natural symbiosis. No one bothered us much during those final weeks, apart from the odd inspection—that was the way we liked it. With a week to go, we were required to attend the drill practices for our own passing out parade. 'It would be a pleasure, Sarge. Thank you for the invite'. So, it transpired. Cadet Keeble became Acting Pilot Officer Keeble. My greatest pleasure, apart from seeing my parents at the parade, was getting my first salute from my drill sergeant. 'Well done Sir'—and this time he meant it.

Lunch was in the officers' mess and Lord Shackleton, the son of explorer and geographer Ernest, was the guest of honour. It was a very special day, one on which I had taken the first step on the road towards becoming a pilot. It had taken me twenty-five weeks instead of the normal fifteen but that was fine. I had made some great friends during this period, ones whom I would continue to be in contact with fifty years later. The sense of camaraderie was tangible and encouraging. The sense of belonging was humbling and inspiring. The sense of achievement was gratifying and rewarding. All in all, I was a happy bunny. It was, however, about to get a whole lot better as I was about to go flying.

David Gledhill

In the 1970s, there were a number of routes via which an officer could be trained. The cadet system still existed at the RAF College Cranwell. Future officers attended a college-level induction that lasted two to three years emerging with a permanent commission having undergone an element of flying training. By far the majority of future officers went through initial officer training (IOT) as direct entrants at RAF Henlow in Bedfordshire. Walking through the gates was, to some extent, stepping back in time. An old flying station, Henlow had an illustrious history dating from the time it was built at the end of the First World War, all the way through to my less than illustrious presence. Home to a series of fighter squadrons, it housed an assembly line for Hurricane fighters during the Second World War before becoming the Officer Cadet Training Unit, or OCTU, between 1965 and 1980. The 'gate guardian' was a historic Mark P1 Lightning prototype, which was the forerunner of the aircraft that entered service and had been used for trials and evaluation. Positioned prominently at the edge of the parade square, it offered a tantalising preview of things to come and a goal to which to aspire.

The domestic site where much of the academic training occurred was set along a main road flanked by barrack blocks and support buildings. Opening out on to the cadets' mess and the parade square, the site had a very military air, emphasised by squads of officer cadets who formed up and marched, smartly, between training venues. Across the road was the former airfield, by then largely unused. Dominated by large wartime-style hangars, the airfield was the venue for much or the leadership training. That it had been used as a set during the filming of *Battle of Britain* said much about the air of the place.

Day one was a blur. The first stop was the station barber to adopt the regulation 'short back and sides'. Whether by accident or design, the barber stepped away, momentarily, halfway through the operation. Looking in the mirror, one side of my reflection sported my hitherto longer 'locks' while the other half might have been from a recruiting poster. The image was psychologically significant and demonstrated the momentous change that was imminent.

The first formality was attestation in which I swore the oath of allegiance to Her Majesty the Queen, a commitment which is limitless in scope. Leaving the room as an officer cadet, it would be the only document that would commit me to at least twenty years of service in the Royal Air Force. As a contract of employment, it was staggering in its simplicity. I am not sure if I had fully appreciated the commitment I was making. I wanted to fly aeroplanes but the implications of a lifetime of service and the fact I had just signed a blank cheque was perhaps lost on me.

An endless stream of administration followed raising endless paperwork, some of which would follow me around the Air Force for many years. I emerged from a visit to clothing stores with kit bags stuffed with uniforms of every hue from working blues to the cabbage kit I needed for field exercises.

Training an RAF officer is a thorough process. The first stage is to break down the personality of those who walk through the gates into constituent parts and then to reassemble them in an approved mould. Individuals were selected for a variety of reasons but had demonstrated traits that were deemed relevant to their future employment. When reassembling the parts, it was important not to destroy the core strengths but important to instil discipline and loyalty. The training was designed to nurture the skills needed to function as an officer in the Royal Air Force. Of prime importance was leadership and this was the basis of all other skills yet the most elusive. There are many tenets of leading a team but to be a leader, one must first be a good subordinate and know when to question but also when to comply.

The four training squadrons were numbered and allocated colours. I was to join No. 280 Initial Officer Training Course, or Yellow Squadron. A new course arrived every four weeks, which meant that Henlow was a busy station and faces changed with regularity. Of the eighty personnel allocated to my intake, only eight were aircrew. Of those, two were pilots, one of whom would go on to become the commander-in-chief Air Command and the other to become 'Red 10', the manager of the RAF Aerobatic Team, the Red Arrows. The rest of the aircrew were destined to be navigators some of whom would become lifelong friends. The remaining personnel allocated to the squadron came from a variety of backgrounds and were to become officers in each of the branches of the Service from administration, through engineering to fighter controllers. The breakdown did not seem significant but I was unaware that the RAF was downsizing and that many serving aircrew had been selected for redundancy at that time. Under the law of supply and demand, I was indeed fortunate to have been offered aircrew at all. As I was arriving, many of my predecessors were leaving in large numbers yet I was still joining a force that numbered about 150,000 people. By the time I retired, that number had reduced to only 38,000—a shadow of its former self.

The cadets' mess was separate to the officers' mess, which housed the instructors. A large sixties-style building, it lacked the style of a traditional officers' mess but provided dining facilities and the public rooms for what would be limited leisure time. Sleeping accommodation was less glamorous and, although I was allocated a single room, military discipline was imposed from the outset. After reveille, I would strip my bed and assemble the sheets and hairy RAF blankets in a 'bed pack'. The pack was arranged in regimented fashion at the head of the mattress. My single wardrobe was also arranged with military precision, and kit was stored in an approved fashion. Most evenings, a strict cleaning regime was imposed and the barrack block was subject to snap inspections. With my experience in the Air Training Corps this regimen came as no surprise but to some of my new colleagues, it was a revelation.

The course began with the predictable academic phase covering diverse topics that Keebs has already described. Nothing was assumed, however, and such was the level of detail that we were even taught the etiquette of formal dining—how to hold your knife and fork.

Leadership training was the start, the middle, and the end of the course, and failure to meet the basic standard would result in suspension. You might have the best aptitude in the world to be a pilot, but if you could not demonstrate basic leadership skills, there would be no future in the RAF. From the early set-piece exercises, where hesitant team leaders persuaded reluctant subordinates to lash together a series of pine poles with greasy rope, the training rapidly accelerated. Scenarios became more complex culminating in field exercises on Stanford Training Area in Norfolk.

One of the most significant characters, perhaps more so than the course's commanding officer was the drill sergeant. Selected for a difficult role nurturing young prospective officers, the modicum of a sense of humour was often hidden—in fact, it was hidden well. He was responsible for parade and ceremonial and weapons training. Drill was a daily event and not only the formal parades and drill instruction. Officer cadets did not amble between lectures and the cadets' mess; officer cadets marched everywhere. Dressed in working blues and wearing the white-banded hats and epaulettes denoting their lowly status, squads of cadets were a defining image. The drill sergeant lurked around every corner and woe betide the cadet in charge of the squad who condoned 'tick-tocking' in the ranks. Precision was expected and retribution followed for offenders. Leadership was not restricted to field exercises.

Like Keebs, one of the defining moments was when my erstwhile inquisitor announced that this would be the first and the last time he saluted his motley crew. His face reflected an obvious sense of pride at the transformation he had supervised. He had indeed transformed a shambling group of individuals into a coherent team and a disciplined formation.

The two set-piece leadership training exercises conducted in the training area were centred on training camps reminiscent of wartime bases, where teams of students were set arduous tasks in austere conditions while under pressure. Sleep and food were deliberately sparse and it was not unknown for one team member to be briefed to adopt a deliberately hostile stance, playing the spy in the camp. Without a doubt, these exercises were the critical stage of the course and a positive assessment would guarantee graduation whereas a negative result might result in a swift return to 'Civvy Street'.

The office simulator was another crucial element of training. An RAF officer would be expected to demonstrate good staff skills both written and verbal and the office simulator gave the means to learn the pedantic standards demanded by the service. Basic service writing, registry and filing procedures, interview techniques, and operational security were all new subjects to most. Happily, the Administrative Branch would shoulder much of the burden on a flying station but even new aircrew were expected to show a basic understanding. How to draft a loose minute and to send a signal were carefully explained and practised. The directing staff proved to be adept actors and SAC Bloggs seemed to have an uncanny desire to book a place in Colchester jail, such were his misdemeanours that the officer cadets were expected to resolve.

As the course progressed, there was one activity that offered a tantalising glimmer of hope. Fittings at the station tailor for my first uniform began. No. 1

Home Dress was the formal uniform for ceremonial duties and the No. 5 Home Dress was the mess dress, which would see me through countless dining-in nights over the years. Each uniform was carefully fitted and tweaked to ensure a perfect fit, a concept alien to a working-class lad from Leeds. Up to that time, off the peg had been the order of the day. Happily, Her Majesty, for the first and only time, funded my uniform costs but that was to be the limit of her generosity and for the rest of my career, I would be putting my hand in my own pocket for replacements. The first time I would wear them would be on Graduation Day, assuming I passed the course.

The final interview in which I heard that I was to graduate on time came as a relief. It had been the greatest challenge of my young life but I had obviously fooled someone and I was to receive the Queen's commission. A formal parade followed by my first Dining-In Night as an officer was a huge milestone in my embryonic career. I suspect that every RAF officer and airman will recall the details of this momentous moment but my commissioning parchment still hangs proudly in my study as a reminder.

The next stop was navigator training.

David Gledhill graduates as an acting pilot officer from the officer cadet training unit at RAF Henlow.

3

Pilot Training:
Primary Flying Squadron,
RAF South Cerney (1966)

Philip Keeble

For once you have tasted flight you will walk the earth with your eyes turned skywards, for there you have been and there you will long to return.

Leonardo da Vinci

Leonardo da Vinci was not on the same course as me but a couple ahead. He certainly had the flying bug and I had it too; it was incurable.

Before I get on to the flying side of RAF life, it would be remiss of me not to mention that after passing out as acting pilot officers, we moved into the officers' mess proper and what a delight that was. We had spacious single rooms with carpets and curtains; even the shared bathrooms could be forgiven because, luxury of luxuries, we had a batman to take care of the general day-to-day essentials of being an officer. There were to be no more 'bull nights' for us.

Those students who already held a private pilot's licence went straight to flying jets but for those of us who did not, it was first to the primary flying squadron at RAF South Cerney flying the de Havilland Chipmunk T.10. We knew the airfield intimately, in that we had run around it many times, we had built great engineering structures on it, ones that the ancient Britons and Egyptians would have been proud of, now we were about to take off from one of its grass runways and soar high above it, rather than slogging along below. South Cerney was an old wartime airfield built on top of a hill in a delightful part of the world on the edge of the Cotswolds. It had a perimeter track, hangars, and a control tower, but it had no concrete runways, which, for the Chipmunk did not matter one little bit, for it had been designed by de Havilland to take off and land on grass. The de Havilland DHC-1 Chipmunk, designed and originally built in 1947 in Canada, was seen as a replacement for the ubiquitous Tiger Moth of the Second World War. It was built under licence in the UK where it was known in RAF service as the T. Mark 10 and described as a 'two seats in tandem, piston engined, primary trainer, with a fixed tricycle undercarriage with a tail wheel'. It had a wingspan of 34 feet and was constructed out of a stressed alloy skin that made up the fuselage, with parts of the wings and the control surfaces being fabric covered. The 'Chippie' may have seemed very flimsy but a tougher, more rugged little trainer you could not wish to take aviating.

It was depicted as a gentle and stable aircraft to fly and was fully aerobatic, but she had her vices and, if mishandled, could bite. It was fitted with a single-piston Gipsy Major engine producing 145 hp that allowed it to cruise at 90 knots with a maximum speed of 173 knots in a steep dive. I should know that fact intimately and if you want to know more, you should read my book *Patrolling the Cold War Skies* for the full hair-raising story of how I inadvertently exceeded that limit.

From my logbook, I flew thirty-two exercises in a one-month period while on the primary flying squadron, giving a total of thirty hours and fifteen minutes, of which five hours and fifteen minutes were solo, with my first solo on trip sixteen in WG306. That may seem a lot of hours compared to the private pilot's licence, but it reflected the rigorous RAF standards as military instructors put a lot more content into our training than an equivalent training course at a civilian flying school. I think that I had the better deal.

An enduring memory was the fifteen dual sorties with my flying instructor, Geoff Dillingham, an ex-Second World War Spitfire pilot, a brilliant flyer, and a fantastic instructor. Geoff and his peers were a bunch of mavericks in the best British sort of way: funny, quirky, irreverent, and idiosyncratic. They had been in the war, they had fought the Germans in dogfights, and now it was their duty to turn raw, trainee pilots into future versions of themselves. I do not know which would have been the more daunting of tasks: fighting the Germans or training us. Anyway, they gave both their best, with humour and skill; in the meantime, they taught us some bad habits—ones that I was more than happy to show my own students in later years.

Before we got anywhere near an aircraft, there were the mandatory lessons: aerodynamics, airmanship, Rules of the Air, meteorology, radio communications, engineering tech, and so on, not forgetting to learn all the flight checks by rote: pre-flight, strapping in and pre-start, start, after start, taxiing, pre-take-off checks, after take-off checks, climb checks, pre-general handling checks, ten-minute airmanship checks, recovery checks, descent checks, downwind checks, finals and pre-landing checks, after landing, and, last but not least, shutdown checks. Each and every checklist was memorised. Flight reference cards were forbidden and there was certainly no navigator calling them out from the backseat. Yes, we flew and got lost all by ourselves with no one to help. I still remember some of those checks to this day, although of note I forgot the shutdown checks later on in my career, much to my embarrassment. The Chipmunk downwind checks were 'MFFHHB', which mnemonically stood for 'My Friend Fred Has Hairy Balls'; it was more properly interpreted as 'Mixture, Fuel, Flaps, Hood, Harness, and Brakes'.

It took hours of preparation before you were ready to sit in that revered front cockpit but come the day on 9 May 1966, I was scheduled for Exercise 1, the 'Dual Familiarisation'. After breakfast, I walked down to Ops: Check in. Met brief. Sortie brief. Strap on parachute and waddle out to Chipmunk WD390. Following checks *in situ* and then thirty glorious minutes flying around the Cotswolds in the front seat, I was the king of all I observed. I loved it, every single second, from the smell of the cordite starter cartridge being fired, to the whiff of the rubber facemask and even the oil fumes from the engine. From the noise of starting up and take off to the silence of the glide, it was bliss. From the bumps of the grassy airstrip and the air turbulence to the calm serenity of being above it all, surveying everything from above, it was perfect. Who could have wished for more? I certainly could not have. I was in heaven and almost before it began, it was over and that was it. I wanted more but I would have to wait twenty-four hours for my next trip.

My logbook entry for that first trip reads: 'Flt. Lt. Dillingham/Self/Ex 1 Famil/ :30mins'. What my logbook does not record is what each trip actually consisted of, which was remiss of me. It states only the exercise number, although having been a Chipmunk instructor in another incarnation, I have a pretty good idea as to what each contained. The exercises that followed provided the fundamentals for all future flying instruction as they are the basic concepts of flying all aircraft—well, most anyway. They are vital to every single pilot who has ever flown anything except a chair. There are two axioms that must be remembered: firstly, in aerodynamics, what goes up must come down, and secondly, in aviation, the number of landings must equal the number of take-offs. Remember those two things and you will not go far wrong. Next follows the 'Aerodynamic Big Four': lift, weight, thrust, and drag. These have a fundamental effect on what is happening to an aeroplane and I will explain more about all this as we come to it. The initial few flying lessons fell into a number of broad categories. These were effects of controls, turning, climbing and descending, climbing and descending using flaps and/or power, stalling, spinning, and normal circuits. For example, trip two covered basically the effects that the joystick and rudder have upon the aeroplane. There are three planes of movement: pitch, roll, and yaw. Directly or indirectly, they are somewhat interconnected, to a greater or lesser degree. Change one and you can bet that one of the others will want to change, but it is important to remember that the axes are relative to the pilot as he sees his world, not as we see it being tied to gravity and a horizon.

A bit more detail to begin with. The control column, or pilot's joystick, moves in two planes (forwards and backwards for pitch control), operating through the elevators on the tailplane and thus making the nose move up and down relative to the pilot. In straight and level flight, that would also just happen to be in relation to the earth's horizon. Pull the stick back and you climb and the houses get smaller; push the stick forward and you descend and the houses get bigger. Moving the stick sideways moves the ailerons on the outboard of the main plane (wings) and you will roll left or right as desired. You can even roll all the way round through 360 degrees if you want. That seems simple, but what happens if you roll upside down and the sky and the ground swap places? Now, if you want to climb, you have to push to make the nose rise above the horizon and if you want to descend you have to pull. That means it is not quite so easy after all. It may be easy on a computer screen but when the sensors in your body are totally at odds with the physics acting around you, and when you are hanging upside down in your straps and pushing against gravity, it can get mightily confusing. For that reason, you practise and practise until you get it right and even then, you can get it horribly wrong. Trust me, I have.

The next dilemma is what to do with your feet while your hands are busy. Your flying boots sit on two pedals; these control the rudder that is attached to the fin (and vertical stabiliser) at the back. They are not used to any great degree in straight and level flight, but they are needed a little and often; there are times, however, when the rudders are desperately needed and they are vital as you will read shortly. Push your left leg forward and the aircraft yaws left, with a sideward slew in the opposite direction, and *vice versa*. The rudders are used mainly to ensure equilibrium in what is known as 'balanced flight'. For example, in a piston aircraft like the Chipmunk, when you change power, the yaw changes, the principal reasons being engine torque and propeller backwash. There is a need to change the rudder constantly to ensure that the aircraft flies in a straight line and does not 'crab' along, which is very inefficient aerodynamically, thereby adding to the fuel consumption of the aircraft and the crew's discomfort. That brings me nicely on to the throttle, a simple device used as the accelerator in the plane. It speaks for itself: power on and you accelerate and once up to flying speed, you get airborne. Any excess energy produced by the power plant can be used to climb and/or manoeuvre. Taking power off, obviously, the converse applies. This would be pretty straightforward except that every time you change power, you must re-balance the aircraft in yaw by feeding in a corresponding amount of offsetting rudder force. Luckily, in most jet aircraft, you do not need to do this very often; and, of course, in modern aircraft, fancy computers do the rudder bit for you— sheer luxury, if you like that sort of thing.

Once the basics are mastered, we have the beginnings of understanding how an aeroplane flies, so the next thing will be how to use the control column, rudders, and power to achieve straight and level flight in the air. Thus, we now move on to the next trip. If we cannot fly straight and level, we will wander all over the sky and eventually disappear into oblivion. Firstly, we need to understand the terms. Straight is maintaining the wings level to the horizon using the ailerons to change the bank if required. Level is using the pitch control of the elevators to stop us going up or down when we decide we do not want to; following lots of practice; once these basics have been flown to the instructor's satisfaction, it is back to base for a well-deserved cup of tea.

Starting trip three, we practise lesson two again before moving on to the new session: turning. Here we begin to use all three controls in order to make a balanced turn. First, we apply an amount of bank using the ailerons to roll to a given bank angle. Then, because of aerodynamic changes, we will have to use some of the lift vector from the wings to generate the force to turn. As the vertical lift vector now reduces so the aircraft will begin to descend, thus we use an appropriate amount of extra pitch to increase the lift to maintain level flight, which stops us from descending. As the aerodynamic forces have increased, we will now need extra power to prevent the aircraft from slowing down but now extra engine power means that the yaw will change as a result. It seems complicated but I managed to understand it so it cannot be that difficult. To add just a little more, other effects are also in play because as the aircraft starts to turn, it will also sideslip into the direction of turn, which is downwards. As it sideslips, we must prevent that by applying a small amount of counter rudder otherwise the aircraft will continue into a spiral dive. It is an exercise in coordination and a good one too. You can now see that nothing is done in isolation. In order to keep even a simple plane flying, if you change one thing other things occur. Practice does indeed make perfect, and you will continue practising until, like all motor skills, sooner or later, things start to make sense and become an automatic reflex. There are, of course, natural pilots and there are those poor unfortunates for whom it will never make sense but for the majority of us, we can achieve the basics even if we have to be taught more than once.

Trip four moves on to climbing and descending but what comes first? Yes, that is right: practising lessons two and three. By now, the basic concepts of flying should be making some sense. Like with anything worth doing, it takes time, whether learning a musical instrument, to drive, or to ski. It does not happen overnight but comes through progression. During this sortie, your flying instructor will give you words of wisdom, which will stick with you over decades. One such mantra is 'PAT': 'Power, Attitude, Trim': the three keys to climbing and descending. If you put power on the aircraft accelerates, the speed of air over the wings increases and the wings produce more lift. You can use that lift to climb by raising the nose by changing the attitude. Conversely, take power off and the aircraft slows and you are forced to lower the nose attitude and descend to maintain a safe flying speed. Do not forget that a change of power and speed means a change in yaw. Levelling off is 'APT': 'Attitude, Power, Trim'. The order is different but the same principles apply. You select a level attitude, adjust the power for the speed you want, and trim the aircraft back into balance. By now, we are in a groove and trip five covers climbing and descending lesson number two, it is similar in format to the previous trip but now we use some of the extra services provided by the Chipmunk, though that really amounted to 'not a lot'. It had flaps, mechanical devices that increase the lift by changing the overall contour of the wing, which were used only at key times for a take-off and landing. Other aircraft have additional aids but it is too soon to mention them.

One important question remains: what happens if you do not have enough lift and gravity does the inevitable and hence you drop out of the sky? This brings us nicely on to stalling, a seemingly unwise exercise where you deliberately allow the aircraft to slow down to the point where the lift being generated by the wings cannot support the weight of the aircraft and so it stalls. In some aircraft, this means a gentle and controlled descent but in others, it has a more vigorous and exciting effect, the F-4 Phantom being a prime example. Having put the aircraft into a stall in the first place, the student must recognise the symptoms and learn how to recover, bringing the aircraft back to safe flight; this is most commonly done by the use of full power and judicious handling of the controls.

The next lesson is what happens if you grossly mishandle the aircraft at the point of stalling and cause it to spin. This can be truly exciting as the aircraft will depart from controlled flight, descend rapidly, and proceed to rotate around all three axes in a somewhat 'robust manner', some might even say showing 'violent behaviour'. This is a little disconcerting at first but, happily, once you have experienced a couple of spins, then like everything else beforehand, it loses its mystique and begins to make sense as it is perfectly controllable. Recovering from a spin is a relatively straightforward exercise and applying the controls correctly brings everything back to straight and level flight, although this was not always so in my case as I have recounted in my first book.

You will be glad to know that very few aircraft spin these days. It was not always so, and once upon a time, it caused the loss of many an aircraft with fatalities. In modern designs, the adverse characteristics are minimised at the design stage with a combination of teaching and clever computers negating the risk; however, there is still plenty of scope to screw up as many aircrews over the years have found out to their cost, even in some very modern and sophisticated aircraft.

We now know how to fly straight and level, how to turn, how to climb and descend, how to stall, and how to spin. Most importantly, we know how to recover from the consequences of our actions and so it is on to the next two phases. Circuits and landings (more of which later) and then most excitingly the 'Sport of Kings'—aerobatics—with loops and rolls to begin with. The combination of these two movements will delight and thrill your soul in a veritable ballet of stunts and manoeuvres that defy gravity and the forces of nature. Let me say that treated responsibly and with respect, aerobatics are as safe as crossing the road, but stupidly, I did not always show them that due respect and as a result nearly killed myself experimenting with a barrel roll. This was a bit like trying to cross the M62 on foot during the rush hour. Again, you can read a whole lot more on not how to do it in *Patrolling the Cold War Skies*.

So now we are ready for solo. Well, not quite so fast. I have covered the exciting bits so far and deliberately have not made mention of some very important aspects of flying. It is all very well getting airborne, but you cannot just bludgeon your way around the skies. You have to know where you are and how to get back to base and, yes, there is plenty of hypocrisy in that remark. You have to keep an eye on the fuel and engine instruments and, additionally, have to be able to read the wind and the weather, understand air traffic rules and procedures, and, of course, how to fly a circuit on arrival back at base in order to make a safe arrival on the runway.

The circuit is a pattern flown around the airfield that feeds aircraft down towards the runway in a sequenced manner, each aircraft landing safely in turn. The circuit needs a great deal of attention to detail and accurate flying for it has specific heights, distances and speeds to fly, places where you do your checks and, importantly, where to make radio calls. That means that everyone in the circuit is aware of the position of each other aircraft. If flown properly, it guarantees safe separation and ensures that your aircraft is set up in a correct and safe manner for touchdown. In the life of a military pilot, they will do hundreds of these identical patterns but even so, complacency must not be allowed to take hold for therein lies danger. Yes, guilty as charged.

At this early stage, we think that we can now fly. We are pilots and are ready to go up on our own. If our flying instructor agrees, he will authorise us to do so but trust me at this juncture, we know next to nothing and are in a very vulnerable place. Later in my career, now as a qualified flying instructor (QFI) I would send young people solo, yet no one was more apprehensive and full of trepidation than I was when watching them from the control tower, for I knew what danger lurked in the skies.

I completed fifteen sorties before being allowed to fly solo, first though a pre-solo dual check on the day with my instructor, Geoff. Satisfied that I was indeed ready he climbed out, patted me on my bonedome, wished me luck and left me all on my own. It was the 20 May 1966 in Chipmunk WG 306 and I was airborne for fifteen minutes. It was just days after my nineteenth birthday and I was airborne on my own without an instructor—just me. I took off, climbed into the circuit, flew one normal circuit, and landed. That was it, my first solo. Congratulations and well done to everyone else who has done it for we have joined an exclusive club. I still remember singing to myself on the downwind leg: 'A Life on the Ocean Waves'. Who knows why? Yet it is true. Maybe I had a secret hankering to be steam catapulted off an aircraft carrier in a Phantom, in the dead of night, into a force 8 storm, with 70-foot waves breaking over the bow and then, assuming, I made it back on to the deck in one piece, spend years away on the high seas being seasick. No thanks, I would stick to land-based runways.

Once solo for the first time, a series of sorties then followed where each of the earlier exercises was practised yet again plus a whole load of new 'stuff'; such as advanced aerobatics and unusual circuits. The last exercise to be taught was navigation. This involved flying out of the local training area and into places where it said on the map, ''ere be dragons'; this was all most exciting but there is always one last hurdle to jump through before being allowed to move on and this was known as the 'Final Handling Check Ride'. On this assessment sortie, your erstwhile instructor handed you over to a senior instructor who then put you through your paces to see if you had absorbed the lessons and were ready to advance on to the next stage of training. I was, and so it was off to jets for me. There were no more cream teas and chicken in the basket in the Cotswolds. Nope; instead, it was off to Nottinghamshire and on to the Jet Provost with its 'variable noise, constant thrust engine'.

4

Basic Jet Training: No. 2 Flying Training School, RAF Syerston (1966–1967)

Philip Keeble

Before the RAF allowed me to get my sticky little mitts on one of the RAF's jets, there was the matter of getting from Gloucestershire to Nottinghamshire via Hampshire. This sounds easy enough, but despite travelling light, getting around was a bit of a logistical nightmare. So, I decided to buy an old Austin Mini, a vehicle that was the opposite of a TARDIS. Getting from Bournemouth to Newark along ancient byways was not too bad, motorways having not been invented yet. I knew that RAF Syerston was alongside the A46 somewhere between Bath and Lincoln so the airfield was not totally impossible to find even for someone as useless as a navigator as myself. It is very handy when airfields are built alongside a major trunk road, other RAF airfields were much better hidden, especially those in the wilds of Yorkshire and Lincolnshire.

I checked in at the guardroom fully expecting my billet to be in the officers' mess but not so fast, for: 'You, Sir, are accommodated in a barrack block next to the parade square'. Never had I expected to hear those dreadful words ever again—a barrack block? Yes, but at least this one had been modified to single rooms. Over the years, as an officer, I have slept in some funny old places: old wartime huts riddled with damp and rats, remote Army barracks with twenty-two men to a room, miles from the main base, and an ex-Second World War RAF mess that was supposedly haunted. I have slept under parachutes in remote places such as in the Bavarian mountains with the temperature at -28 degrees Celsius, and under pine branches on the Troodos Mountains in Cyprus. A whole room to myself was not too bad on reflection. It was just that I was expecting a bit more, it seemed to be a backwards step even from my recent experiences at RAF South Cerney. Here at Syerston, we even suffered the ignominy of having to march everywhere in flights and to salute the officers on the permanent staff, including pilot officers from air traffic control; that, especially for the flying officers on my course, was definitely a backward step. However, as a bonus, right next-door to our block was the WRAF block and the compensation of having thirty nubile young ladies right next door seemed to make up for any minor inconveniences. What could possibly go wrong (or go right)? Much depended on your point of view and how successful you were at chatting up the lasses and here I certainly do not wish to digress.

On the first Monday morning at 8 a.m. sharp, we reported for duty, which began with four weeks of ground school lessons, where we quickly refreshed the basics that we had already been through and then the lectures stepped up a gear going to a much greater depth. There was a lot to get through. Aerodynamics covered the effect of Mach number upon the aircraft. Tech (short for technology) told us to forget all about piston engines and switch instead to jet propulsion and their associated systems. Meteorology covered new things like icing, upper clouds, and high-level winds, something we had been shielded from up to now. We even drew our own weather charts and tephigrams, something that computers now do for the Meteorological Office today. The level of detail was quite extraordinary and I could now see why maths and sciences qualifications were so important, most of it was absorbing and fascinating yet, at times, complicated and difficult.

The worst subject of all for me was learning Morse code. One dot sounded just like a dash and put more than three together and I was totally flummoxed. Oh, how I hated Morse. That is probably why I wanted to fly with a navigator because he could deal with all that 'dah dit dah' stuff. Actually, at that time, I wanted to be posted to single-seat jets but I have to say nice things about navigators to foster a spirit of collaboration given the theme of this book. I am sure I would have muddled through Morse code somehow without them.

Some things were easier; there was no more PT in the snow, but we still kept up with the sports on a Wednesday afternoon and a Saturday, I even tried running around the games field in the evenings in a vain attempt to keep fit, but that did not last long, despite the fact that the track ran right past the WRAF block where the occupants would often sit outside and sunbathe.

Once it was deemed that we knew enough to be able to understand the workings of a jet aircraft, something that could fly higher and faster than anything we had experienced before, we were sent up to the flight line to meet the Jet Provost Mark 3 and our flying instructors; this was where we would begin the basic jet flying training syllabus. The Hunting Jet Provost first flew in 1955 with the Mark 3 coming on to strength in 1958. It was fitted with side-by-side ejector seats and a retractable tricycle undercarriage, with a nose wheel. The Armstrong Siddeley Viper Mk 102 turbojet engine produced 1,700 lb of thrust, which could drive the little trainer to about 380 knots and 30,000 feet. It had an electrical starter system and a number of other features that differed from the humble piston-engined Chipmunk. It boasted systems including hydraulics, breathing oxygen, a basic navigation aid called distance measuring equipment (DME), a full instrumentation, and a central warning panel to warn the pilot of any emergencies, such as a fire, oxygen failure, or icing. It may all seem a little primitive by today's modern standards, but, at the time, the 'JP' (as it was universally known) was a pleasure to behold and to fly. Its systems and performance were a quantum jump forward and flying it properly would test the abilities of many student pilots to the limit and some beyond it.

Ground school continued and rotated with flying either in the mornings or the afternoons. The airborne syllabus followed a similar pattern to that on the primary flying squadron—namely, the effects of controls through general handling and eventually on to spinning and aerobatics. It was an intense programme, as it was meant to be. A new feature of the Jet Provost was that the undercarriage had to be raised and lowered by the pilot, a fact that some forgot. Luckily, at the threshold of the runway sat the runway controller in a brightly painted truck or caravan. His job was to check that any aircraft coming in to land had lowered its undercarriage; if not, he fired a red flare from a Verey pistol to warn the pilot to go around and try again. In my encyclopaedia of mistakes, I am glad to say it is not one I ever made, but there was always the chance and so it was check once, check twice, and check thrice. A 'wheels up' landing would lead to review action and most certainly to suspension from the course, known in RAF vernacular as 'getting the chop'. There were many reasons why a student might be suspended but for most, it was the inability to learn at the required rate of progress. Once flagged up by his instructor, a remedial package was set in place to aid the student and at the end of that review action would be taken either to continue training or to suspend the poor unfortunate. Again, I was sufficiently average to proceed but I could see the poor wretches who were struggling. The review process was likened to being under a spotlight and it must have felt like the eyes of the whole establishment were watching you for any infractions. I failed the odd trip but nothing serious and nothing that a refly could not fix but we lost a few of our fellow students along the way. It was not a nice thing to happen—to come this far, get a taste of jet flying, and then have to leave. Later in life, one of my own students was forced to leave the RAF because he was dyslexic but he actually went on to join British Airways—you have been warned.

Looking back in my logbook, I flew a total of 115 exercises, logging 145 hours on the Jet Provost, of which forty-seven were solo. My instructor was John Delafield, who had been a British gliding champion and was another all-round good bloke. I was averaging two out of two for excellent QFIs so far, so I was doing well (but sadly, that would not last). The first major milestone was going solo in Jet Provost XM426 on 27 July 1966, worryingly on trip number thirteen. It was another one of those joyous moments when you say goodbye to your instructor and set off down the runway all on your own. Some people might get lonely not having anyone else in the jet with them to talk to, but if that was the case, they were in the wrong job. For me, it was a liberating experience, especially not having a propeller spinning on the nose; flying as a passenger is all so mundane and uncomfortable, especially if travelling by budget airline but in the cockpit, as the pilot in charge, nothing could be less dull and routine. It was excitement all the way from start to finish. There was not anywhere else in the world that I would rather be and it was a great office to work from. I even have mates who tell me that the Boeing 747 was great to fly; I am sure it was. However, there is only one civilian jet that I would have liked to have flown and that is Concorde, which was simply the best civil airliner ever built. I suspect it would have made an even better RAF bomber but again I digress.

With our first solo behind us, we got down to the business of being taught totally new lessons. Some I loved, such as formation flying, which I will come to shortly. Some I never got to like much, such as instrument flying. Tell me who in their right mind wants to fly in cloud and not see the view. Well, if you are flying in Europe, you had better get used to the grey, wet, claggy stuff and I did, even becoming an instrument rating examiner (IRE), but for the record, I never ever enjoyed it or felt relaxed, which was probably a good thing.

After a basic handling test (BHT) came phase two where we moved on to the relatively punchier Jet Provost Mark 4 with its more powerful Viper engine pushing out 2,500 lb of thrust. Now here I was introduced into the whole new world of formation flying, and I loved it right from the get-go, just as much as I did at the end of my career; it was challenging, strenuous, exciting, and was everything I wanted in flying until I discovered air combat, of course. I had always wanted to fly in a jet aerobatic display team but never achieved those giddy heights—not for the want of trying, I might add. Learning and practising formation flying was not just for the hell of it because it was an intrinsic part of operational flying, of which I will say much more in later chapters, but it was here that I received my grounding in the skills needed.

A Jet Provost T Mark 4, XP554, of the Central Flying School.

Philip Keeble shown during his basic flying training.

First, as with all new modules, came the formation phase brief where the whole of our course was introduced and briefed as to what was involved in formating on another aircraft. It covered how to take off and land in formation, how to fly an echelon position and in line astern, and how to move safely from one to the other. The brief also explained how to handle an emergency when near to another aircraft. After the phase brief came the individual sortie briefs, which covered the specifics for each formation trip. The first sortie would be flown as a pair, but later in the phase, a third ship would be added. An instructor briefed us on a myriad of important details, such as the aim of the sortie, the weather, the airfield and runway state, the training area, frequencies, callsigns, emergencies, and so on. He would also cover the salient features and format of the exercise; this pre-flight brief would last about half an hour or more before it was time to walk to the jets. Nervous? Yes. Apprehensive? Yes. Enthused? Oh yes, and I was not to be disappointed.

As I said, flying in close formation is a thrill that I never ever tired of. Flying at 10,000 feet just a few feet away from another aircraft while moving along at 300 knots had a frisson that is difficult to describe, so I will not; 450 knots at 100 feet, locked and loaded in a F-4 Phantom down the Falklands was even better.

The first exercise we flew alongside the lead jet, about 6 feet apart and swept back slightly in a position called echelon. With just two aircraft at this stage from echelon starboard (right), we would be taught how to move safely back, down and across the leader to arrive in echelon port (left). All this was done while flying straight and level. Next came the same move while turning, then when climbing and descending, and so the sequences went on. After echelon came line astern, which at first was a lot of swinging from side to side behind the lead aircraft. It was very easy to over control the aileron inputs and start oscillating violently; once settled in, the turns began followed by flying the same manoeuvre while climbing and descending.

Just as you thought that you had got the hang of it, a third aircraft would be added into to the mix and now we have a 'Vic' formation, which is a leader with two wingmen, one on each wing. Echelon port or echelon starboard was pretty much the same but with the two wingmen on the same side, it was not too bad just as long as the inside man was 'Rock Steady Eddy', but if not, you had to try and ignore him and take your cues from the leader. Line astern became a whole lot harder if you were number three in the line, especially if number two was making distracting errors; the trick was to try to concentrate on the leader and ignore what 'matey' was doing in between. That was easier said than done and, occasionally, poor old number 3 would be spat out of the back and have to re-acquire the formation once more and execute a safe rejoin.

Formation flying would become our daily bread and butter in the future. Later on, we flew formation in cloud, necessary for a recovery into an airfield; for this, we would close up as tight as possible and hope that you did not lose visual with the leader, which if you did could get more than a tad hairy.

Then came the cherry on the cake—tail-chasing, a three-dimensional exercise of 'follow my leader', flown first with two aircraft and later with a third. Only 300 yards separated each aircraft and the aim was to try to maintain that separation. Whatever the lead aircraft did and wherever he went, you followed his manoeuvres as closely as possible. If the leader pulled up into a loop, the following aircraft did the same. Here was where it became interesting because if number one is pulling 3 g, then number two is probably pulling 4 g to keep up, which rippled back down the line if there was a third jet. Equally, if the leader is doing 150 knots over the top, then the followers will be probably be slower and, therefore, have to be very aware of the minimum speed. While being taught formation tail-chasing, I learned another bad habit; that was 'cloud bashing', which is finding a delightful looking, puffy, cumulous cloud and flying around and through its valleys and canyons chasing one another. Not all clouds are nasty, wet, claggy blankets of visible moisture in the atmosphere and thank goodness cumulous clouds are made for pure enjoyment. It would have been a sin not to use them for that purpose; the only minor problem was finding someone else with the same idea coming the opposite way through a gully. It never happened as far as I know, so all was well; in fact, any opportunity to bash a cloud was taken. While tail-chasing sounds like enormous fun, and trust me it was, it had a purpose and that was to give the student pilot experience in 3-D orientation and the effects of 'lead and lag'; this was our first introduction to these terms—ones that were to become fundamental to an air defence pilot. Lead and lag were methods of varying the range between jets by cutting the corners (lead), or extending the turn (lag), to increase or decrease the separation range between aircraft without the use of changing speed and power. Lead and lag are very much as they sound—if you lag behind in a turn the separation distance between yourself and the aircraft ahead will increase and, conversely, if you lead a turn the separation distance will decrease. Flying the most efficient flight path saves fuel, which is significant, especially if you are flying a jet with reheat. This, of course, was a basic building block for something that lay ahead—intercepts and combat. If we were extremely lucky, our instructors would indulge in maybe a slightly illegal 'practice combat' for their own benefit and for our education. Bring it on. There is much more of that to come.

There is a famous poem entitled 'High Flight', written by Canadian pilot John Gillespie Magee, Jr, Royal Canadian Air Force, in which he encapsulates the sheer joy of flying with phrases such as:

> Sunward I've climbed and joined the tumbling mirth of sun-split clouds, and done a hundred things you have not dreamed of. Wheeled and soared and chased the shouting wind through footless halls of air.

His work is probably most recognisable from his most famous line: 'Oh! I have slipped the surly bonds of earth.' He himself slipped the surly bonds of earth for one last time in a mid-air collision while in his Spitfire over Lincolnshire in 1941 and, as he so eloquently wrote in the last line of his famous poem, 'Put out my hand, and touched the face of God.' It is a truly beautiful poem.

The next series of exercises was about navigation. We had learned rudimentary lessons back on the Chipmunk at an eye-watering 90 knots but now we were stepping it up a gear or two. First of all, the speed was increased in stages—in phase one of the course from 180 knots, then to 240 knots, and eventually to 300 knots in phase two. That is 5 miles in one minute. Get confused by flying a wrong heading for two minutes and you are many miles away from where you thought you were. This is enough to be officially 'lost' and not just 'uncertain of position'. There were methods to extricate yourself from this unfortunate scenario, and sometimes, they even met with a degree of success.

At medium level, we used a basic navigation aid called DME. Beacons were scattered across the country transmitting signals to onboard aircraft equipment, which would receive them and calculate how far away the aircraft was from the beacon. This information was displayed to the pilot as a range on the DME instrument. Hypothetically, if we were 30 miles from a beacon, we could be anywhere on an arc of 360 degrees of a circle, which is 188 miles in circumference—north, south, east, or west. Thus, we needed a second refence beacon for a more accurate position, a crosscut. If we were 30 miles from beacon 'A' and 20 miles from beacon 'B', where the two ranges intersected, or overlapped, that is the place where we must be. However, they cross over in two places, which still gives us a largish area of uncertainty, so to narrow it down even further, a range from a third beacon is needed to give us an accurate cross fix known in the trade as a 'cocked hat'. A three-beacon overlap is, of course, more accurate and most desirable, but DMEs were sparse and, therefore, this was not always possible. Dave discusses this in more detail in his chapter on navigator training. In the tight confines of a Jet Provost cockpit without a plotting table, it was difficult to envisage the range circles in the mind's eye to aid us in our navigation, so before we went flying, we drew range rings on our pocket maps radiating out from every local DME beacon. A quick glance at the map would show us where those circles overlapped and by plotting them thus give a reasonable position; it was a crude but effective technique, of course, at low level, we were below the line of sight of most of the beacons so, therefore, navigational visual techniques took over. Low-level techniques were not so very different from reading any map, for example as when in a car, just a tiny bit faster. Look ahead at the features coming up, look at the map and try to make sense of it all. Ground to map, not the other way around.

These basic techniques may seem primitive by today's standard of navigational instruments, but modern systems using the Global Positioning System (GPS) actually use principles not too far removed from DME only satellites fix the position rather than radio beacons and the accuracy is vastly different. Although a satnav does it all for you, I still use an old-fashioned paper map on any journey as I have seen too many mishaps when relying on modern technology, such as drivers turning up at Newcastle-under-Lyme rather than Newcastle upon Tyne, or getting stuck down narrow lanes, or ending up in the middle of a river ford. In an aeroplane, that is not such a good idea.

Despite everything I have said about navigation, I have been uncertain of my position many times in the air but never actually lost, of course. That would be apart from when trying to find the island of Gan in the middle of the Indian Ocean with no navigation aids at all. On that occasion, I had to revert to centuries-old techniques as used in the canoes by the Polynesian people, by finding clouds that were higher than the rest they were therefore rising up from heated ground beneath, and so it was possible to pinpoint the various island landmasses. The other stalwart navigation technique was called 'The Shackleton Principle': Turn right, find India, and then turn left. Eventually, you will come to the Maldives. This is scary stuff when you are running short of fuel but I digress yet again.

Back at the basic flying stage, we are progressing from pure flying to applied flying and are not that far from being able to call ourselves proper pilots and to receive our flying badge (wings). We can fly in cloud, we can do basic formation, and we can do low-level navigation. It was time to up the pace yet once again, so we did some of these exercises at night. Night handling and circuits were followed by night navigation and night instrument flying. Happily, night formation would have to wait some fifteen years before I felt its deathly touch. I admit I never ever got to like night flying despite hundreds of hours flown in the dark during my career but it had its compensation. On a clear night, you could see the lights of towns and villages for hundreds of square miles around and on Bonfire Night, the view was truly spectacular. One of the positives of night flying in Flying Training Command was that there was always a night flying supper and a barrel of beer waiting for us after landing. Now that is my sort of flying. On reflection, though, I consider it was some sort of clever psychology to make us think that it was fun. In other words, it was a bribe but then I am easily bought. Landing from an air defence sortie at 3 a.m. during the night and having to make your own cup of tea in the crew room was a whole different ball game.

Intermingled with the serious training were moments of relaxation. We were stationed not far from Nottingham where some of the best night clubs and working men's clubs in Britain were to be found and, of course, Nottingham is noted for having the prettiest girls in the land. How could a good-looking, young pilot go wrong? That is for another book—one that will not get published.

Unfortunately, there was no escape from the officer training and leadership exercises, which continued with us climbing up frozen waterfalls, yomping across snow-covered moonscapes on top of the Derbyshire Peak District, and sleeping under a parachute while huddled up for mutual warmth, but all good things must come to an end and a year later, we were deemed to have learned enough to pass out as pilots worthy of our RAF wings. I cannot think of a finer moment in my career than pinning that famous flying badge on to my No. 1 uniform. My mum and dad were there to see it and were as proud as punch, Pa especially, being an ex-pilot himself. There was still one small fly in the ointment. I never did pass my Morse code examination; in fact, five of us were still sitting in the exam room on the morning of our passing out parade, desperately trying to make sense of random and incomprehensible bleeps and blips as the others were getting dressed up in their finest. The band was practising and we were in panic mode; eventually, our examiner said, 'Push off you lot and go and get your wings'. 'Thanks, Sir', and we were gone like a rat up a drainpipe.

Morse code, like musical crochets, demi-quavers, or even a breve, never made any sense to me but an aircrew brevet certainly did; I now had one and I still wear it on my dressing gown with pride.

Before we moved on to the next phase of training, our course was streamed. Our next postings were generally sorted out in line with our final positions on the course and our suitability; we would be going either to fast jet training at RAF Valley in Wales or to heavy, twin pistons at RAF Oakington in Cambridgeshire. The top ten went to fast jets and the rest went on to piston training. I was not in the top ten; in fact, I was somewhere down the middle of the course, yet I was posted to RAF Valley. It was not because I was good enough to fly swept-wing supersonic fast jets but because they did not trust me with heavy aeroplanes—ones that flew with a crew and/or passengers. Actually, my humility prevents me from telling it as it actually was.

I was going to RAF Valley so I could fly the fabulous Folland Gnat and that was all that mattered.

5

Advanced Flying Training:
No. 4 FTS, RAF Valley, Anglesey
(July–December 1967)

Philip Keeble

Before I could fly the Gnat, I had six weeks to wait because of a backlog in the training system so I took a month's leave and spent two weeks holding at RAF Bicester with Oxford University Air Squadron. While I held there, I could keep my hand in flying so after a quick dual check in the Chipmunk, I was airborne again. Certainly, the Chipmunk was better than nothing and, in fact, I must say it was an absolute delight to be at Bicester. The mess was wonderful and run on proper old school lines, the flying was relaxed and enjoyable and I flew eleven trips, of which three quarters were flown solo.

My short stay was not uneventful and I experienced a moment of embarrassment when on returning from my first dual trip, I was sent solo straightaway after a running change, that is without shutting the engine down. After my final landing, I could not remember for the life of me how to close the engine down with the cut-off switch. I knew that there was a lever somewhere but could not seem to find it among the hundreds of other knobs, switches, levers, and dials in the cockpit so I called across to the ground crew and asked him how it was done. He gave me a look that said, 'This is a bleedin' spoof, right?'

In fact, he was slightly more polite but I could see that he thought I was pulling his leg. 'Nope, sorry, it isn't a joke, where is the cut-off?' Sure enough, it was tucked away up under the coaming out of sight and out of memory. Having been shown, I soon I had the old girl safely silent and climbed out, but I could almost read his mind, in that I had been up there flying this aircraft on my own and did not know how to close the engine off. Despite the hiccup I flew a further seven solo trips that went without a hitch, thank goodness.

Assembling back at RAF Syerston for our departure, those of us who had been selected for fast jet training formed a convoy and headed off across the moors and mountains for darkest Wales. Although bodily we all made it, our four-wheeled camel train lost a few of its members along the way as they abandoned their vehicles alongside the A5 between Shrewsbury and Bangor. Most were recovered as scrap metal sometime later. I survived the first journey but my Austin Mini expired on the Shrewsbury bypass some months later, venting steam and water by the roadside. They did not make very good cars in those days, or if they did, we certainly could not afford them. I would add that the roads were not very good either and what should have been a journey of about 4 hours probably took twice as long. As lunchtime approached, we were somewhere in the Ogwen Pass just outside of Betws-y-Coed and decided to pull over at a pub for a pie and a pint. We were wrong; Wales was 'dry' on Sundays and the pubs were closed. 'What, no beer on a Sunday?' we cried. Nope, not a drop was to be had anywhere for a weary driver and his passengers. 'What sort of primitive place is this?' we asked—a sober one, apparently which meant that we would have to wait another couple of hours for refreshments. Those in the know knew that there were certain local hostelries where a drink could be found, one being the officers' mess at RAF Valley. The officers' mess at RAF Valley was built on more modern lines than the old style of wartime messes (which were known as the 'Binbrook' model) as it was planned to be used as a holiday hotel if the RAF should ever pull out. It would be our home for the next six months and soon we were unpacked and having a well-deserved pint in the bar. More importantly flying once more beckoned.

Our new mount was the Folland Gnat, a swept-wing, supersonic, two-seat, tandem training jet. It had also been produced as a lightweight single-seat fighter and was exported to other nations, notably India, as a fighter variant but never made it into operational service with the RAF. It was beaten in a competition to provide a new, agile fighter by the Hawker Hunter and I feel that was probably the right outcome. Nevertheless, the Gnat was an outstanding aircraft to fly and had flight instrumentation similar to that fitted to the English Electric Lightning and the Blackburn Buccaneer. The idea of compatible cockpits would not catch on again until some forty years later.

As a trainer, it was superb. It was fast and nimble and the cockpit was compact, even 'snug'. In fact, it was tiny. People were said to 'strap it on' rather than 'strap into it' and yet a 6-footer could sit in the back seat without needing to be a contortionist. It was, to my mind, a bit like a Caterham R500 sports car in that it had truly superb performance; if it had only been fitted with reheat, it would have been the best aircraft in the world, even if it would have only done a ten-minute sortie—yet some ten minutes that would have been. As it was, the average trip was around the hour mark, which at 7-plus miles a minute was pretty good going. The Gnat was a lot more complicated than many jets of the age and in trying to pack such a lot into such a small airframe, the designers must have experienced more than a few headaches. Nevertheless, they did a great job with the technology available.

Before we started the ground school, our course had been split into two groups, the greater portion of us going on to the Gnat with a smaller group going on to fly the Hunter F6, which also operated with No. 4 Flying Training School at the time. I am not sure who got the better deal but having experienced both jets over the years, they each had their own merits and I consider myself very privileged to have flown both types. The ground school was heavy on the technical and went deeply into high-speed flight, a new aspect of aerodynamics looking at what happens as you approach and go beyond Mach One (or, as it is colloquially known, 'The Sound Barrier'). Factors such as supersonic shock waves make fundamental changes to the aerodynamics and the way an aircraft handles and performs; breaking Mach 1 was still a relatively new concept in 1967, and flying at those speeds was still pretty exciting, especially for a young twenty-year-old.

In addition to the technical stuff, the course touched on politics and world affairs and the inevitable leadership training continued, albeit, this time in the hills of Snowdonia, which, if you have never visited them, are beautiful. If you are travelling on foot, as we were, the hills were fearsomely steep in places and set new challenges. Sports continued either down at the gym if it was wet or on the local beach if was nice. Happily, that summer, it was nice.

RAF Valley was also my first experience of sea drills, referred to as 'dinghy drills'. Taken out into the Irish Sea in an RAF Air-Sea Rescue launch, we were thrown into the 'oggin' and, once in the water, went through our survival drills. First climb into a tiny, one-man, rubber dinghy, bale it out, do lots of other things, and then wait a couple of hours for a Whirlwind helicopter to come and lift you out and return said wet and cold pilot to the rescue craft. In the UK, the sea temperatures rarely go much higher than 10 degrees Celsius, so it is always nippy out there; when you add to that a stiff breeze, large waves, and a feeling of nausea, you can probably understand why I did not enjoy the drills very much. They were to become part of my RAF life as we would complete a drill every year and, although some were better than others, some were pure torture largely depending on the outside air temperature. Let me also say that I also hated helicopters; they are nasty, draughty, uncomfortable, and noisy beasts that should never be able to fly—more on that later.

Eventually came the time to fly the 'Pocket Rocket', as it was affectionately known, and it fitted its description perfectly. It was tiny but it went like a 'bat out of hell'. This phenomenon was something they refer to in the manuals as 'thrust over weight ratio' and in the words of one of my fellow students, 'For the first month it flew you around. You just pointed the pitot tube at the sky and followed it. The second month got better'. I must agree with him totally because it was staggering in its performance—the rate of roll was impossibly quick at 360 degrees a second, which is head-spinningly rapid. It is worth noting that the Red Arrows Gnats rolled at 420 degrees per second; I do not think there was an aircraft with a faster roll rate anywhere in the world at the time. One twitch of the stick and the world revolved at a bewildering rate; however, like all things, you soon got used to it and learnt to be judicious with control movements.

It also pulled over 6 g, and that could also catch you out. I once experienced GLOC ('g-induced loss of consciousness') where the blood is dragged down and away from the brain, causing cerebral hypoxia. With such extreme g force, the brain is starved of blood because it pools in your legs, firstly causing 'greyout', shortly followed by 'blackout', and then finally unconsciousness. There were ways to overcome the risk by compressing the muscles in your stomach, abdomen and thighs to prevent too much blood from sinking into your boots. A 'g suit', a tightly laced pair of trousers, aptly nicknamed 'turning trousers', was specially fitted to your lower body, helping enormously in aiding your tolerance. Without one it would have been mightily difficult to operate a Gnat to its full performance. High-performance flight certainly brought on new challenges.

While on 4 FTS as a student, I flew a total of seventy-four hours, of which twenty-one were flown on my own; the first solo was on trip number eight. I loved every sortie but best of all was going supersonic for the first time, just like those boyhood heroes of mine: Neville Duke and Peter Twist. I had seen the Pathé newsreels of the Farnborough Air Show on a number of occasions and had watched them put their aircraft, such as the Hunter and the Fairy Delta 2, through their paces, even to the extent of going supersonic over the crowd. Unfortunately, air show regulations were sparse in those days and, sadly, there were horrendous accidents during a few of those demonstrations; however, for me, watching the Mach gauge creep up to Mach 0.9 and on through to Mach 1.0 and beyond was just a total and utter thrill. It was something to write home about for I was buzzing with excitement. Years later, along came Concorde and you could do the same thing while having a gin and tonic at the same time. It may have taken some of the glamour away from the pilot in favour of the passengers but then it was a huge buzz. It would be a long while before I had a go at achieving Mach 2.0 in a Tornado F3 fighter but that is yet another story.

In addition to going very fast at a high level, we also went very fast at a low level, flying 'navexes' around northern England and Wales. Departing from RAF Valley and heading into Cumbria, we would first fly up the Irish Sea, home to the pirate radio station 'Radio Caroline' and fair game for a flyby. Speed and height had no limits and thus presented no problems as no one was going to report us for the crew on board could not and I recall Johnny Walker, during one of his programmes, announcing that the ship was being buzzed by a Gnat. I hope that they enjoyed it because we certainly did.

They were long hot summers, flying high, flying low, and flying fast with time off on the beach with the girls in miniskirts and bikinis—what more could a young man want? Formation was what a young man wanted, and lots of it; accordingly, that is what we got. Close formation in the Gnat was tricky until you got the hang of how sensitive the controls were. It was almost a case of manoeuvring by thought control but students adapted quickly. Next came tactical and battle formation. Flying in a package of three or four aircraft in standard close positions is unwieldy and makes it difficult to manoeuvre quickly and efficiently, but now space the aircraft out to somewhere between 50 and 300 yards, and now the formation is much more flexible and dynamic. In this way, the formation could respond rapidly to changes in direction and height; it was a follow-on from the tail-chasing we had learnt on the Jet Provost.

It was all beginning to come together as we headed slowly towards operational flying duties; to that end, we were constantly assessed for our future suitability. It would not be long before we would be streamed for the next stage of training; some of the best students would be 'creamed off' via the Central Flying School to become flying instructors, poor souls, as it would be some time before they would serve on an operational squadron. Some would go directly to the Canberra Operational Conversion Unit at RAF Bassingbourn, with the remainder going to the Tactical Weapons Unit at RAF Chivenor in Devon to fly the Hunter on the pre-fighter course.

Most of us would eventually go on to front-line operational squadrons, but there was an ominous cloud hanging over the course in that the V Force might even take one or two pilots to fly the Vulcan bomber, aiming to improve their 'gene pool'. Luckily for me, it was to be flying the Canberra in the reconnaissance role. This was not too bad at all as I certainly felt that it was a step up from the Canberra bomber. Whether the Canberra crews agreed or not was another matter entirely, but my instructor had been an ex recce 'puke' and made a good case for the job. So that is what I aimed for, and that is what I got. It would be some years before I eventually achieved my true goal and receive a posting on to fighters and the mighty Phantom; for now, I would experience the PR Canberra as the first step in my operational career.

With yet another backlog in the system, I had a six-month wait before arriving on Number 231 Operational Conversion Unit at RAF Bassingbourn in Hertfordshire. By this time, I had met a local girl on Anglesey, whose father was also in the RAF and, as we were getting serious, I asked if I could hold at RAF Valley, which was approved. I waited for my course holding with Flight Operations, giving me a chance to pick up quite a few extra trips (some solo and some dual). I logged a further forty-five hours on the Gnat, which was just great; however, not having an instructor around meant that I got into some bad habits, which were soon discovered. As a salutary lesson, I was sent for a short spell at the School of Refresher Flying at RAF Manby in Lincolnshire on the Jet Provost. This was supposed to remind me of the proper way to do things. The staff at the Jet Refresher Squadron was bemused at my arrival to 'refresh' having just flown the Gnat. They played along for a while before getting fed up with me wasting their valuable flying hours and sent me back as 'redeemed'. Was the lesson learned? For a while, I guess it was.

6

Navigator Training: RAF Finningley

David Gledhill

My earliest recollection of RAF Finningley is as I parked my car and entered the guardroom to sign onto the station for the first time. 'Acting Pilot Officer Gledhill,' I announced proudly to the orderly corporal. His amused sneer and slightly dismissive directions to the officers' mess deflated my newly ignited pride over the award of my Queen's commission.

One of my first acts after 'warning in' to the mess was to check the noticeboard. My arrival pack told me where to be and when for the arrival briefing in the morning. Perhaps a quick glance at the messages posted on the board would give me an insight into what goes on in a mess? The first notice highlighted with a huge Day-Glo arrow was headed 'Briefing for Officers Taking Redundancy'. What is this redundancy of which they speak?

In the early 1970s, like in recent years, the RAF faced a surfeit of personnel and a redundancy scheme had been initiated to balance the numbers. The fact that my officer training course had only two pilots, six navigators, and that the remaining seventy-two officers were destined for ground trades was beginning to make sense. As I was arriving, a large number of aircrew officers were leaving the service, surplus to requirements. I began to suspect that it would be no easy ride and that failure to meet the nominated standards might mean an 'early bath'.

Navigator training on No. 6 Flying Training School in the 1970s was geared towards producing a traditional navigator with plotting skills to man the V Force. By far, the majority of postings were to the Vulcan in both the plotter and radar operator roles. The RAF still operated a broad variety of types, from Buccaneer and Phantom fast jets, through Canberra reconnaissance and target towing variants, to the Hercules transport and the Shackleton airborne early warning aircraft.

I was fortunate to have a short time awaiting the start of my course, and my logbook records a number of familiarisation flights in both the Varsity and the Dominie. The crew environment is alien to most trainee aircrew, particularly given that I had started life in a twin-seat, light aircraft. The simple luxury of seeing how a crew operated together was an invaluable insight before I was thrown in at the deep end as a fully fledged student.

Mess life was less military service and more 'pseudo university'; it was a far cry from the mess on an operational station. Filton Block (as the accommodation was known) was an annexe to the main officers' mess. A gaunt 1960s structure that has since been demolished, it was a sharp contrast to the traditional 1930s building that housed the permanent staff and mirrored the type of officers' mess I was to become familiar with later in my career. We would use the public rooms in the main mess but live in Filton Block. Life during the week revolved around the academic syllabus with intensive lectures throughout the day interspersed with flying and simulators. Private study in the evening was inevitable to cope with the workload and to meet the required progress; it was rare to spend much time in the bar. Being close to my hometown of Leeds, weekends were spent away from base, arriving back late on a Sunday ready for the next round of training.

In those days, life was a little more formal and dress for training was a No. 1 Home Duty uniform now only worn for parades and special occasions. The No. 2 'woolly pully' had yet to be issued and the days of 'hairy blues', the battledress style uniform, were long gone. As we were introduced to each other during the opening session of our course, each student was asked which aircraft he hoped to fly on graduation. My choice was the Nimrod, which had recently entered service. It was to be an option that I would review over the coming months.

In his excellent book *Observers and Navigators: And Other Non-Pilot Aircrew in the RFC, RNAS and RAF*, Jeff Jefford recalled the scope of the navigator training syllabus. Aeronautical studies underpinned the whole course, and a total of sixty-two hours were spent in the classroom learning the fundamentals for that topic alone. A significant amount of time was spent on general subjects, such as combat survival, intelligence, meteorology, electronic warfare, space, weapons employment, general service training, and fitness training. Leave and administration was built in and amounted to 292 hours alone, although it seemed less generous at the time. In total, including flying time, a massive 1,728 hours were spent learning just the basics, leading to the award of a navigator's flying brevet.

Aviation medicine training prepared the students for the rigours of flight on the human body. Oxygen is a vital commodity and is sparse in unpressurised aircraft or at height. Understanding the symptoms of hypoxia, or oxygen starvation, was a new and vital piece of knowledge. Early on, we would be subjected to the barometric chamber in the aviation medicine school at RAF North Luffenham where academic lectures were underpinned by practical demonstrations in the hyperbaric chamber. The fact that thirty-six hours was devoted to the topic emphasised its importance. Crucially, the confines of a fast jet cockpit and the ergonomics of aircraft (such as the Buccaneer) meant that all torsos were not born equal. Critical anthropometric measurements were taken using cockpit rigs representing the combat aircraft. As an example, the distance from backside to knee was critical in a Buccaneer. Too long in the leg and the potential navigator risked losing a knee to the Martel instrument panel. The least understood aspect was that, seemingly, 50 per cent of my mental capacity dumped itself at the door of the aircraft and refused to return until the engines stopped. Regrettably, this phenomenon continued late into my career.

Aviation-based topics were the core of the syllabus and included aircraft performance, aircraft systems, airmanship, compasses, navigation systems, and radio and radar. Applied techniques were another significant section, including astronavigation techniques and dead reckoning navigation. The flight briefings and airborne time were naturally the bulk of the effort and amounted to an enormous 148 hours in the air, split roughly equally between the Varsity and the Dominie but with only twelve hours on the Jet Provost, arguably the most important phase for a potential fast jet navigator.

The first phase of training was conducted on the Varsity, a twin-engined trainer procured to replace the Wellington. This fact alone puts the nature of navigator training in the '70s in context. Adapted from the Valetta transport, the tail wheel was replaced with a nose wheel and therein lay the first problem. Affectionately known as 'the flying pig', the nickname was apt and crewing-in was an experience never forgotten. The massive pole positioned under the rear fuselage was not only for cosmetic purposes but acted as a solution to a basic issue. The pilots boarded first to ensure that a large weight was positioned at the front extremity of the aircraft; I will say no more. The two student navigators and the instructor followed in turn, taking up their stations close to the main spar and the centre of gravity. Failure to adopt the strict routine would result in an ungainly descent of the tail towards the tarmac. As the engines fired up, the noise was staggering and the lightweight 'G-type helmets' worn by the crew were scant protection from the cacophony. The Shackleton was often described as 'a hundred thousand rivets flying in close formation' but the Varsity ran a very close second.

The Varsity really was a throwback to a bygone era. The pilot's cockpit was dominated by a pair of leather armchairs and acres of glass, giving an excellent view of the outside world. The flight instrument panel was traditional in design, grouped around the usual six instruments. A modern dial, delivered in glorious technicolour, provided the pilot with radio navigation information from the TACAN system. It was apparent that the gentlemen up front did not entirely trust the student navigators down the back; and understandably so. At Finningley, the aircraft was operated by a single pilot with an air electronics operator acting as pilot's assistant. The engine instruments were grouped in the centre with throttles and pitch controls on the centre console. The relatively modern IFF box looked oddly out of place.

Immediately behind the cockpit was the signaller's station, where the radios might have been transferred from the cockpit of a Lancaster. An archaic navigation system known as Consol was often pressed into use to provide a position line for a 'fix'. By listening to a series of dots and dashes, the navigator could translate this into a line on a chart; GPS this was not. Below the cockpit was a bomb bay fitted out as an observation area. Lying flat on the stomach and peering forward through a panoramic window, the navigator could use visual navigation techniques to find his way around. Regrettably, this was an option not offered to the student during the Varsity phase, confined instead to the rear cabin, facing backwards, in the dark. An early impression was forming.

The main spar dominated the rear compartment running, transversely, across the space. Fitted with a bank of electrics controls, it was a constant impediment to moving around the cabin. The navigators' stations were towards the rear and faced aft with the 'First Nav' closest to the window and the 'Second Nav' inboard. The 'Screen Nav' did not have a dedicated station, choosing instead to roam around the fuselage with an all-seeing eye. The equipment was a mix of eras. Centrally mounted was a small scope known as 'Gee'. Designed during the Second World War, 'Gee' was a radio navigation system that measured the time delay between two radio signals to produce a fix, with quite amazing accuracy. By the '70s, it was obsolete with the number of ground stations dwindling. The main panel was dominated by the two position indicators. The first was an air position indicator and took the airspeed, heading, and time to compute a position in the air. The second, the ground position indicator inherited from the V Force, worked in tandem with the onboard Doppler system. By computing the heading, speed, and drift, dials read out the latitude and longitude of the aircraft dynamically.

Other more modern navigation aids were available. The ADF (automatic direction-finding) gave a single bearing to a radio beacon after carefully tuning in the frequency. The TACAN (tactical air navigation system) was under the control of the pilot and gave a precise fix by giving a range and bearing from a beacon on the ground. Given that this information would allow a student navigator to actually know where he was, the two elements were never on offer simultaneously. The student could ask for either but never both at the same time. Many deception techniques were tried to elicit both vital parameters but never successfully. Where TACAN was not fitted, twin VORs achieved the same capability by providing bisecting radials on an instrument. Some but not all airframes were fitted with the Decca radio navigation system, but this would not be used by the students until the advanced phase on the Dominie. We would occasionally watch the screen navigator plot his position using the rapidly gyrating dials, but it would be a mystery for some time yet.

The sextant protruded through the roof of the cabin and was an act of vengeance on a 'baby' navigator. Used by V Force crews on long 'blue water' oceanic legs, the sextant could be used during daytime to 'shoot' the Sun. A measurement was taken to determine the angle between the astronomical object—in this case, the sun and the horizon. After plotting the position of the Sun in the heavens using a series of calculations and information from *The Air Almanac*, the student navigator ventured towards the dreaded object—the sextant—having warned the pilot that 'astro' was in the offing. Most Varsities still had an astrodome with the sextant mounted in a transparent cupola. Others, and certainly the Dominie, had a more modern 'through the roof' fit and by manipulating a heavy handle, the periscope was pushed into the airflow. The pre-calculated settings were applied to the instrument and with a long countdown, a series of sun shots were taken over a one-minute period, during which the pilot held a precise heading. Any deviation induced more errors over the inevitable errors the technique produced. Once measured, the navigator could calculate the latitude and taking the result back to the plotting table, the figure could be translated into a position line on the chart. A result somewhere in the Northern Hemisphere was cause for celebration. One student realised that should he wish to plot a perfect astro position line, perhaps he should extend the periscope into the airflow. His navigation career ended abruptly, with his morals called into question.

A little-used instrument was the drift sight, another throwback to former times. Located on the port side close to the door, the sight was a small telescope that extended vertically downwards through the fuselage. Evenly spaced parallel lines were projected on to the background image and a grid was rotated until objects on the ground or the wave tops moved parallel to the lines. The measured angle indicated the drift angle due to the wind velocity and could be used to calculate the ground speed.

Without a doubt, the most bizarre navigation aid was known as Consol; the concept stemmed from a wartime navigation system developed by the Germans known as 'Knickebein'. A Consol station was tuned-in on the huge radio at the signaller's station, thankfully by the pilot's assistant, and after hearing the beacon's call sign, a number of dashes merged into a continuous tone switching to a series of dots. By counting the number of dashes before the tone, the bearing from the beacon could be calculated. The Consol chart was marked with circles radiating from the beacon and numbered with the number of dots or dashes that would be heard before the continuous tone. The time taken to interpret the dots and dashes, the potential inaccuracies, and the time to locate the line on the chart made it the most unwieldy technique and it was feared almost as much as astronavigation. Navigating using traditional means was no mean feat.

One of the earliest tasks on the ground is to learn the language of aviation. When aircrew get together, whether in a flying environment or over a beer, talk rapidly turns to flying and an innocent bystander might easily think that the conversation is being held in a foreign tongue. Acronyms and abbreviations abound which had their genesis in earlier times. The 'Q' code originated during the Second World War and allowed aviators and controllers to pass simple instructions using three letter codes. For example, QSY meant change frequency. Some of these codes still exist in a modern flying environment. The term QNH still means the altimeter setting that will register a height above mean sea level. Others have passed into legend, such as QDM, which was the old radio steering facility that gave a bearing towards the home airfield. This has long been replaced by GPS and inertial navigation systems that can be bought for a few hundred pounds.

A Varsity T Mark 1 at RAF Finningley 'At Home Day' in 1969.

The cockpit of the Varsity.

The navigator station in the Varsity.

A navigator student wearing a 'G' helmet at the second navigator's station in a Varsity. (*Jeff Jefford*)

The phonetic alphabet has become more familiar in recent years, but it was an essential tool in the air. Beginning at 'A' for alpha and ending at 'Z' for zulu, the words would become the basis of all discussions over the radio. Odd conversations ensued as students struggled to assimilate the language. Ironically, the fidelity of a modern digital radio has, probably, reduced the need for such precise annunciation.

Meteorology is not only an academic skill in understanding the principles of weather patterns, high- and low-pressure systems and frontal patterns but it also had its own language. Produced hourly by the resident met forecaster, a METAR (meteorological actual report), was a coded message that broke down each aspect of the weather situation to allow aircrew and supervisors to analyse the precise details of visibility and cloud base to allow aircraft to operate safely. A METAR looked something like: 'METAR EGXC 051853ZMar 04011KT 300 FZFG BKN003, 1017, 1019, Red/Red'. This translated as the actual met report for Coningsby on 5 March at 6.35 p.m. GMT is wind speed 040 at 11 knots, visibility 300 metres in freezing fog, a broken cloud base at 300 feet (if the met man could see through the fog) with a QFE of 1,017 millibars and a QNH of 1,019 millibars, the colour state is red forecast red.

In earlier years, the cloud base was measured in oktas or eighths, but the code changed over the years to make it more intelligible by introducing terms such as BKN or broken, but the basis remains. The colour state in itself was a code giving colours from red to blue broken down by increasing values for visibility and cloud base.

I had a slight advantage over my peers in the first few weeks, having had a brief flying course as I qualified for my private pilot's licence. That slender advantage was rapidly eroded as the complexity of the new language was passed on by seemingly gleeful instructors.

Even nowadays, one of the strangest requirements is to be able to read Morse code, the series of dots and dashes that form an alphabet. Most of us cope easily with that famous signal of distress—'SOS', which translates as dot-dot-dot, dash-dash-dash, dot-dot-dot. At that point, it becomes much harder. Navigation beacons transmit their identification codes in Morse and it is a wise aviator that identifies his navigation beacon before relying on the information. Careers have been made by homing on to the wrong one. Although I became quite adept at listening to and understanding the unintelligible strings during my training course, I have to admit that I carried a decoder on my kneeboard should I ever decide to identify a TACAN beacon in the air.

With the basics of the language mastered, we moved on to the dialects. An instrument approach into an airfield was a GCA (ground-controlled approach) controlled by an 'air trafficker' (air traffic control officer) using a PAR (precision approach radar). A pilot may elect to control his own approach following the localiser, down the glide path using the ILS (instrument landing system) down to his DH (decision height) where he might land or overshoot into the circuit (the visual traffic pattern). Such terms became commonplace but the learning curve was steep.

The most fundamental part of training was to learn traditional chart-based navigation techniques that worked on a principle known as the triangle of velocities. An aircraft flies across the ground along a track but is diverted from that track by the wind. The wind blows from a certain direction and at a certain speed so the distance an aircraft is diverted depends on the wind velocity. To compensate, a pilot flies a heading which ensures the aircraft follows the track. Simple. The air position is the point the aircraft will reach in still air. The ground position is the point to which it is blown by the wind. If the wind velocity is accurate, the ground position is correct but, if not, the two positions diverge. The role of the navigator plotter was always to know the correct ground position yet many things conspired against him.

The fundamental fixing technique was known as a three-position line fix, but, unlike Keebs in his JP cockpit with his DME, the navigator community made it much harder by simulating austere conditions. Each of the instruments provided a single line of bearing and the ideal solution was to choose three sources, which would bisect each other roughly 120 degrees apart. Two parallel lines were useless as they did not cross and could not determine a position on the ground. Once measured, the lines were plotted on a navigation chart but because it was impossible to measure them simultaneously; each line was then transferred forward on a chart to a point a few minutes ahead of the aircraft using the actual ground speed. In an ideal world, all three lines would intercept precisely giving a position on the ground. Invariably, there were errors that meant the aircraft's position was within the sector marked by the three lines known as a 'cocked hat'. Using geometric techniques, a 'most probable position' (MPP) was calculated, allowing the ground position indicator to be updated. The new information was recorded on the navigation chart using a protractor, dividers, a parallel ruler, and a pencil. Each annotation was carefully marked on the chart and recorded in the flight log. At this point, the whole fixing cycle began again.

The training course began with the inevitable ground school phase, which was a feature of any RAF flying course and was liberally punctuated with academic subjects on non-flying days. The flying syllabus was only ten sorties long, beginning with Exercise V1, the familiarisation sortie. Starting flying on 25 July 1974, my first sortie was as first navigator, flown in WF372, which survives to this day at Brooklands Aviation Museum. Paired with another student navigator, we took turns in the primary and secondary seats with the second sortie following immediately. Two weeks of academics and simulators ensued before the tempo increased with the next events following in short order, moving to two flying events each week, firstly as first navigator and then repeating the same sortie profile as second navigator. The first five sorties taught the basic principles of navigating and fixing one's position using the variety of aids available. By Exercise V6, night flying was introduced, although I was beginning to appreciate that in the rear cabin of a Varsity, night and day were remarkably similar and I had little time to look out of a window.

Each sortie was roughly four hours long and followed a similar cycle. Planned the previous evening, a plotting chart was crafted using the nominated route and the shell of the sortie was entered on to the pre-prepared flight planning log. Only the last-minute aspects were left to the morning briefing including the domestics such as callsigns, our place in the 'stream', diversions, and the weather. The flight plan winds were taken from the weather briefing for the route and headings were calculated, completing the plan. The real wind would make that plan obsolete. There were a number of standard routes that the 'stream' of Varsities followed and the pilots could fly them, in all likelihood, in their sleep. The student's route brief, undoubtedly, would not impart any startling revelations.

Changing into flying suits and collecting survival gear was the last event after the customary pre-flight meal; the norm on a V Force or transport squadron but an unheard-of luxury on the fast-jet equivalent where a biscuit was an extravagance. Again, unlike a fast jet squadron, a crew coach ferried us from the ops complex to the aircraft depositing us, conveniently, at the door of the waiting Varsity. The routine was not too far distant from that experienced by wartime bomber crews although the 'flak' over Cornwall was, thankfully, absent.

Start-up, taxi out, and take-off were carefully timed, particularly as any astro calculations were based on an expected position and time around the route. On a real transatlantic trip, V Force navigators would have time to calculate fixes in the air. For the student navigator, the fixing cycle was so intense that pre-planning was vital. Unexpected delays caused no end of consternation to a student who had planned his sortie to match the precise details of his route and a replan was a sight to behold. The whole course flew the same event on the same day so a stream of up to six Varsities taxied out and followed the route at ten-minute intervals. On climb out, the student was allowed the luxury of homing to a radio beacon so at least at the start of the sortie, he would know his precise position. The NDB at Langar became a friend. Once on the first leg, the fixing cycle began immediately with, normally, two cycles per leg if memory serves me. There was no let-up in the tempo and after the first position lines had been gathered, a predicted ground position was calculated and a 'most probable position' determined. This was no reflection on the skill of the 'baby' navigator, rather the appropriate term for the projected position. At that point, a new wind velocity was calculated and a revised heading to the next turning point was passed to 'Biggles' and 'Algy' in the front, hopefully bringing the Varsity back to its planned track.

The most important check of the sortie was the 'top of descent fix', which determined how easy the return to base might be. A precise fix led to an orderly descent and arrival. With controlled airspace in close proximity, mistakes could be more than embarrassing and the supervising instructors paid close attention at that stage for fear of an ATC violation. Of course, in the front cockpit, the pilot had the luxury of following a VOR or a TACAN radial towards Finningley but was sworn to secrecy by the screen navigator.

After landing, the short ride in the crew bus was a positive luxury, allowing the student navigator to check his charts, shortly before it was revealed at the debrief, where the aircraft had actually flown.

The navigation simulator that prepared students for each event was a rudimentary affair with the training stations being based on a generic navigator's station rather than either of the main training types in service at Finningley at the time. As with most of the prevailing technology, what would run on a small desktop computer today demanded numerous banks of electronics in large cabinets. It was hardly a simulator in the true sense that today's aircrew would recognise but more a procedures trainer; however, it did allow the profile to be practised on the ground ahead of the flying event. The instructional cubicles were enclosed and solitary and the only link with the outside world was via the headset. Although the performance of both the Varsity and the Dominie could be represented quite well, the isolated environment was unrealistic and did not represent the world in the back of a Varsity at all, particularly in simulating the noise levels. In keeping with normal RAF training routines, each flying mission was preceded by the same exercise in the simulator, allowing the event to be rehearsed in the relative calm of a shirt-sleeve environment. Unlike the real event, invariably the simulator would suffer an airborne emergency requiring a diversion *en route*, although as training progressed, the student was expected to be able to cope with the demands of in-flight emergencies and to position the aircraft for a safe return to *terra firma*.

As the end of the phase approached, training gave way to assessment. Exercise V9 was a consolidation sortie leading to the final check ride, the dreaded Exercise V10, in which everything could, and would, go wrong. This was not only the end of phase check ride but an interim progress check to see how our plotting skills had developed. The use of navigation aids had been progressively restricted simulating navigation in areas less well served with radio aids. Aircraft emergencies were introduced requiring diversions from track simulating a diversion to an *en route* airfield. These drills were terminated before the descent and the pressure cooker atmosphere returned as the fixing cycle, now horribly compromised by being out of position and off track, had to be replanned. The infamous check ride, V10, had an almost mythical reputation among the students. The challenges were more demanding, the equipment failures more punishing, and, significantly, the marking schedule was more rigorous, making a pass mark harder to achieve.

Suffice to say that young Gledhill had not demonstrated adequate skills to convince the course mentor that moving to the next stage was warranted. Happily, there must have been a hint of promise because a re-course to the following course was offered. The setback was a shock but after a short period of revision in the simulator and a refly of exercises V9 and V10, something clicked, the appropriate standards were met and a temporary respite beckoned.

As my former course colleagues progressed to the next stage, there was another necessary evil to endure known as Exercise Moor Trek, which would introduce the concept of combat survival techniques. This was part of the general service training syllabus and focused on teaching the skills needed to survive in the event of an ejection or a crash behind enemy lines.

The students piled into a fleet of Land Rovers and decamped to the wilds of the Peak District, the staff opting for the luxury of a local hostelry while the students 'opted' for life under canvas.

The first day began with learning basic survival skills. The assumption was that we, as survivors, had ejected and had landed with the contents of a survival pack available to us. As the parachute would already have served its basic purpose, the technique of converting the individual gores from which it was constructed, into a para-tepee became fundamental to survival. Shelter was the first basic tenet and the ability to build a simple lean-to shelter, under which to sit out the first hours following an ejection, was a vital lesson.

The time immediately following ejection into hostile territory with the associated risk of capture, prompted the second element of training, namely evasion. A jet crashing to earth is never subtle and the first few hours, during which time enemy patrols would be dispatched to the area to find the survivor, was critical. Immediately firing up one's personal locator beacon and transmitting an emergency signal, as would be the norm in the North Sea, might be ill-advised and lead to capture. After a quick exit from the immediate area, the priority would be survival from the elements and a rudimentary structure of sticks, tied together with parachute cord, was the basis of a temporary respite. Once the framework was fixed to a suitable tree or wall, gores of parachute material stretched across the frame and tied to the framework provided shelter from adverse weather. Awaiting friendly search and rescue forces, hopefully dispatched quickly, the survivor would need to avoid the attention of hostile troops and wait out until help arrived. Understanding the art of concealment during this time might be the difference between escape or capture.

My group was deposited in a small wood and given thirty minutes to build an evasion shelter or to find a hiding place, after which time the directing staff would seek us out. My new colleagues found thick bushes and other suitable places to hide and one even climbed a tree, disappearing into the upper branches out of sight. After a brief search, I fell across a gem—a low, dry stone wall that had toppled over the years, extended from below a deep thicket. Pulling the stones away, I found a natural hollow and, by rearranging the stones into an improvised wall, the cavity was more than enough to conceal my slim frame. A carpet of branches spaced across the stones formed an impenetrable roof and, climbing inside, I covered myself from view and waited.

Sometime later, the noise of the staff crashing through the trees was punctuated by shouting and the beating of the bushes as each member of the team was systematically apprehended. The noise of them being returned to the Land Rovers ended their freedom.

The allotted hour for the exercise extended to two and I may have been guilty of nodding off in my comfortable burrow. The racket from my pursuers had diminished following the sounds of Land Rovers being driven down a track and disappearing into the distance. I was becoming slightly anxious but still distrustful, suspecting a ruse to flush me out from my hiding place. Time passed and the sound of returning engines came as something of a relief as the isolation was becoming disturbing. This might well have been a realistic symptom of a real escape and was a lesson well learned.

Ordered out of hiding by a disgruntled staff leader was clearly not a ruse and I emerged from my hidey hole, stiff but pleasantly satisfied. The subsequent discussion seemed perplexing. Being a lowly student, I was clearly in the wrong despite my demonstrable skills and, although I had just proved the ability to survive, the inference was that I had somehow done wrong. I steeled myself in the knowledge that I had achieved an unusual success, albeit at the expense of a few egos. It appeared that a head count before the Land Rovers departed had been botched and that my absence had only been noted sometime later. Being a new member on the course, recently re-coursed, I was not yet well-known even to my new colleagues so my absence had not been missed. It appeared I had work to do on making my presence felt.

Learning to forage and to make the best use of available food was another fundamental skill but the food source came as something of a challenge. A live chicken was a setback for a city boy but, if we were to eat, it had to be dispatched with all due haste. One of our numbers professed to have butchering skills from his former life but his attempts to wring the hapless bird's neck and remove its head with an aircrew survival knife proved less than effective. While such acts occur in factories around the country on a daily basis, when the object of attention is the only source of food and is the difference between a full stomach or starvation, its destiny becomes personal. As the decapitated bird was laid out ready to be butchered, it took off at 10 knots through the surrounding trees closely followed by a dismayed band of 'survivors'. Thankfully, its escape was short-lived and it was dispatched properly before being taken back to the camp. A 'headless chicken' became an image that would stay with me for a long time.

I was told later that the chicken had really met a peaceful end and that its gyrations had been a natural reaction, although 'Mike the Headless Chicken' was a bird that survived for eighteen months in Utah after a farmer's axe removed the bulk of its head but missed the jugular vein, leaving one ear and most of the brain stem intact. Our own bird's determined effort to escape and evade might have led to a very different outcome the following day had we begun the exercise on empty stomachs.

The directing staff had secured the use of a cottage as overnight accommodation, located just a short distance away from our makeshift camp. The sounds of alcohol-induced camaraderie and the smells of a tasty evening meal were not lost on the 'survivors'. With the chicken dispatched to meet its maker, a cooking pot seemed like an essential requirement if the meal was to be edible rather than unappetising. A raiding party was dispatched on a reconnaissance and, finding the rubbish bins behind the cottage, retrieved not only a discarded jumbo-sized can that had formerly contained baked beans but the remnants of a few vegetables joined the chicken in the pot. Back at the tented camp, the carefully plucked and jointed chicken fitted neatly in the improvised pot and produced the most appetising meal that I had ever eaten. Even so, I was learning that survival could be a trial.

The climax of the week was the escape and evasion exercise. After a thorough search to ensure that stray Mars bars had not been secreted judiciously around the person, groups were released from a start point with interim objectives and a final rendezvous. Time was of the essence, meaning that some compromise was needed if the gate times were to be met leading to more risk. Patrols of 'enemy' infantry were tasked to look for the escapees and to apprehend them and return them to an earlier checkpoint. Unlike operational escape and evasion courses, happily, there was no interrogation if caught. Armed with only a map and compass, it was a stiff test, both physically and mentally demanding. Add to that the fact that the previous day's meal was a long time ago, the search parties were extremely professional and aggressive and the task took on a very realistic air.

Over the years, many efforts to avoid the worst effects of a survival situation had been made. The broad exercise area was a poorly guarded secret, although the specifics of where the individual exercise was to be held for each 'Moor Trek' was a closely guarded fact and the venues were varied. Students sought to ameliorate the effects of hunger in many ways. One enterprising officer had visited the area in advance and secreted a cache of food to make life more tenable. Another officer hid cash in a secret hiding place and invited his team to drop in at the pub during the evasion phase. This ruse had evidently been tried before as the landlord had been warned not to serve bedraggled officers wearing soggy flying kit. Their initiative failed and their thirst went unquenched.

My lasting memory of the exercise is returning to the officers' mess at Finningley for a long soak in the bath and the first proper meal of the week, although why I chose a ploughman's meal rather than a heaped plate of hot food is an eternal mystery.

Exercise V10 had been a salutary lesson that there would be no free ride on an RAF training course and that standards were high. Even so, it may be evident that, so far, the focus of navigator training was of limited value to an embryonic Phantom navigator, albeit at this stage none of us had any inkling of which type would feature in our operational futures. My first taste of failure had come as a surprise and I questioned whether life in the back of a large aircraft, pointing backwards in the dark, was where I wanted to be. It was a huge relief that life on the airfield waterfront on the Jet Provost Squadron was to be a breath of fresh air. I soon met my instructor, an aged gentleman called Vin with a massive handlebar moustache, to whom I immediately warmed.

'Which aircraft do you want to fly?'

'Nimrod, Sir'.

'Wrong answer,' he replied, repeating the question.

'Well,' I responded, hesitating, recognising the twinkle in the eye. 'Fast jets,' I replied.

'Come with me,' he said; there began my metamorphosis.

As the Varsity phase had reflected life and operations on a Vulcan squadron, the Jet Provost phase was designed to reflect life on a fast jet squadron. Dress of the day was a flying suit and life revolved around the squadron. Planning was done on the day, flying the sortie immediately. Gone were the navigation logs replaced by annotations on the map and using a stopwatch in the jet. This was more like it.

It was New Year in 1975 when I climbed into a Jet Provost T4, XP556, which also still survives today at the RAF Cranwell Heritage Museum. My pilot, a relative youngster took me airborne for the first familiarisation and I felt immediately at home, if not a little green around the gills. Sadly, he was killed a few years later when his JP hit the water in a reservoir during a low-flying exercise.

As a navigator student, I would occupy the left-hand seat and be responsible for operating the radio and avionics kit, avionics being a relative term. More importantly, it was the first time I had strapped into a Martin-Baker ejection seat. Designated a 0/90 seat, this meant that you could eject on the ground, namely zero feet, but only when the aircraft had picked up flying speed and was travelling at over 90 knots. Designed as a pilot trainer, there were dual controls with a throttle box in the centre and on the left-hand console. Painted the obligatory black, the instrument panel was of a conventional layout, positioned in front of the pilot in the right-hand seat. Directly in front of me was remarkably uncluttered and dominated by the radio box. It was equipped with simple radio navigation aids that would form part of the syllabus to come. Most importantly, the broad windscreen and slightly bubbled canopy allowed a good view both ahead and around the jet, albeit the low mounted wings obscured the downwards view. This I would find out would not be an issue because while the Varsity had droned along in straight lines, with the experienced pilots on the JP Squadron, the wings were often exceptionally dynamic.

The syllabus was a scant twelve sorties that was designed to impart the skills needed to fly and fight below the radar. Low level is a hostile environment. Close to the ground, thinking time is limited and mistakes are harshly punished. Flying aloft, ground features are easily interpreted and the horizon is a long way distant. At 250 feet, the trees are close and the horizon even closer, making it hard to define your position. One of the early skills is to use features with 'vertical extent', which will stand out, even when flying in the weeds. When flying at 240 knots, the aircraft will cover 4 miles every minute, so simple mental arithmetic ensures that the progress down the carefully plotted track can be monitored. A planned heading, based on the expected wind, can be adjusted once the actual wind velocity has been calculated, normally by finding out that the actual position over the ground is different from the one you had expected. By now, I was appreciating that navigation is the art of working out why you are, not where you hoped you would be. Flown in the local low-flying areas known as Areas 6, 8, and 11, the basic concepts of low-level navigation were refined. Skills such as visual fixing, track adjustment, and timing techniques would become ingrained but it was here that the first lessons were taught. It was also the grounding in fuel management and awareness. Careful fuel calculations were made before ever getting airborne. Constant monitoring, including a continual awareness of how much fuel was needed to get home, became second nature. Airmanship, knowing what your pilot was doing and why, and being aware of the aircraft in its environment was important and anticipation was critical. Once behind the jet, catching up was hard.

By sortie nine, we had progressed to flying as a formation with the impressive call sign 'Fantan' and had ventured further afield to the Lake District, which was known as Area 17. This began to introduce the concept of a fighting pair, which would be the baseline for all my future flying. A wingman is vital in combat in order to provide mutual support against potential threats. For a bomber squadron, it also allows force to be massed to ensure the maximum weapons load is delivered to a target in the shortest time. For a fighter squadron, the fighting pair is the basic element. The JP may have bimbled along at slow speeds but it was plenty fast enough for me at that time, and I was rapidly adapting to new tactical concepts.

The culmination of the phase was to plan a landaway to RAF Leuchars in Scotland and it was here I was to see the jet that I was destined to fly. Home to the Lightnings of No. 23 Squadron, it also housed the Phantoms of the RAF's No. 43 (Fighter) Squadron and those of 892 Naval Air Squadron. Flying northwards through Yorkshire and Northumbria, the brief visit was inspirational. Returning via the NATO low-level route that started at the famous Bell Rock Light and threaded its way through Northumbria, past Leeds Bradford Airport where my love of aviation had been born and back into South Yorkshire, we landed back at Finningley. The progress had been remarkable and rapid. By 24 January, the short introduction to fast jet flying was over but I had earned the coveted fast jet recommendation and was newly motivated. I had learned how to navigate at low level but, as yet, had still not begun to understand the skills I would need as an air defence navigator. Those would begin to be taught when I next encountered the JP Squadron.

Returning to the Navigation School Headquarters, I felt an air of gloom reassert itself but after an introduction to the syllabus, I was to be pleasantly surprised.

The Dominie was a much more pleasant working environment and I was delighted to find that my nominated instructor had previously flown Phantoms in the ground attack role. A truly nice man, Pete Simpson became my inspiration and I was fortunate enough to cross paths at many times in the future. It was a good omen.

The Dominie entered RAF service in 1965 and was the backbone of the advanced training squadron. Based on the Hawker Siddeley 125 twin-jet business aircraft, it offered cruising speeds and heights more representative of operational bombers and transport aircraft as well as an endurance of approximately three hours, although typical training sorties were about two hours long. Even at a low level, it was able to fly at higher speeds but a typical sortie was much shorter due to the increased fuel burn at lower altitudes.

Not only did it provide the platform to train new navigators but also other rear crew including engineers, air electronics operators and loadmasters, although not on the same sortie. Entering through a broad front door, the cockpit housed a single pilot and a pilot's assistant, normally an air electronics operator, who acted as co-pilot. The two navigator students were supervised by a 'screen' navigator, one of the instructors from the flying training school. I remember Pete commenting that he still could not see how five people could fit in such a small aircraft. The Dominie seemed quite large to me at that time, but when I was finally acquainted with the 'Mighty Phantom', I took his point.

The navigation suite was a major upgrade from the austere suite fitted to the Varsity. The basic configuration in the 1970s was still for the two navigators to sit side by side facing backwards. The navigators' station was dominated by the ground position indicator in front of the first navigator. The second navigator controlled the ADF with other systems sitting between. The most prominent was the small display and controls for the EKCO 190 'cloud and clonk' radar, which could be used to home to a feature on the ground or to take a precise fix from a significant geographical point. A new-fangled radio navigation aid known as Decca, after its manufacturer, allowed the precise location to be plotted by taking three readings from a series of dials and plotting them on a Decca chart. Coupled with a VOR/DME radio system, the Dominie was a quantum leap.

Much later, the aircraft underwent an upgrade programme with the installation of new avionics systems and a redesigned cabin configuration. A new ground-mapping radar replaced the ubiquitous EKCO 190 and was integrated with a more modern avionics suite, which used multicolour displays and a main computer. Such precision was an unheard-of luxury during the Cold War. The Dominie served in the training role until 2011, when it finally retired after forty-six years of service.

The standard high-level training routes were shaped like an elongated triangle and flown around Flight Level 350, or 35,000 feet. After a climb out to the Langar radio beacon, the route went initially eastwards out to the 1-degree east line of longitude before turning westerly and heading across the crowded airspace of southern England, across the West Country, and into the Southwest Approaches. Turning back easterly, the route headed for Flamborough Head, climbing higher as the fuel burned off, before making a descent back into Finningley.

The advanced navigation phase began with the obligatory familiarisation to become used to the new navigation systems. Quickly, we were expected to work with limited systems as equipment was deliberately failed. By Exercise 5, we were introduced to using the EKCO 190 to navigate at a high level. Using the radar as a fixing aid, life became much more realistic and relevant. Two intermediate sorties also introduced the totally mind-blowing concept of navigating at night using the stars, or 'night astro'.

It was in the Dominie that the influence of the V Force was most marked. The concept of first navigator and second navigator, which pervaded the training, was based on the roles in the Vulcan and Victor. Modern navigation techniques using GPS systems and inertial navigation systems simply did not exist at that time and the thought of a constellation of satellites guiding navigators around the skies was alien in more ways than one. A more fundamental constellation provided the means by which position could fixed—namely, the stars in the heavens. A

A Dominie T Mark 1, XS709.

A navigator student 'shoots' Astro in a Dominie. (*Jeff Jefford*)

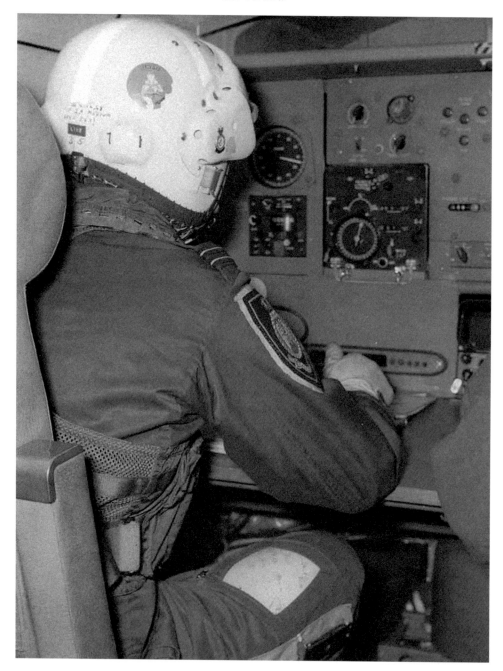

A navigator student wearing a Mark 2 bonedome at the second navigator's station in a Dominie. The ground position indicator and the ADF gauge and control panel can be seen in the background. (*Jeff Jefford*)

traditionally trained air navigator would be as familiar with the stars that made up the constellation of Cassiopeia as he would be with how a VOR beacon generated its radio signal.

This was the way a Vulcan crew would expect to fly a long-range transcontinental profile outside the range of radio navigation aids. The navigator plotter would shoot astro lines using the Sun and the stars, supplemented when available by fixes taken from prominent or sometimes obscure features on the ground. In the middle of the Atlantic Ocean, the position of the aircraft might be less precisely plotted with the course only being refined once known features on the coast came into range and the navigator radar was able to plot a radar fix to refine the accuracy. In the Dominie, this teamwork was replicated by the first navigator, plotting the progress using position lines and the second navigator using the EKCO 190 radar to provide radar fixes. It said volumes that the Vulcan was retrofitted with an inertial navigation system in order to allow the crew to navigate accurately across the South Atlantic Ocean when the aircraft went to war during the Falklands conflict.

'Night Astro' was a term that generated fear in the mind of a student navigator. On this sortie, the sole means of navigating was to use three position line fixes plotted from a series of position lines captured through the sextant. The cycle began back in the comfort of the student's room in Filton Block. First, the track was marked on the plotting chart, which would be used on the night and the flight planning log compiled to decide the headings, heights, and speeds to fly. A fuel plan would be carefully worked out. Most importantly, the planned take-off time, along with the forecast winds, would determine where the aircraft would expect to be at any moment around the route. This would be the basis of the planned flight. Next, the navigator would select certain stars around the route, which would give bisecting position lines when measured in the air using the sextant.

The principles of celestial navigation were established by famous navigators in times gone by. To work out the position of a star, the angular difference of the body from the celestial equator to the hour circle passing through the star is calculated. This gives the 'hour angle', which can be measured either from either the Greenwich Meridian or the local meridian. The terms sidereal hour angle and local hour angle became tools of the trade. When paired with the declination of the body, a precise location can be calculated using data from *The Air Almanac*. Once these readings were set on to the sextant, the navigator would peer through the instrument and, if all had gone well, a star would appear in the centre of the scope. If not, a blank patch of sky would result in generating a feeling just shy of panic. By collecting three position lines from different stars and predicting forward to a future point in time and space, the navigator would produce the 'cocked hat', which would determine his position on the ground.

Celestial navigation was an imprecise art and even under ideal conditions, the size of the cocked hat could be huge leaving a broad variation on the 'most probable position'. Surprisingly, the record for the most wayward route was not held by an *ab initio* crew during my time at No. 6 Flying Training School.

The accolade went to a crew on a refresher course, which comprised of aircrew returning to operational roles after ground appointments. Setting off on their night astro refamiliarisation, their calculations left a little to be desired. Coupled with unexpected winds, rather than track to their planned turning point somewhere off the Scilly Isles, the crew drifted well to the south and into French airspace. Myth and legend have it that the pilot and his trusty assistant spent a good deal of time negotiating handoffs to the French air traffic control agency rather than receiving the usual service from London Military. Naturally, nothing more was said of the incident, (allegedly), but sales of French wine topped Yorkshire ale in the mess bar for a number of nights.

Thankfully, towards the end of the homeward leg, the navigators were allowed to use more precise fixing aids to home in on the top of descent point with somewhat more confidence. Without this concession, descent into Finningley would have been less than organised.

The use of advanced navigation techniques known as grid navigation was one of the penultimate exercises and proved to be one of the most bizarre concepts invented and utterly alien to an embryonic navigator. The map maker cannot represent the globe, which is a sphere, on a flat surface without distortion, so it is formed using a process known as chart projection. Depending on the type of projection, a different type of map is produced. Maps and plotting charts fall into two major categories known as Mercator charts or gnomonic map projections. The latter displays great circles as straight lines, these being the shortest route between two points on the earth's surface. The most common of these had the grand title of a Lambert conical orthomorphic projection. Most maps in use are Mercator projections, which show rhumb lines as straight lines. This is an imaginary line on the Earth's surface that cuts all meridians at the same angle and, therefore, shows as a straight line on the map. This is by far the easiest route for an air navigator to follow using a magnetic compass. Although a great circle is the shortest path, it is difficult to navigate because the bearing changes constantly. It was crucial for the navigator to know which chart he was using, as a great circle route—and being the shortest route, normally, it was the preferred route—might be a straight line or a curved line depending on the map type.

The system worked reasonably well at the lower latitudes from the equator up to around 70 degrees north or just inside the Arctic Circle. As the globe merged to the single point at the North Pole, the lines of longitude converged and the traditional projections ceased to work. Much smarter navigators than me determined that it was possible to expand the area close to the North Pole back out into a square grid using a conical projection and then to provide a means by which a heading could be flown. Using a magnetic compass referenced to the magnetic north pole, it was possible to fly a heading that was not really a proper heading at all. This technique was known as 'grid navigation' and explains why all sensible navigators avoided the polar regions at all costs. Happily, my forays north, even on QRA missions in the Iceland–Faroes Gap, stopped at about 67 degrees north just inside the Arctic Circle. The 'Blue Nose' certificate I awarded to my crew—well my pilot—during a deployment to Iceland was purchased quietly in the American Base Exchange at Keflavik and records the epic voyage.

The words on the certificate may have been a little flowery but, thankfully, my forays south did not extend beyond the waters just south of the Falkland Islands, a balmy 55 degrees south, and well clear of any magnetic anomalies from the south pole. Nevertheless, it is safe to say that grid navigation was a truly scary concept.

A series of exercises known as Dominie Low Radar (DLR) saw the radar once again used as a navigation aid. Returning to low level, a further two exercises introduced us to navigating along a low-level corridor that passed through the heart of the country but this time using the radar to steer us. For the first time, the training was more operationally focused and used techniques that were similar to those adopted by the V Force and perhaps the Buccaneer Force. The exercise introduced CMRP (continuous map radar prediction) techniques. At that time, a Vulcan crew would expect to fly a pre-planned route to a target in Eastern Europe to deliver a nuclear weapon, probably on a one-way mission. Plotting techniques at low level were the least effective means by which to navigate, and a combination of radar navigation and visual map reading to provide fixes was the more efficient method. The navigator radar would use the pre-planned radar predictions, which showed the view he would expect to see on radar along his defined route. With the predicted radar returns extending up to 10 miles across track, he would see bright spots and radar 'holes'; for example, a village would be a bright spot whereas a ridge line would show as a defined line with a dark area beyond where the radar beams could not strike the ground and be reflected back. If matched to the actual radar picture in the air, radar predictions could give a precise position in relation to the planned track.

Sadly, the quality of the EKCO 190 'cloud and clonk' radar fell somewhat short of the superb performance of the H2S navigation bombing system in the Vulcan and Victor. While a Vulcan radar navigator could pick out a church tower in a village, a Dominie navigator might struggle to recognise the town of Brigg but for a simple system the EKCO 190 was extremely capable and a useful training aid. Even so, the tiny rectangular picture was somewhat harder to interpret using CMRP than even the normal picture used for area navigation. Crucially, to be useful, the Dominie had to fly relatively close to the planned track in order to match up the prediction with the actual radar picture in the air. In the world of the 'baby nav', this was by no means certain and some carefully prepared CMRP traces proved utterly useless as the Dominie drifted off track. This was where carefully briefed codes between the navigator staring disconsolately at the radar and his peer, happily watching progress from the right-hand seat up front, could prove invaluable. Sitting in the right-hand seat was introduced to begin the process of learning to operate as a crew. Although the role was merely monitoring the navigation, sitting in the seat and being involved in operating the aircraft was a vital skill to assimilate. Learning this new lesson that 'a peep was worth a thousand sweeps' would hold me in good stead in the back seat of a Phantom throughout my air defence career.

The final event on the course was the overseas landaway, flying a planned route via the European airways to a selected destination. For us, it was to be the exotic Mediterranean island of Malta. The route was practised in the simulator before ever venturing outside UK airspace and circular routes around the island of Sicily seemed commonplace. For the first leg from Finningley to Istres in France, I would act as first navigator before handing over to my teammate and taking the second leg onwards to RAF Luqa as second navigator. On the return journey three days later, the roles would remain the same with me picking up the first leg before handing over in France. Not only was the trip professionally stimulating, but it was also my first opportunity to sample the delights of overseas detachments, and what better venue?

By the end of the course, I had amassed the heady totals of eighty hours and ten minutes on Varsity, twelve hours and fifty minutes on Jet Provost, and sixty-two hours and fifty minutes on Dominie. Some of the hours had been tedious, some frustrating, and some downright terrifying, but a few of the hours had, actually, been fun.

Postings night was a blast and a blur in equal proportions. Some would end the night in a euphoric state but some would resign themselves to a lost opportunity and a readjustment of ambitions. The types on offer reflected a snapshot of the Cold War. The promise of an operational tour on the Buccaneer or the Phantom was the highlight. Canberra slots were rare as, by then, the bomber had retired and the photographic reconnaissance, electronic warfare support, or target towing variants were the only options. A Nimrod posting was highly prized but less popular were postings to the Vulcan either as a navigator plotter or a navigator radar. The Victor had reroled as an air-to-air refuelling tanker as the last maritime recce. squadron was wrapping up, leaving the Hercules and an occasional Andover posting representing the transport world. By far the least popular option was the venerable Shackleton, which soldiered on in the airborne early warning role.

Much beer had already been consumed before the first candidate was given a piece of paper with his posting appended. For the ten newly confirmed navigators, there would be one Buccaneer slot, one Phantom, and one Shackleton, but by far the predominance was V Force and mostly Vulcan; half the course would begin operational life at Scampton or Waddington. Whatever the emotions, there was a huge sense of relief that we had emerged from the mill relatively unscathed.

I graduated on 6 June 1975, earning my coveted navigator's brevet. The ceremony was held on the aircraft servicing platform at RAF Finningley and the reviewing officer was Air Marshal Sir Neville Stack, KCB, CVO, CBE, AFC, RAF, then the air officer commanding Training Command. I was yet to appreciate the acronym soup of his post-nominals but I knew he was important and what was more, he held my brevet. I was to graduate alongside my original course mates from No. 189 Air Navigation Course with my new colleagues on No. 190 Course. No. 55 Air Electronics Operator Course and No. 55 Air Engineer's Course graduated on the same day.

It was a huge event and Finningley rose to the occasion and even though it was a regular feature on the calendar, they made it seem special. To receive a flying brevet awarded by the Royal Air Force was a huge privilege and represented more hard work than the average university degree course and, certainly, a much larger investment. We had arrived from a variety of backgrounds. Some were 'chopped' pilots, some held university degrees, and some like me had arrived straight from school. Whatever our background, we were united in our love of aeroplanes and a shared sense of achievement.

We formed up in front of the review dais, which was backed by family and friends looking out on to the parade ground decked out with a Varsity flanked by two Dominies and two Jet Provosts. The parade commander was bordered by the navigators from each course and flights of NCOs from the AEO and Air Engineers courses. An RAF band provided the music and I confess to a slightly teary moment as the RAF March Past rang out. Happily, we were spared too much drill, unlike the parade at Henlow just a year earlier. As my brevet was pinned to my uniform, I felt a totally euphoric sense of achievement. I was not the first, I would not be the last but for me, it was the moment when all my efforts, thus far, came together. Becoming an officer had been special but becoming a qualified aircrew officer had been my ambition.

The celebration was short-lived and it was only a beginning but I had a posting to No. 228 Operational Conversion Unit to fly the mighty Phantom in the air defence role. In true Air Force fashion, there would be a delay waiting for my course.

The graduation parade for Nos 189 and 190 navigator courses, as well as 56 AE op and air engineer courses. (*UK MOD Crown Copyright [1975]*)

David Gledhill receives his navigator brevet from Air Chief Marshal Sir Neville Stack. (*UK MOD Crown Copyright [1975]*)

7

Life Between Training Courses

David Gledhill

Training pilots and navigators was a complex and lengthy process involving different phases of training at different flying training schools. Scheduling such a complex jigsaw meant that, inevitably, delays would occur. It was more marked for a pilot who had to move from elementary flying training to basic flying training, then to advanced, and then on to the tactical weapons course before finally reaching an operational conversion unit. With navigator training and lead-in training centred on RAF Finningley and running sequentially, a navigator faced only one potential bottleneck—namely being allocated an OCU course. Sure enough, I faced a six-month wait and this was known in the trade as 'holding'. My postings officer showed a remarkable sense of humour as I was to hold on a single-seat Jaguar squadron at the legendary fighter base at RAF Coltishall in Norfolk.

Although seemingly wasted time, experience gained during this short interlude would prove to be vital. A squadron runs in a very specific way. The wing commander, squadron commander is assisted by two flight commanders and a series of specialist executives. The flight commanders control the aircrew and, normally, supervise the daily routine such as coordinating the tasking, delivering the flying programme and the leave programme, training the aircrew, and making contact with the relevant headquarters. A specialist qualified flying instructor (QFI) is the expert on handling and systems for the specific aircraft type which the squadron operates. He carries out dual checks and annual check rides as well as providing advice on systems and procedures. The qualified weapons instructor (QWI) acts in a similar capacity for the weapons system and the weapons the aircrew employ. A senior engineering officer (SENGO) controls the engineering

effort assisted by a junior engineering officer (JENGO) and commands the
ground crew. The aircrew are allocated to one of two flights and the peacetime
establishment is set at just over one aircrew member per aircraft on strength. This
would have increased in wartime. For a Jaguar squadron, this meant ten aircraft
and two flights of about six pilots, including the executives.

One of the flight commanders controlled the daily flying programme assisted by
a programmer drawn from the aircrew. The operations room—the hub of daily
activity—was run by an operations officer and an ops assistant; I was to assist the
ops officer on a daily basis, acting as general gopher. It was a formative period
as I learned how to adapt my newly learned skills into an operational setting. I
learned quickly that academic navigator training had little day-to-day application
on a bomber squadron.

Later, a dedicated Ops Support Branch was to provide officers and NCOs to fill
the vital functions but at the height of the Cold War, no such structure existed so
personnel were drawn in from all branches of the service to fill these important but
more mundane roles. Often, master aircrew, the remnants of the wartime NCO
pilot and navigator cadre, ended their service in a more sedate manner running
operations desks. Many of them had a lifetime of stories to tell and experiences
to pass on and during quiet times on the desk, I learned of aspects of flying that
I would never experience in the high technology world I was to join. Life in a
bomber over Germany was somewhat different from life on a fast jet squadron.

The ops desk was the hub of the squadron. The daily flying programme reflected
the task which had been set by the Group Headquarters and well in advance, the
boss in discussion with the flight commanders and the Senior Engineering Officer
would agree to a broad flying rate based on the myriad of tasks. Exercises, both
at home and overseas drove the activity. With a deployment to Decimomannu
on the horizon, where the squadron would practise weapons delivery profiles
using live and practice weapons on the range, lead-in exercises and work-up
sorties would prepare the pilots for the main event. Check rides and simulators
would be scheduled to ensure that the squadron could concentrate on the main
activity without distraction. Night flying would ensure that all the pilots were
current before leaving the UK, although at that time, the Jaguars had no declared
night role.

Once a rough plan was agreed, the shell would be passed to the programmer,
an aircrew officer fulfilling the task as a secondary duty in addition to flying.
He would massage the plan, adding the details to the skeleton and nominating
everyone to specific tasks as varied as aircrew medicals, through simulators and
ground training as well as flying.

The availability of pilots drove the flying day. A typical flying day would be
to fly three 'waves' with the first launch planned as early as was reasonable
to avoid the local populace being disturbed over their cornflakes. With only a
limited number of airframes, which were temperamental and prone to breaking
at regular intervals, the sortie rate reduced during the flying day. Whereas the first
wave might be eight aircraft spread over thirty minutes, the second wave around

midday might reduce to six with a final wave of four later in the afternoon. If night flying was needed, and, thankfully, that was rare on a Jaguar squadron in the early days, the whole day would shift right as there were simply not enough ground crew to man two full shifts. Again, to mollify local residents, the aircraft would be put to bed by 11 p.m., even if the rectification shift might work on into the wee small hours.

It not only included the glamorous events such as a live weapons drop on Cowden range but the programme contained the mundane. Pilot X would need to have an annual medical or pilot Y would be away on leave and each minor commitment had to be taken into account to ensure that each cockpit was filled with current and qualified aircrew. Every aspect was woven into the plan and, eventually, after a good deal of head scratching, the crossword puzzle was finished and would be devoured by the pilots before leaving the squadron in the evening. That meant via the officers' mess bar before heading home.

No flying programme could run without the efforts of the engineering staff which would be required to produce enough serviceable airframes to meet the sortie rate. A day shift would support the flying operations and rectify immediate problems with aircraft on the line. If a snag could be fixed by changing a black box at the expense of a minor delay, all well and good but often the problem was more complex meaning the jet was pulled into the hangar for rectification. Ideally, a spare would take its place but as the day wore on, spares became rarer. The night shift would take over from the day shift towards the end of flying operations and would work through until enough airframes had been fixed to meet the following day's programme.

Such detail was lost on me during my first months and my principal duties were to ensure that the information the pilots would need was readily available. One of the key aspects of planning a sortie was accurate information about the state of the airfield and local diversions. The main displays showed the airfield state, the recovery state, and any likely warnings affecting the flight. A colour state board that showed, at a glance, the weather states of key airfields around the country used a simple colour code, which could be interpreted in terms of visibility and cloud base and gave an instant picture of weather patterns. The passage of a cold front was easily recognised by the poor conditions on the front shown in reds and ambers and the traditional post-frontal clear weather shown in blue. More importantly, the weather diversion and the local crash diversion were listed, showing which airfields would be used if pilots could not recover to base. Next door in Engineering Operations, the states of each airframe were toted showing any limitations affecting the flight.

It was during this time that my academic training was translated into real experience in how to operate combat aircraft. The duty authoriser was the lynchpin in the execution of the daily flying programme. An experienced aircrew officer, he was responsible for overall supervision of the daily flying activity. Each flight of an RAF aircraft is entered into a document known as the authorisation sheets recording the details of who will fly, for how long, adding the basic parameters of speeds and heights, and expanding on the sortie content. The duty section may include an authorisation for low flying, to drop weapons or to operate against an opponent. By signing the document, the captain of the aircraft accepts the task but the authoriser signs to acknowledge that the supervisory aspects have been completed and are in order. Most importantly, the authoriser must satisfy himself that the crew is fit to fly and competent to fulfil the demands of the sortie. This might be as simple as whether the pilot had too many beers in the bar the night before but it could be whether he had completed his annual tactical check and was certified as competent.

Aircraft were lost in service far too often during the Cold War, victims to operational accidents for many reasons, including simple human error. Recognising the potential risk is a skill developed over years of training and experience. The reason for the loss might be a mid-air collision, but the president of the board of inquiry would wish to satisfy himself that the pilot had signed group Air Staff orders and that his instrument rating was up to date. Neither may have had a direct effect on the accident but the authoriser is the final arbiter and would be called to account.

While I was not expected to exercise any original thought at this stage of my career, watching experienced colleagues run the squadron was preparation for when I would be given the responsibility later in my career. It was to be a skill that would be used on a daily basis and, even though there were formal courses to prepare you for the responsibility, it was learned best by osmosis. Watching experienced aircrew running the programme and making routine decisions about flying operations would be a part of my life, whether it was running the desk on my own squadron, running my Tornado F3 flight in the Falkland Islands, supervising the formal training programme for the Tornado F3 Force in its entirety or orchestrating operations over Bosnia and Serbia as the senior operations officer at the Balkans Combined Air Operations Centre. Each role was different and the responsibilities markedly diverse but the principles were the same.

An aspect that would feature in my future career was deployments. In their war role, the Jaguar squadrons deployed forward to other NATO bases to be closer to the potential operational areas. Being allocated to No. 38 Group, for the Coltishall Wing, that would be either Norway or Denmark.

Moving a squadron falls to the logistics officer, normally the JENGO. For a planned detachment, the preparation began some months before with a visit to the forward operating base—the so-called site recce. For the Coltishall squadrons, the venue was well-known and the facility from which the aircrew and ground crew would work had been used on previous occasions. Even so, the mechanics of moving the aircraft, the personnel, the engineering support, and the spares were complex and detailed. Leaving a single vital component behind might prevent an aircraft from joining the flying programme. Lists of equipment were prepared in advance and, if air support was allocated, the material was assembled into loads known as 'chalks'. These would be laid out in a hangar ready for dispatch, although because air transport flying hours were so precious, often, they had to be loaded on to trucks, delivered to the air transport bases at RAF Lyneham or Brize Norton and flown out from there rather than from the squadron's operating base. This was a feature of life that was to frustrate me endlessly later on, when I became involved in deployment planning on my own squadron. For a relatively short deployment to a nearby NATO base, it was often more effort to move the kit to the airhead and fly it out than it was to undertake the whole move by road and cross channel ferries. For real, had a Third World War broken out, this might have been a more likely scenario as the transport aircraft would have been tasked on higher priority, more remote deployments. As air transport assets declined throughout my career, the problem was exacerbated.

In the operations room, I was to assist my sage mentor, a master pilot, to prepare for the move. Being a deployable squadron, spare copies of each of the essential documents—such as order books, data operating manuals, and even classified war plans—were already packed in a container but, in true air force fashion, the checklist was compared against the contents. Trivial items—such as spare authorisation sheets, pens and pencils, and flight supplements—joined the growing list. As preparations continued, the squadron still had to function at its home base.

On this occasion, air transport had been allocated and the sense of excitement grew as the date approached. What might have been a swift channel crossing and a brief drive to the base at Tirstrup in Denmark turned into a voyage of epic proportions worthy of Vasco da Gama. The bus left Coltishall at 'O dark early', arriving at Brize Norton mid-afternoon; RAF fifty-seven-seater coaches were not the sprightliest forms of transport. A lengthy convoy of equipment followed in our wake. A night in the transit accommodation known affectionately as 'The Half-Star Hilton' beckoned, before the movements staff called us at 4 a.m. sharp, to be well prepared for a mid-day take off. Being loaded into the cramped cargo bay and allocated an austere parachute seat was a blessing. By the time the C-130 transport landed at the Danish base mid-afternoon, the party which left for the sea crossing was already setting up the facility. Logic clearly fell foul of policy and dogma in the modern Royal Air Force.

The detachment flashed by in an instant and, spending long shifts on the ops desk, I saw little of life in the cockpit as the Jaguars were dispatched on missions to the simulated forward edge of the battle area. Missions were briefed in closed briefing rooms and the pilots emerged only to sign out and disappear for a number of hours to complete the task. It was frustrating for a newly qualified navigator and I would have preferred to join them, eyeing the empty back seat in the twin-sticker enviously, but these were operational sorties and I was not qualified for the role. My role was to watch and learn making sure not to screw up in the meantime.

Not only did I learn operational lessons but I found out that there was a healthy rivalry between pilots and navigators, and I was at the centre of attention wearing my shiny new navigator's brevet among pilots. It was to stand me in good stead in the future. A few of the pilots had flown the Phantom in the ground attack role and sprang to my defence when the banter became too strident. Other 'dyed in the wool' single-seat mates were less charitable. It was a baptism of fire for a young navigator, alone and unafraid amid a sea of testosterone but immense fun.

There was to be a final event which would provide motivation among the darker days ahead as I moved into the final stage of training. I was fortunate to be given a passenger ride in the Jaguar T2 flying with one of the flight commanders who later went on to command the Air Warfare Centre where I would be based in my later career. It was a seminal moment.

Flying in the Jaguar for that first time was an anticipated but still unexpected treat. Hitherto, the limit of my experience had been when strapped to a Jet Provost travelling at 240 knots. Although it was similar to a fast jet cockpit, the reality in the Jaguar was poles apart. The tandem seating meant that I was remote from my pilot for the first time, communicating only through the intercom system. The isolation generated a new experience. As a navigator sitting in the rear seat, you place total trust in the pilot when flying close to the ground or at the limits of performance. In a Jet Provost, I could see the hands flashing around in steely, fighter pilot fashion and see the world outside responding. Alone in the confines of a tandem cockpit, the only warnings were from the front seat or from the instruments, and single-seat pilots were less used to commentating before manoeuvring. The new 'office' turned upside down with gay abandon and the effects of *g* became more relevant, although the new-fangled *g* suit helped me cope with the stresses. With experience comes healthy scepticism and a huge increase in the need to monitor the other's actions. At the formative stages, complete trust was implicit.

It would have been easy to be discouraged by the way in which the navigation system appeared to be rapidly making my hard-won skills irrelevant. Given that I was scheduled to train on the Phantom, the need ever to employ a sextant or a three-position line fix in a cramped cockpit seemed unlikely. There was, however, a redeeming factor. The early Jaguar Navigation and Weapon Aiming System (NAVWASS) incorporated a large circular map display in each cockpit. The circle representing the present position sat in the centre of the circular display set on top of the moving map. Happily, the location of Coltishall airfield had been misplotted on the map so the position circle sat some distance outside the airfield boundary. My navigational prowess was restored as the trusty 'analogue' map in my pocket confirmed I was indeed on the aircraft servicing platform at RAF Coltishall. My confidence restored it was a valuable lesson that navigation systems should not always be believed. Mind you, nor should navigators.

Strapped in and listening to the litany of checks from the front seat and the interaction with the ground crew, I realised that operational jets were significantly more complicated than the venerable Jet Provost. In the latter, the engine was fired up and, after a few checks, we would be taxiing to the runway without fuss or drama. Aligning the navigation system in the Jaguar was a lengthy process and the checklist now extended to multiple pages of pre-strap-in, strap-in, start-up, post start-up, pre-take-off and finally after take-off checks. At that stage, I was a passenger. As I converted to my new aircraft type, the Phantom, I would become an integral part of that process. Not only would I be responsible for my own checks, but I would also be responsible for ensuring that the pilot had completed the essential safety checks on a 'challenge and response' basis. For my first sortie, I could sit back and relax somewhat.

The Jaguar rear cockpit was a comfortable environment with a good all-round view and, as a dual control trainer, equipped with all the relevant role equipment. I had just as much insight into what was going on around me as the pilot in the front cockpit. This was a different concept to what I would become familiar with. In the Phantom, the rear cockpit was optimised for the role of the navigator. Apart from a few airframes, most British Phantoms were not fitted with flying controls and the equipment was different front and back. The weapon system was the core, set around the radar controls. In the Jaguar, everything was replicated to allow the rear-seat pilot to monitor the front seat occupant and when acting as checker or safety pilot, to take control *in extremis*. The noises were new and unfamiliar as was the need to wear the complex flying clothing such as a g suit and an immersion suit under the life jacket.

After take-off, the jet stayed at low level, heading north towards the Wash, coasting out at Blakeney Point on the north Norfolk coast. The immediate impression was the speed at which the ground passed beneath the jet, a massive increase over the Jet Provost. That said, the tiny circle on the NAVWASS now tracked our progress with precision and I found myself barely looking at my map. Operating as a singleton we headed north completing a low-level navigation exercise with absolute ease. It was a far cry from my own efforts thumbing along a track marked in grease pencil on my low-flying chart and it was a tantalising taste of the contribution of modern avionics to my historic profession.

The sortie was over far too quickly, logging a mere one hour and fifteen minutes. It was not to be my last flight in a Jaguar and I would fly as an air combat leader, assisting Jaguar pilots to assimilate the intricacies of air combat manoeuvring later in my career. Nevertheless, it proved to be a formative experience and underlined my desire to succeed in the fast jet arena.

I left RAF Coltishall much the wiser with a grounding in the real world. I had seen what life could be like on a squadron but I had yet to prove that I had the skills and tenacity to join the elite. For me, it was a return to the training mill.

8

Pilot Fast Jet Refresher Training and the Tactical Weapons Unit

Philip Keeble

No. 3 Flying Training School, RAF Leeming, Yorkshire, 1980;
No. 4 Advanced Flying Training School, RAF Valley, Anglesey, 1980;
and No. 2 Tactical Weapons Unit, RAF Lossiemouth, Moray, 1980–81.

By 1980, I had completed two Canberra PR9 Reconnaissance tours—one in Malta and one in the UK. I had done my stint as a QFI on Chipmunks and Bulldogs on Birmingham University Air Squadron and had completed a tour on the Jaguar as a simulator instructor; while there, I had been given the golden opportunity to fly the Jaguar GR1 solo, my first single seat jet. Nearly eight years I had waited—eight long years of waiting patiently. I had been patient, but now I had a fast jet posting in my hands. I was back on track to becoming a fighter pilot. I was posted to the Tactical Weapons Unit at RAF Lossiemouth to fly the Hunter. The boy was back in the game. I admit I was a little carried away with the excitement of it all; in fact, I was excited as an excited fox that has just been made a professor of excitement at the University of Oxford, on a particularly exciting day (apologies to Rowan Atkinson). Yes, I was pleased; I had served my time, done my best both as a flying instructor and as a simulator instructor and now came the reward.

The first stop was the Refresher Flying Squadron at RAF Leeming to fly the wizard BAC Jet Provost Mark 5, which was a vast overall improvement on its predecessors, with its more powerful Viper 201 jet engine, a pressurised and streamlined cockpit, and improved avionics. Inside and out, it was revamped, which all added to its general appeal. This was a very nice little jet to fly and I thoroughly enjoyed whizzing around in this updated version. I spent eight weeks on the refresher course and flew forty hours from RAF Leeming, buzzing

Philip Keeble strikes a pose with his Chipmunk at the University of Birmingham Air Squadron.

Philip Keeble poses with his flying colleagues at the University of Birmingham Air Squadron.

BRITISH AIRCRAFT CORPORATION
DASSAULT – BREGUET AVIATION

This certificate is to mark
the first solo flight
in an Anglo/French
JAGUAR

By........**FLT LT P W KEEBLE**...............

On ....**29 Nov 78**.................

Officer Commanding Jaguar Operational Conversion Unit
RAF Lossiemouth

.... **Wg Cdr**

Philip Keeble's certificate to mark his solo flight in a Jaguar.

around the beautiful Yorkshire countryside honing my skills in general handling, instrument flying, formation flying, and low-level navigation. The course was well designed and the instructors were well attuned to what was needed for the days ahead. The beer was not too bad either as the Black Sheep Brewery was not far up the road.

With that 'tick in the box', I set off once more across the mountains, now in a rugged Saab 95, for RAF Valley, this time to fly the Hawk T Mark 1; as an added bonus, this time, the pubs were open on a Sunday. The car might have been a vast improvement on my earlier Mini but the roads were still much the same. The Hawk refresher course was an intense period of flying—twenty-four hours in three working weeks—majoring more on the front-line skills, such as tactical low level and formation flying and, dare I say it, something akin to air combat. Naturally, it could not officially be called combat as the rules prevented that so let us call it extreme tail-chasing involving large amounts of *g* forces, often with a fairly constant 7 *g* at times. I seem to recall that I was gasping for breath as I got used to the high strain manoeuvres once more. I have already described the tensing and grunting routines performed under *g* to prevent *g*-force-induced loss of consciousness (GLOC). It was not a nice experience and the cause of more than a few crashes. However, something that was new to me was blood pooling in the crook of my arms, causing dozens of tiny blood blisters to appear under my skin as the capillaries burst. It was disconcerting at first, but 'quite normal' said my instructor, which was nice to know. The Hawk was a terrific aircraft to fly and cleverly designed to be as placid or as exacting as needed, depending on the training syllabus. It was also a nifty little weapons platform and carried a variety of weapons so I can see why it sold so well overseas; more fool those who did not buy it as they missed out on one of the great trainer/fighter aircraft in the world.

My time at RAF Valley passed all too quickly and it was over in a flash. I moved back north, away from deepest, darkest Wales and back into deeper, darker Scotland where I arrived at No. 2 Tactical Weapons Unit; they operated the magnificent Hunter FGA9, which was getting a bit long in the tooth by 1980, the first marks having seen service in the early 1950s; nevertheless, the more modern variants were still a very effective way of delivering weapons. It too made for a perfect training aircraft as it was relatively easy to fly and technologically not very complicated, which meant that the student pilot could learn how to operate it in challenging ways without having to contend with black boxes and their associated complications. In its time, the Hawker Hunter was a fine interceptor, day fighter, fighter-reconnaissance, ground attack, and close air support aircraft—a true multi-role platform. Nearly 2,000 Hunters were built and operated by twenty-two different nations, which is an exceptional record. It saw operational combat service in around a dozen different conflicts, where it equipped itself very well indeed. With exceptional performance in its day, it was capable of taking on the earlier marks of the Canberra, apart from the PR9.

The Hunter armament included four 30-mm Aden cannons plus a ranging radar, which meant it packed a punch as a fighter. It was also able to carry a variety of other weapons, including four Matra rocket pods, thirty-two Hispano rockets, a lethal selection of bombs, and two 200-gallon drop tanks, which gave it a ferry range of 1,600 nautical miles and a combat range of over 400 nautical miles. The export models were fitted with air-to-air and air-to-ground missiles. Combine all that with a high-top speed of over 600 knots and you had a truly outstanding fighter for any air force. It was robust, reliable, and easy to maintain; therefore, it suited many overseas customers. In short, it was an iconic fighter. Had the RAF ever fitted their Hunters with a pair of Sidewinder AIM-9Ls, as once proposed, it would have been a superb option for mixed fighter force operations (MFFO) alongside the Phantoms, or the Tornado F3s, in a combat engagement. With a few additional bits of kit, it would have been a worthy addition to the RAF's inventory. Sadly, no further modifications were funded, but it would have been an ideal weapons platform to have. Eventually, the role was given to the Hawk, but the Hawk ran out of puff at high speeds when carrying missiles and the tactics had to be adjusted to cater for their limitations.

The Hunter was replaced in the RAF by the English Electric Lightning and later the Phantom; however, it continued in RAF operational service with Nos 43 and 8 squadrons in the Middle East during the Radfan campaign flying against insurgents in the fighter bomber, close air support, and tactical reconnaissance roles. It was withdrawn from Aden in 1967 and from Bahrain not long afterwards. It soldiered on in RAF service in various training roles and in an aggressor support role, doing much the same role that 100 Squadron does today. It served into the 1980s as a two-seat trainer on Buccaneer squadrons, where it remained as an ideal trainer for tactics and weaponry, the only downside being that it had little in the way of navigation aids, and this meant that just about everything relied on visual navigation techniques or mental dead reckoning. It had an ADF, but the principal use for this unwieldy kit was to tune into the BBC World Service and listen to the cricket scores while blasting around Scotland getting lost. Out of interest, in my yet-to-be-published first novel, *Battle of the Baltic*, part one of the 'Combat Ready' trilogy of books, I write about a scenario that features Hunters supporting Phantoms in a MFFO against the Russians.

Anyway, here I am at Lossiemouth and raring to get my hands on a Hunter. The Tactical Weapons Unit had been known as No. 229 Operational Conversion Unit for a while when it was based at RAF Chivenor in Devon. In the 1960s and 1970s it had a fearsome reputation for being excessively punchy and for taking no prisoners. Not only was it the OCU for the front-line Hunter squadrons based around the world but it was the lead-in course for the Lightning fighter. Stories abound of the overly aggressive atmosphere. Allegedly, students phoned in after crashing their cars in the snow to be told 'you had better make it in or else'. There was little or no sympathy in those days but, fortunately, things changed for the better. In 1980, the TWU at Lossiemouth was a much more civilised place to be, thank goodness; it was the best flying course that I ever attended without a doubt. Over the years, the TWU flew a mixed fleet of Hunters and later Hawks. It split, rejoined, and moved around from Chivenor to Brawdy to Lossiemouth and back again, eventually being swallowed up by RAF Valley in 1992. The TWU now flies the Hawk T2 with its glass cockpit, sensor simulation, and a brilliant avionics suite.

The TWU course was a fundamental link in the training chain for Cold War fast jet pilots so I will take time to explain what went on. The syllabus covered weapons familiarisation and combat preparation with a focus on operational practices for the front line. As such, the training syllabus was common to all fast jet aircraft types in service within the RAF. Later, once our strengths and weaknesses had been discovered, our course would be streamed into air defence or ground attack postings; if I was to be uncharitable, I might think that like many RAF manpower plans, the impetus was to post students to empty slots rather than reflecting any deeper development. Our eventual choices would be Lightnings, Harriers, Jaguars, or Phantoms; there were no Buccaneer postings with the jet slowly coming to an end of its life. Metal fatigue had resulted in accidents after the loss of a wing section, leading to fleet grounding and lengthy get-well programmes. Its replacement, the Tornado GR1, was on the horizon; it was still too early for 'newbies', as the force first built up using experienced crews. Fortuitously, there was not a bad posting among the choices but we all had our dreams and desires of what we wanted to go on to fly.

As was customary, firstly came the ground school phase with the simulator rides running alongside, eventually leading to the first ride in the T-bird, the T7. It was a nice enough aircraft to fly but a right old hulk when the hydraulics were turned off and reverting to manual mode, forcing us to fly for the practise. After two trips in the two-seater, the moment came that I had been waiting for all my life: the chance to fly the single-seat Hunter, the FGA9, which in my view was the perfect version of the Hunter (along with the FR10). This first solo was a sortie to be savoured and was a whole hour of pleasure—sixty minutes of joy, 3,600 seconds of nirvana, 3,600,000 milliseconds of heaven. Other aircraft were excellent in their own right but this was truly special, remembering when I was still in short trousers watching the Hunters practise their formation displays, I had nursed that passion to fly one for some twenty-five years, now, here I was on my own in a single-seat fighter and achieving my boyhood dream. Not many of us are fortunate enough to be able to say that.

The Hunter was not quite as nimble as the Hawk nor as agile as the Gnat but, nevertheless, it was highly manoeuvrable while retaining a feeling of real solidity. It gave excellent feedback to the pilot in that it felt like a proper fighter, one that meant business; it could do the business for sure. In some ways, it felt a bit like a cut-down, single-engined version of the Canberra PR9, another aircraft that I cherished flying. If allowed only one word to describe the Hunter I would say it was 'purposeful'; 'hard-hitting' and 'rugged' would be equally apt, so obviously one word is not enough, nor is three to be honest.

Two more rides followed then back to the T7 for the 'boom run', the supersonic demonstration, before returning to the FGA9 for the solo high-speed supersonic sortie. The Hunter needed a little encouragement to break through the sound barrier but once there it was a dream. Returning to the T7 for two more general handling trips, then followed a third for my instrument rating test (IRT), with a couple more GH solo sorties in the single-seater. Next, we moved on to tactical manoeuvring flying as a combat unit in battle formation. A solo trip was followed by a further dual trip and then a further two solo formation sorties leading up to the first trip as a four-ship. The curriculum was very intense and the learning curve was intentionally steep. Just as you were getting the hang of one exercise it was on to the next stage.

The weapons phase began with Exercise 'WC1', Weapons Cine, flown initially dual before a following eight solo sorties. 'Cine weave' was an exercise designed for two things; firstly, it allowed student pilots to operate the Hunter's gunsight in a dynamic situation and, secondly, it taught how to follow another aircraft, through a pattern of three-dimensional manoeuvres, while closing the range into a gun's tracking solution. This was the culmination of all that tail-chasing so long ago in basic training. Two aircraft would climb up to around 15,000 feet into clear airspace where the leader would set up at 360 knots with the student some 1,000 yards behind and slightly above. The student would begin a shallow dive, picking up speed until 800 yards astern where he would call 'Commence'. On this call, the leader entered a level, 60-degree turn to port and after a short amount of time would roll off the bank while holding the back pressure on the stick. Entering a 30-degree climb as the speed decreased, the lead aircraft would roll to starboard and when upside down, would spot roll back into straight and level flight. The student would follow this manoeuvre closing the range down from 800 yards until into guns range at 300 yards, all the time trying to keep the target pipper (aiming point), in the gunsight, tracking the cockpit of the lead jet. If the student got too close to avoid going inside minimum range, he would back off the pull and, with a small amount of lag, allow the range to increase to a safe distance once more. If stretched and drifting outside of the parameters the converse would apply and the pilot would take lead and close in. Performing lead and lag manoeuvres would mean that the target pipper would not be tracking the target at all times thus the idea was to close into guns range, stabilise the speed with the use of power and airbrakes, and try to resume steady tracking. All this was filmed on the gunsight camera, hence the term 'cine'; after landing, the wet film from the gunsight would be taken away for processing. Later, it was assessed by a weapons instructor who would look at the tracking and debrief the student's handling capabilities accordingly. The QWI would consider the ranging and the use of lead and lag and the amount of time that the pipper had actually been effectively tracking the target. A score was then awarded that would be used to assess overall progress.

Once upon a time, the Hunter had an ARI 5820 ranging radar in the nose that would lock on to the target and feed information through to the gunsight gyro. The radar had long since disappeared and ranging was achieved visually by manually using a twist grip on the throttle. Known as 'stadiametric range finding' (see below), this was a classic exercise in hand-eye coordination and it took quite a while to get the hang of it. In earlier fighters, an even more primitive fixed gunsight was in use so this technique was a relative improvement. If the radar had been retained it all would have been so much easier; however, at the time, the weapons instructors made it harder by introducing a high-level version of 'cine weave' flown at 40,000 feet and Mach 0.9. I avoided that ordeal but I can only imagine how tricky it must have been handling the aircraft at that height.

So how did stadiametric ranging work? The pilot would dial in the known wingspan of the target into the gunsight processor, he would then control an illuminated reticule in the gunsight by manually twisting the range grip, on the throttle, to keep the reticule markers (known as 'diamonds') fixed on the wing tips of the target. Through a system of calculations of arcs, radians, and the target's known wingspan, the gunsight would work out what the range was and alter the torque in the gunsight gyro, damping down the movement of the pipper as you got closer. It was a tricky old business because, at long range, the pipper bounced around like it was on the end of a rubber stick, whereas at shorter ranges, it calmed down and became more stable. That is how I seem to remember it all but I stand to be corrected by a QWI.

All this attention to gunsight handling obviously had a major purpose, the first being to prepare for the live weapons phase on the range, the second for air combat and the third to sharpen up the pilot's handling prior to the air-to-air gunnery phase. Going to the live firing range was a big event in my calendar. I had been before in the Jaguar's back-seat and the Canberra to drop night photoflash flares but that was hardly the same as at night, where we obviously could not see the target. Unfortunately, that meant that I had been known to drop ordinance outside the range on one notorious occasion, which led to myself and my navigator receiving a 'formal warning' from the Air-Officer-Commanding No. 11 Group. Formal warnings were a sort of 'yellow card' system, which was entered into your logbook in red ink and would be used in evidence against you in later days. They were intended to prevent further infractions and were extremely serious. Night photography was fun in the strange sense of being able to turn night back into day but it was no match to that of hurling your little pink body at the ground in bright daylight and unleashing death and destruction upon the surrounding countryside.

Air-to-ground gunnery was first up on the programme where we would be firing the 30-mm Aden cannons against the gunnery targets on Tain Range in Ross and Cromarty, Scotland. It began with a couple of dual rides leading on to four solo events. The first dual sortie would be flown with a QWI in the other seat of the T-bird and was limited to filming dry runs, concentrating on the joining procedures, the topography, the range pattern, the target and, of course, the essential safety checks. The Hunter was notorious for having a right old mishmash of weapon selectors so it paid to check and check again. The second dual sortie was in the T7 with a live load; I was in a gun-armed aircraft.

The Hunter had a brilliant system for loading and unloading its Aden cannons using a pre-loaded, removable, gun pack that could be winched up into the aircraft armaments bay and be ready to go in just five minutes. It carried four-gun packs which sat just behind the cockpit, each pack holding 150 rounds of high-explosive/incendiary (HE) rounds; in our case just the one pack was loaded and that with inert ball ammunition. Each cannon had a rate of fire of 1,200 rounds per minute that gave each gun pack a firing time of 7.5 seconds—not long, but long enough to do considerable damage even with inert rounds. Ammunition links and spent shell cases were ejected through slots out into a fuselage pod called a 'Sabrina' which collected them before they fell to earth. The added bonus was that when the guns fired the cordite fumes drifted into the cockpit where they smelt superb. It was an evocative smell and one that still lingers in the memory to this day, especially on Bonfire Night. Luckily on practice sorties, we only flew with the one gun pack loaded; otherwise, I think that I might have died from sensory overload.

Entering the range, we overflew the target in a clearing pass to make sure that it was safe and get an accurate height check using the range pressure setting. The pattern began after a pull up from the first pass, turning through 180 degrees on to the reciprocal heading entering the pattern at around 1,000 above ground level. I cannot remember the exact height at the start point but it was important to get it right because a good guns pass began from the correct position downwind. Drift was assessed and applied, height checked, speed checked, weapons checks complete and a radio call made. Watch the target as it began to drift behind your shoulder and at the right spot, start a descending turn on to the final attack heading. Make a radio call, either 'In hot' or 'In dry', depending on whether rounds would be fired or not, and receive clearance to proceed. Acquire the target, check the height, check that the switches were now live, allow for any crosswind by applying a touch of bank to correct the line for drift, check the target distance, check the height again and acquire the target in the gunsight. When coming into range, start the commentary: 'tracking, tracking'; 'pause'; 'in range'; 'pause'; and 'squeeze, fire'. Just a short burst of twenty rounds or so, a mere spasm on the trigger, then recover vigorously from the dive up into a climb and start all over again, and again, and again. On my first run, I scored five hits. Surely it deserved more, but that was what the RSO had seen on his acoustic scorer and that is all I was given. On the next run, I got only three hits. Words failed me. The third run was eight hits and so it went on slowly getting better with each pass. In all, I fired 150 shells at twenty to thirty rounds per pass to begin with and then a more refined ten to twenty later on. They do not last long and there was no round counter in the cockpit so everything was assessed on general feel and experience. At least the fuel gauges gave some idea that time had passed in what seemed like a mere blink of an eye. Finally, it was: 'Downwind, last pass and depart', and all too soon, it was back across the Moray Firth to land at Lossie and debrief the film to see what improvements could be made. The bad news was that all it took was small errors to compound themselves into poor scores; conversely small corrections to technique were all that were needed to improve the scores. In the following four solo gunnery sorties, I spent a wonderful time trying to blast the targets on Tain Range to kingdom come but just as I was getting the hang of air-to-ground gunnery, it was all too soon on to 'WR1' ('Weapons Rockets'), air-to-ground attacks with SNEB rockets.

SNEB was the acronym for the French-made Societe Nouvelle des Establishments Edgar Brandt, otherwise known as the Matra Type 116M/155. This was an unguided 68-mm, air-to-ground rocket with a variety of lethal warheads. Different heads could be fitted depending on the type of target, including high-explosive, anti-personnel (flechette darts or fragmentation), anti-armour, smoke, flares, and finally an inert training round, which is what we used on the TWU. This phase started with the inevitable dual check followed by three solo trips firing the SNEB rockets. We all like firing rockets into the sky at night but firing them from a moving aircraft against a ground target was enormous fun as you could watch the rockets leave the jet, their smoke trails snaking their way downwards towards the ground and impacting spectacularly. The Type 116M was a relatively cheap, disposable pod holding nineteen rockets, which automatically jettisoned after the last projectile had gone. The Type 155 was a reusable metal container with a fluted nose through which the missiles exited. The Type 155 carried eighteen rockets in the pod and they could be fired singly or in a salvo with a 33-millisecond spacing. Fired with live warheads, they were an excellent weapon, not terribly precise it must be said, but accurate enough to be extremely effective against the right kind of target. We were fortunate to be able to take a day trip out to visit Tain Range to see them fired from one of our own Hunters. The thing that I remember most was the loud crack that they made as they went supersonic in the descent, almost immediately after firing. It would certainly have kept me hidden away in my bunker had I been a grunt on the ground. The final sortie, WRG 5 (Rockets & Guns), was a mixed weapons profile and one that gave plenty of room for getting the infamous Hunter switchery wrong. The cockpit was an ergonomic nightmare and the rockets/tank jettison switch was a fine example of how not to design a switch. It could be fitted upside down, and inevitably had been, thus on more than a few occasions pilots had jettisoned the tanks instead of firing the SNEB rockets. Even after a safety critical modification programme you had to check the switch position very carefully indeed. The composite rockets and guns sortie was even more fun than firing just the guns. So that was the SNEB, and just as you were once again getting the hang of that, once again it was time to move on. Bombing was next.

Bombing is not a job for the faint-hearted for there is a purpose to all this enjoyable training; while it seems like good sport, there is a deadly intent and it was getting a bit late in the day to have any qualms. By now, you should have sat yourself down and figured out the moral dilemma of being in the armed forces where the role is to dispatch targets with expediency and efficiency. It does not matter if you are front line aircrew, a supporting engineer, an administrator, an air trafficker, or a caterer, everyone is part of that same big chain from the munitions factory to ground impact and it does not matter what the slick recruiting adverts want you to hear for all members of the armed forces are responsible, in their own way, for delivering the weapons, that can be all too easy to forget sometimes.

Deterrence is the basic aim of all military thinking in the UK and we fervently hope that it is effective and that force will not be required, but there will come a day when threats no longer work and it is time to take off the gloves and fight to kill—that is the bottom line.

Aerial bombing has been around a long time since the first bombs were dropped from balloons by the Austrians in 1849. The first bomb delivered by an aeroplane was by the Italians in 1911. The Royal Flying Corp's DH9s and FE2Ds dropped the 'Bomb HE', otherwise known as the 'Cooper 20 lb' and the 'Mark II-B' 25-lb weapon. The bombs rapidly increased in weight and explosive potency, leading up to the 550-lb weapon in the First World War. During the Battle of the Somme, the RFC dropped some 14,000 bombs, but it was not too long before that figure had gone up to 25,000 bombs a week. The bomb, and thus the specialised bomber aircraft, were here to stay, culminating in the bomber offensive of the Second World War with the massive 12,000-lb Blockbuster. Although that was a big bomb, come the nuclear age, everything changed once more. Even so, here we were in 1980, training with something that had not changed much over all those years—we were dropping dumb gravity bombs, more of which later.

Operationally, weapons have changed apace and now there is a whole array of smart bombs and guided weapons designed to be deadly accurate and, therefore, cost-effective. If that sounds like a job for an accountant, in some ways, it is. Matching the weapon to target is the skill of the operational planner. There are many options to choose from, ranging from nuclear to high-explosive bunker-busting, soft target cluster, and incendiary munitions; it is the job of a specialist to analyse the target and match the right weapon to the job. Let us not beat about the bush here, all weapons are designed to kill and destroy as best they can with as little collateral damage as possible, weaponeering is a deadly game.

The phase began with 'WB 1', level bombing with two dual rides preceding three solo sorties, which included composite bombs and guns missions. The bombs that we were dropping from our Hunters were cousins of those earlier First World War bombs; they still weighed 25 lb but had been designed to match the flight characteristics of a 500-lb operational weapon. The 25-lb practice bomb was 4 inches in circumference and 22 inches long, made of sheet steel with a solid, cast iron nose, fitted with a striker head that ignited a flash/smoke charge of gunpowder on impact. This allowed the RSO to spot the impact point in daylight and to mark the drop. You will be pleased to hear the round had a variety of safety wires and pins to prevent it from going off on the ground if accidently dropped. So here we are on the day, armed with a few of these 'eggs' slung underneath the wings, in a bomb carrier, hanging from the hard points and ready for the range. They would be delivered from a level pass at a set height, which if memory serves was 150 feet. The racier 30-degree dive-bombing was not yet in the syllabus but came sometime later.

Once again, you would arrive at RAF Tain, get the range QFE (the pressure setting giving height over the ground), and overfly the target for a minimum height check and to make sure that the target was clear and available. You would pitch up and off the target and up into the range pattern. Why did the bomb circle always seem like such a large target until you tried to hit from the air? There were always a number of dry passes to begin with and, when deemed competent to proceed, it was 'In Hot'—with a 'Clear Hot' from the RSO and the event began for real. There were so many possible errors: the incorrect drift, too much yaw, wrong line up, too high, too low (which triggered a guaranteed yellow card from the RSO), too fast, too slow, and so on. The biggest variable of them all was pitch up or pitch down at the last second when just the tiniest smidgeon of pitch could send a bomb off into no man's land. Bombing called for a steady hand and a cool head.

Hearing 'One hundred at four', meant a bomb of 100 yards at the 4 o'clock position from the target centre point (i.e. slightly short and right), 'Seventy at eleven' corresponded to too much compensation from the previous one. 'No Plot' was a dreaded call and meant that the drop could not be scored as it was off the plot because of a terrible release on the bomb picture, or a 'pansy pickle' which was not actually depressing the release button down far enough to release the weapon, worse was pressing the bomb release button in haste and having the bomb drop well short, but worst of all was a 'hang-up', which initiated a raft of drills to be carried out inside the range area. First, a check that all the switches were in the correct position and if a 'switch pigs' had been committed then admit it by telling the RSO who would, hopefully, allow you to continue. If not, scuttle back to base staying over the sea and avoiding built-up areas. Once on the ground, await the armourers to check out the system and investigate the reason for the hang-up.

There was plenty of potential for things to go wrong with weapons, as a friend of mine found out when he lost a few bombs somewhere between Wainfleet Range on the Lincolnshire coast and RAF Waddington near Lincoln. He went into the range with four bombs, tried to drop one without success, which the RSO did not 'spot'; a hang-up was assumed. He then diverted to the nearest armament-nominated airfield. On checking his aircraft after landing, he was short of all of his weapons, which were presumed lost as none of the weapons were ever found, which in a way was a good thing as they must have come off over the sea, or at least that was the outcome of the inevitable Unit Enquiry.

Eventually, the thrilling day came with the magical call from the RSO: 'DH', a dead hit. Now, this was one of those special events in bombing and one to be celebrated with a small 'whoop' of joy. Other DHs would follow but the first was the best. Like all events, the penny dropped and life got easier but you guessed it, as soon as that happened, it was on to something new. 'No peace for the wicked, nor the student', as the old saying goes.

I should explain the term 'switch pigs', which was a student's mistake and was recorded on a 'pigs board' in the squadron. For each error committed a financial penalty was levied on the offending student and the fines were cashed in at the final end-of-course party in of the purchase of beer. Predictably, an end-of-course party could be an expensive event but it was all taken in good spirits and fun.

So that was bombing in its basic academic form, although there was one final sortie of bombs and guns known as WBG 6 (Bombs & Gun). None of the sorties in my logbook seem to mix any other combination; mixing bombs and rockets, I understood could not happen as they both took up the same hard points and rockets and guns would cause confliction in the use of the gunsight.

It would not be long before we were doing first run attacks on the targets; there would be no overflight, or practice, just straight in, drop the bomb and get out. There was a lot to look forward to, barring cock-ups. As the course progressed, most days involved two or three trips, which in themselves were not a hardship except for the interminable debriefs in the darkened cine cubicles trying to convince the QWI that my 'DHs' were not a fluke but a blend of skill and aptitude. Equally, I had to convince him that my 'no scores' were a failure of the RSO to spot the impact, or that he had given me the wrong wind vector, or that the gunsight was at fault, or perhaps something else? During all this intense excitement, if the weather on the range was unsuitable for weapons events, there was no point sitting around getting bored and drinking coffee in the crew room as there was still plenty to learn with an extra instrument flying trip or a bit of general handling.

The next phase was low level, but I will come back to that later as it makes sense to stick with the weapons, and to jump ahead to air-to-air firing. As if hitting a static target was not difficult enough, now things got really tricky because we had to hit a moving target, the one in question being the 'banner', also known as the 'flag'. It was a 30-foot length of coarse material 6 feet wide, which was towed on a long cable behind another Hunter. The idea was to aim at the centre circle marked on the flag and to try to put as many rounds through it as possible. The problem was it was simply not possible, not to begin with anyway; however, the more you practised, the luckier you got. To aid us in the task, we had our old friend the optical gunsight, once again using the stadiametric ranging calculations. By now, the cine weave practices made more sense as things tied in together. The target towing Hunter launched with the banner behind and would fly off to Danger Area D809 to set up in a racetrack pattern. A series of armed aircraft would follow and begin to puncture holes in the flag. Each aircraft had the nose tips of its shells painted a different colour, the theory being that as each bullet passed through the material of the banner it would leave a trace of colour and thus could be scored. Many an argument was had discussing whether one hole was red or a more purple colour, or was that blue or a just a green grass stain obscuring a yellow shell hole? What fun it was before the advent of technology. What we needed was a Moray CSI team to help us out. Once all pilots had taken their turn, the target was flown back to the airfield where it was dropped on the grass and brought back in a Land Rover to be laid out in front of the squadron for all to see. Then began the forensic search for the tell-tale traces of the various colours, a degree of imagination would be called for and vociferous arguments of ownership ensued.

Back at medium level with safety checks made and the target acquired, some poor soul was towing the target and waiting for 'Joe Numpty' to shoot at the banner and not at him. The fighter was above the target by 1,000 feet and would watch the banner go around the pattern, making sure that it was flying straight and not canted over to one side. With weapons checks made, roll into towards the banner, put it on the centre line of the canopy, pull just enough *g* to inflate the turning trousers, as the *g* suit was now known and keep the pull on to get the pipper ahead of the target. Close the separation distance while adjusting the target ranging in the gunsight, then with the range reducing at a suitable rate, and while watching the banner ahead bobbing and weaving around, let everything settle down, wait, and then when at the correct range with the pipper in the right position, let off a very short burst of 30-mm rounds towards the intended victim. To begin with, it was virtually impossible and scores of zero hits were not uncommon; nonetheless, one day and by some miracle a round from my gun actually penetrated the flag and was later scored as a hit. It was followed by a few more and by the fourth, fifth, and sixth trips, the numbers were up to double figures. It was time to quit while ahead. This air-to-air stuff was a proper challenge involving a number of talents, hand-eye coordination being the chief among them. Gunnery at that time was primitive stuff and was not much more advanced than the techniques used by the Spitfires and Hurricanes of the Second World War. It would be some years before the computed-controlled, hotline sights in aircraft such as used by the Tornado F3 revolutionised the art. These later aircraft had much more technical ways of finding the target using radar but, nevertheless, the same basic handling skills were still very much required.

Having started the course at the beginning of July, by the start of September, we had finished the air-to-air gunnery and we were about to step up another gear into the air combat manoeuvring (ACM) and the simulated attack profile (SAP) phases, which would exercise all of the skills that we had learnt so far. The simulated attack profile sorties and the air combat sorties were flown concurrently with both types of training flown on the same day. This was crunch time as this was where we were finally assessed in our capabilities to see which role we would be best suited for when the postings were announced.

Air combat manoeuvring began with the inevitable dual ride before moving on to six solo sorties. Now, this was more like it—man against man, machine against machine. It was glorious dog fighting, the stuff of air aces, pilots like Albert Ball, James McCudden, Edward Mannock, and William Bishop to name but a few of my childhood heroes from the First World War. Even my boyhood fictional hero, Captain James, Biggles, Bigglesworth, RFC, flew fighters. Well he did in the W. E. Johns book anyway, and they are a must read for any aspiring pilot, aged seven to seventy. During the Second World War, particularly during the Battle of Britain, other great fighter heroes came into the public eye. Famous pilots like Douglas Bader and Paddy Finucane became household names. The two top scoring pilots of the war were Sergeant James (Ginger) Lacey—born in Wetherby, Yorkshire, where he attended King James's School, Knaresborough, and later trained as a pharmacist—and Pilot Officer Eric Lock—born at Bayston Hill, near Shrewsbury, Salop, who went to four local schools before working on the family farm mending machinery. These two aces were not public school 'toffs' as so often portrayed in the popular media but they had something in common. They both loved flying and joined the RAF Voluntary Reserve before the outbreak of the war, meaning that they had skills to offer before the conflict began.

Then there were the night-fighter aces like John 'Cats Eyes' Cunningham and John Braham, the latter awarded a Distinguished Service Order and two bars, a Distinguished Flying Cross and two bars, an Air Force Cross, and a Canadian Forces Decoration (CD). Although they well deserved their due recognition, no one really remembers their crewmen who aided and abetted their tally of kills. These were the brave radar operators in the night fighter Mosquitoes, heroic aircrew such as Bill Gregory who flew with Braham and Jimmy Rawnsley, who flew with Cunningham. Theirs was not an enviable job but they too have a story to tell of enormous valour and courage. They were the forerunners of the 'fightergators' that I was proud to fly with, guys like Dave and many others.

After the war, many pilots of the Royal Air Force and the Fleet Air Arm, went on to pioneer jet flying and some (such as Roland Beamont, RAF, and Peter Twiss, RN) became household names. Last, but not least, a mention for the great fighter ace and test pilot Neville Duke, RAF, who incidentally was rejected by the Fleet Air Arm; after the war, he worked for Hawkers, becoming the holder of the world air speed record in one of their jets. There are far too many other heroes to mention. Some became famous and others remained in obscurity but they all did their duty and fought for what they knew was right—we proudly salute them all.

For me, it was now my time to have a go at air combat and luckily no one was shooting back, although that might change in the future. Officially, I had not done any combat training up to that point but unofficially, that was a different matter. I had done a fair bit of vigorous tail-chasing and some unauthorised turning and burning, especially on my refresher courses and that was about it. That is, apart from the one occasion when I suckered a pair of Lightnings into my 12 o'clock while I was flying against 74(F) Squadron out in Singapore. The plan was to fly as high as I could in my Canberra PR7; as the two fighters approached from behind, following my contrails, I hauled the jet into a climbing turn and promptly and inadvertently flamed out both engines. This manoeuvre was quickly followed by a steep descending turn into thicker air. The manoeuvre eliminated the contrails and threw the fighters into total confusion as they try to sneak up on me. By the time everyone has sorted out what the hell was happening, my engines were relit and by then the Lightnings were crossing my nose in a perfect position for me to claim a 'simulated' guns kills. While I might have enjoyed the pyrrhic victory, I was not popular with my two navigators who thought that their day in the air was about to come to a very wet finish in the South China Sea. After I had bought both of them copious amounts of beer, and we had taken the piss out of 74 (Fighter) Squadron in the bar in RAF Tengah officers' mess, even they lightened up and entered into the spirit of things. As the old saying goes, 'a kill is a kill'. You do not think fighting fairly works, do you? Air combat is not a job for gentlemen but for 'rough men who stand ready to do violence', as George Orwell once said.

Now I was being introduced to the reality of what air combat really was and, more importantly, what it was not. There were plenty of new techniques to absorb. It was all guns stuff so far, with no proper missile tactics taught at this stage, other than a passing mention. Some of the basics like lead and lag had been introduced many years previously as a way of increasing and decreasing ranges between a target and a fighter but that had been fairly basic 2D stuff. Now we were about to go three dimensional, so words like 'Hi Yo-Yo' and 'Low Yo-Yo' were bandied about with lots of diagrams. Then there was the 'Barrel Roll attack', the 'Slow Speed Scissors' and the 'Rolling Scissors' (my own personal *bête noire*). It was all offensive stuff to begin with in order to be able to get into guns range on the target; next came the defensive countermoves to avoid being shot down by another fighter and so the deadly game of chess was developed as we progressed as tyro fighter pilots.

After that came the techniques of how to enter a fight with a definite advantage and just as importantly how to get out of a fight if things did not go according to plan. Other tactics followed like climbing up towards the sun, hoping to blind your opponent, or entering a spiral dive down to base height, trying to sucker your opponent into flying below it, thus achieving a ground kill. The Hunter was an excellent aircraft on which to learn combat, especially the single-seater because it handled so very well and had good visibility all around. It had a good amount of power and I found that the staff liked to use a couple of notches of the flap in a slow turn, 'just to help'. Fair enough, two can play at that game. Not for the last time did I discover that the weapons instructors were sneaky blighters and were not averse to cheating, until their little games were discovered.

Flying like *versus* like combat where the same type of aircraft is pitted against the other meant that it was down to the individual to determine who won. Some pilots were naturals in the aerial battle arena, some were not. Most of us had to learn the hard way and that was to keep slogging away until it became natural. I thought it terrific sport but I had an awful lot to learn and I do not think I ever stopped learning until the day I hung up my flying helmet. Once the basic skills were stored away, then began sorties of two *versus* one and one *versus* two, which introduced yet more skills to be mastered. Now we needed to be able to fight, look out in multiple directions, and communicate and plan coordinated tactics with your wingman—all at the same time. On top of this, pilots had to remember the basic air combat skills, the gunnery techniques needed to track the target at gun range should the opportunity present itself, and all this while keeping an eye on the fuel, your geographical position in relation to base, the weather and general airspace—just in case an uninvited stranger flew by. The term a 'one-armed paper hanger' seemed most appropriate. It was busy, and I mean mega busy, but it was a wonderful way to spend fifty minutes in the air, just as long as it was only for practice.

Reality set in as we headed back to base for the debrief. I forgot to mention that you had to remember everything that had gone on in the fights (plural) and to be able to reconstruct them all on a whiteboard. The manoeuvring was mapped out in detail and each action and reaction explained, both good and bad. How did we do this without any electronic aids? Simple. On the kneeboard of our flying suit, we carried a stack of clear plastic inserts plus a chinograph grease pencil. At the end of each engagement, as we repositioned outbound for the next engagement, we scribbled down all the relevant parameters of the fight and the moves that had been made. Once complete with all the important data carefully captured, it was tucked safely away behind a plain, plastic whiteboard, leaving a new clear board on top, ready for the subsequent engagements. No one said that it was going to be easy, and it was not. I seemed to do pretty well at it and got my fair share of kills but interspersed between all of this 'Biggles shoots down the Red Baron' stuff came the SAPs at low level. These simulated attack profile sorties were extremely hard work and I could see that I was going to have to be issued with a bigger brain at this rate.

You have guessed the format: another dual into five solo sorties. If air combat was a martial art, then ground attack was an applied science. During the morning, I was a fighter ace in the making, but by the afternoon I was preparing maps for a sortie where I would be learning how to navigate at low level, cross into enemy territory, find and overfly a hostile target, drop a bomb on a first run attack, 'get the hell out of Dodge', and live to tell the tale. By now, I was suffering from mental and physical overload; in fact, I felt every sort of overload known to man but at least there was now something that I was able to relate to from my past experiences while flying on the recce force except that I had no navigator to assist me, and we should not forget that there was virtually nothing in the way of navigation aids in the Hunter to help either. However, I rapidly quite got to like this single seat-seat, reversionary style of flying and even though later aircraft I flew had fancy navigation aids and computers they were nowhere near as much fun to fly as the rudimentary Hunter.

The instructors of No. 2 Tactical Weapons Unit were terrific to a man. The unit had a tremendous boss and his attitude and leadership permeated the unit. We were there to learn and they were there to teach; all of them were ex-front-line squadron pilots from a wide variety of backgrounds. Between them, they had flown Lightnings, Harriers, Buccaneers, Phantoms, and Jaguars; some had even flown the Hunter operationally before that. On reflection, I think that it was easily the best training unit that I had ever been on as they treated us well, they were dedicated professionals, and they were fun socially. What more could you want? I only wish that all training schools were of the same calibre but history and the future proved that not always to be the case.

Returning to SAPs, we were given a target and a target time, a number of timing gates and waypoints, and a pile of maps; we were then told to go away and plan a route and an attack profile. Of course, we were shown how to do it first with two duals and then five solos. A third dual sortie came later, to introduce the speciality known as forward air control (FAC). On return, the film would be marked to assess the success of our mission. Sometimes, a member of staff would be sent out to follow us around the route and check on our height-keeping and timing.

Later in the sortie, the member of staff would act as a 'bounce' aircraft to keep us on our toes. This pilot would act as a hostile enemy fighter intent on shooting us down and, failing that, he would try to make us deviate from our route and thus disrupt our timings. 'Timing trombones' were added to navigation legs whereby if you were late you could cut off a part of that leg and get back on time once again. If you think of the slide mechanism of a trombone, it has parallel tubes with a 180-degree curved bend at the end. Each leg of the trombone up to the turning point was marked in one-minute segments. Now imagine that if you fly along one of these trombone-shaped legs and you are one minute late, then by making a180-turn across the gap one minute before the planned turn by reversing back on route you make up that lost minute. Different points on the leg could make up more time as required with earlier short cuts. The FAC sorties introduced vital operational procedures. The FAC was a military person, usually RAF aircrew on a ground tour, equipped with a radio who could call in an air strike on to an enemy position. The FAC would be close to the forward edge of the battle area and when a call for help came in from the ground troops, the FAC would request air support from an available fighter/bomber. Giving the pilot the latitude and longitude of the enemy forces, it was his job to talk the pilot on to the designated target, keeping him and his weapons away from friendly forces. This was almost going back to First World War stuff again, only then they used flares and signal panels to direct the pilots until radio communications were developed and became more effective. It had been, and still is, a very effective way of offering close air support to the troops on the ground and was used to great effect in conflicts such as Bosnia, Iraq, and Afghanistan. Nowadays, the technology is more advanced with laser designators 'illuminating' the target and an aircraft laser receiver showing the target position in the pilot's head-up display. Add to that a guidance unit in the weapon that allows it to guide on to the reflected signal and a much more accurate delivery is possible.

Eventually, the end of the course approached and the final event was the infamous SAP 7, the culmination of all we had been taught and practised. It was crunch time. It was the equivalent of the final handling check during earlier training, only this time carrying bombs. First came the planning along with a time on target (TOT) for Tain Range with a live first run attack dropping a bomb from level flight. All this meant working out what time to walk, start-up and taxi to make the take-off time and thus the TOT. After a successful drop, there would be a variety of timing gates and secondary targets, some of which were for simulated attacks at a specific time but some were for reconnaissance overflights. The staff was scattered around the operating area both in the air and on the ground, the former to upset our carefully laid plans using the bounce and those on the ground to observe the accuracy of our timings and positioning. There was even a FAC in there somewhere, but to be honest, it was all a total haze of feverish activity I have forgotten. In the event, I was just glad to get the bomb away and make it around the route making a successful attack and collecting the intelligence, and avoiding being shot down. This was a true 'working your balls off' sortie and there much that could go wrong. In the event, we had been trained exceptionally well and every member of my course made it through. It was a 'DCO' (duty carried out).

With SAP 7 in the bag, our postings were announced. Not everyone was going to get their first choice but, generally, we hoped that we would get an aircraft or a role that we fancied. My posting to the Phantom suited me just fine; although I would have been pleased with Jaguars, I think that on balance my skills were more suited to air defence than to ground attack, although in the event, I found the Phantom Operational Conversion Unit a lot harder than I expected, and I will talk about that in the next chapter.

I had a short wait until I could start my next course and I wondered where I could go. My family were living in married quarters in the City of Elgin and we could not move until after the New Year, so there was only one choice really; I asked if I could stay at Lossiemouth for a couple of months and offer my services on the Hunter simulator. Maintaining the *status quo* would suit me just fine and it was a win-win situation as their simulator instructor was posted and I would step in and run the simulator rides for the next tranche of students coming through. As a bonus, I could keep my hand in flying in the Hunter as and when spare sorties were available. I managed to get three dual sorties and ten solo sorties during that time with a variety of profiles ranging from air tests, to a survival scramble during an exercise, and a little night flying was thrown in for good luck, but best of all I was given an introduction to the art of practice air intercepts by ex-air defence instructors and flew three sorties working with the Buchan Control and

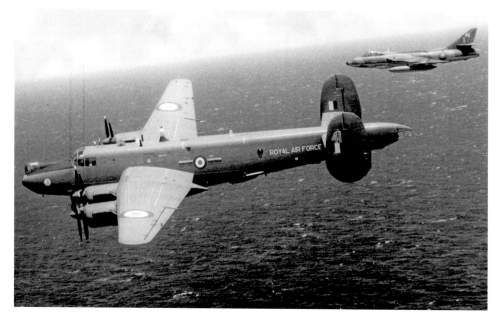

A Hunter flies in close formation with a Shackleton AEW aircraft. (*From the collection of Winston 'Scruph' Oliver; courtesy of the Oliver family*)

Reporting Centre doing one *versus* one and two *versus* one PIs. It did not seem all that difficult at the time but, as I have said all along, I still had a lot to learn.

In my time at the Tactical Weapons Unit, my total flying on the Hunter amounted to eighty-two hours, of which fifty-two were solo. It had been a total work-up of ten glorious months of jet training on three different aircraft types. It had included air combat, low level SAPs, guns, bombs and rockets all fired, dropped and whooshed for the first time in my career. Who could want more?

Who said, 'reheats, a Gatling gun and eight missiles'? Well, you might just be right. Maybe there was more.

9

Navigator Lead-In Training

David Gledhill

My first foray into lead-in training after the normality of life on a squadron was a return to the Jet Provost Squadron at Finningley. A different atmosphere permeated as, newly qualified, we were given the recognition of our achievements. Life was a little more relaxed and the stiff formality of basic training gave way to a more laid-back regime. Well, it was all relative.

Not only was the staff experimenting with a new syllabus but a new aircraft had been drafted on to the squadron in the form of the Jet Provost Mark 5B, or JP5. Fitted with tip tanks to give greater endurance and modified with a pressurised cockpit, which gave the airframe a radically different look, the JP5 was a huge step forward over its predecessor.

The JP5 was procured to replace the JP4 to give better performance in areas such as high-altitude training but an enforced early retirement of the JP4 saw the JP5 taking on more responsibilities sooner than planned. A new avionics suite, the prominent spin strakes under the forward fuselage, and modified wing leading edges distinguished the new type. The JP5A entered service in 1973 but the full capabilities conferred by the tip tanks had to be sacrificed to meet the earlier introduction into service. The version that arrived at Finningley would be the first fitted with the tanks and was dubbed the JP Mark 5B, but the spinning strakes were absent on the Finningley jets. For the first months, the two marks would operate in tandem and some sorties would be flown on the older JP4.

Internally, the JP5 was a huge improvement being more spacious and cleaner with a more logical layout of the instruments. More importantly, the view from the cockpit was much improved with the greater expanse of Perspex of the bubble-shaped canopy enclosing a pressurised cockpit.

The failure to teach relevant lessons for a future Phantom navigator had already become apparent and we were to become the guinea pigs for a new exercise known as 'rat and terrier'. Not only would the traditional visual navigation techniques be reinforced but voice commands to control the aircraft using standard air defence terminology were introduced. The exercise was flown as a pair with each JP setting up at planned navigation points in the low-flying area some 15 miles apart and, once the exercise began, converging on pre-planned tracks. The student navigator in the 'Terrier' would attempt to spot the 'Rat' and set up a visual intercept using suitable commands to his pilot. The student navigator in the 'Rat' would attempt to spot the incoming 'fighter' and call the pick-up to his pilot. For the first time, we would be offered something that was directly relevant to our future employment learning the skill of voice commands and the difficulties of detecting other aircraft visually at low level.

The phase began with some general handling to ease back into the confined cockpit environment in the JP and to blow away the cobwebs of the enforced break in training. The first six sorties were flown in the JP4 and began with simple perch work manoeuvring into a kill position behind the wingman. The next sorties set up basic 90 and 180 attacks, which were the fundamental building blocks of air interception techniques. On a 90 attack, the target crossed the fighter's track at 90 degrees, whereas on a 180 attack, the target approached head on—in other words, 180 degrees apart. With the advent of the JP5, there were more basic low-level navigation exercises interspersed with general handling to introduce radio navigation using VOR/DME. Using a simple kneeboard map and mental dead reckoning techniques, fixing one's position in a JP was a long way distant from the structured techniques in the back of a Dominie. The final exercise was a pairs landaway to RAF Leeming to give an insight into turning a jet around, unassisted at an unfamiliar flying station. After a further fifteen hours in the air, my academic flying training was complete and life was about to become much more operationally focused.

The V Force had not yet loosened its grip even on fast jet navigators and one final phase beckoned before being let loose on the mighty Phantom. No. 230 OCU at RAF Scampton operated a small fleet of three Handley Page Hastings transport aircraft that had been fitted with the H2S radar to train Vulcan radar navigators. Perhaps business was slow but a short course to show the techniques of navigating using radar had been offered to the Phantom force. It may even have been relevant in the days of Phantom ground attack but for an air defender, it rapidly became obvious that this was another diversion with little operational relevance.

I arrived fresh from an operationally focused Jaguar squadron back to a sleepy hollow in the darker confines of RAF Scampton. The strictures of the academic training environment were back with a vengeance yet the topic was still irrelevant. As the H2S was deemed to be superior in quality to the Phantom mapping radar, a cardboard mask was placed over the radar scope to limit the visible sector to an area ahead of the Hastings and out to 60 degrees. With its slow rotation rate, the time base swung lazily across the screen every ten seconds or so. It

A Hastings T Mark 1 TG517, operated by the radar flight of 230 OCU at RAF Scampton.

was totally unlike the rapid 'wig-wag' of the AN/AWG 12 with which I was to become intimately familiar. Although I had no experience yet, radar navigation in a Phantom for air defence purposes was straightforward—select pulse mode, maximum range scale, and point the scanner a few degrees down, then, lo and behold, the coast appeared. We would then wind down the gain until the coastline faded, leaving bright spots, which represented cities. Even I could find Skegness or Ipswich on radar and steer inbound. Another reasonably obvious feature was a minor geographical point known as Flamborough Head, which stood out like the proverbial dog's doo-dahs. I was even known to select mapping mode on occasion—total heresy for an air defender. Before I was allowed the luxury, there was a final penance.

The course members climbed aboard the venerable transport and over a four-hour flight navigated around a rectangular route across the north of England before returning to Scampton. Each of us had a short session at the radar scope following a track and adjusting the headings using radar information. It was a technique that had no application in the air defence world so I freely admit to a lack of dedication to this brief course given the readily apparent lack of relevance to my future role. Imagine my surprise when I was invited to return for another attempt at the course. I decided to pay more attention the second time around, and it proved to be a bonus when we stopped at RAF Machrihanish for a pick-up of smoked Salmon supplies. The training, regrettably, was equally extraneous. With hindsight, I now have eighteen hours and thirty-five minutes in the Hastings rather than eight hours, which confers modern bragging rights and my progress was unaffected. The value I gained from the course remains high on my list of the totally irrelevant.

One of the risks of flying a temperamental Phantom over the North Sea was that, if it decided to stop working and the crew decided to 'jettison the aircraft', you would be spending a few hours in the luxury of a single-seat dinghy mounted, considerately, in the seat pan of the Martin-Baker ejection seat. Although seat familiarisation would come later at Coningsby, the challenges of finding yourself suspended below a swirling orange, green, and white parachute were enormous and relevant. The Combat Survival and Rescue Centre, at that time based at RAF St Mawgan in the West Country, was the venue for this new and worrying discipline. Amid a comprehensive academic package covering diverse survival techniques, the meat of the course was the dreaded sea drills.

Ejection is a traumatic and sobering experience according to those who have experienced it. From the warmth and comfort of a cockpit, the ejected man finds himself separated from the seat, which has saved his life and is suspended in a parachute over cold, dark waters. There are a number of immediate actions to set up for a water entry, such as removing the oxygen mask, which might otherwise funnel sea water into your mouth, lowering the survival pack and inflating the life jacket. Back in the Cold War, these were all manual functions and crews had to learn the drill by rote to ensure they were executed flawlessly under pressure and in the dark.

Once in the water, the dinghy was pulled carefully towards the survivor and inflated giving a modicum of protection from the elements. With its inflatable floor, inflatable canopy, and baler, it was possible to generate a semi-hospitable microclimate within the dinghy, generating enough body heat to offer a chance of survival. With a range of only 90 miles, the venerable Whirlwind helicopters might be out of range of some of the operating areas. Relying on boats or the more capable Jolly Green Giants from the American bases in Suffolk, it might be a long wait.

It was the role of the survival school to introduce these drills and then put them into practical use using one of the RAF marine craft based at the school. Climbing aboard the blue and white vessel, the 'survivors' were taken out to sea and, after being towed behind the launch for some time, simulating being dragged by a parachute, they were dumped unceremoniously into the sea to practise the skills. With the survivors neatly placed around the boat, there were a few remaining challenges. Firstly, the launch would cruise past at 'ramming speed' to generate waves. There was nothing simulated about them. These were good old-fashioned metre-high waves that threatened to swamp the dinghy and deposit you back in the water. The ultimate ignominy was to be returned to the 'ogg splosh' and have to start again.

The final event was the helicopter winching exercise. Generally flown with an RAF search and rescue Whirlwind, later the Wessex, a winchman was lowered alongside with a rescue stop and went through the process of disentangling you from the dinghy, attaching you to the strop, and lifting you into the cabin of the 'demented egg beater'. The first and most important lesson was to ensure that the winchman grounded himself in the water before lunging to the rescue, otherwise the jolt of static electricity could disrupt even the strongest heartbeat. The second was to make sure you did not try to help him. A compliant survivor stood the best chance of rescue. The experience was exhilarating, terrifying, and heartening in equal measures.

The experience was not yet over once we were in the warm and inviting cabin. With all the survivors aboard, we were then, individually, winched back down on to a heaving deck on the end of the winch reacquainting ourselves with the marine launch.

It was only later on a wet and windy day in Lincolnshire with a raging gale blowing and a sea state seven predicted for our operating area when we asked the obvious question of our local SAR colleagues. To find that, they would start engines in a hangar, taxi out and take off in any conditions in order to attempt a rescue was truly humbling. A number of us questioned whether we would deliberately jump into the sea without an immersion suit, knowing the answer. It became apparent that we were taking an even bigger risk by operating in strong winds that might limit our prospects of surviving a parachute descent into water.

The final event in preparation for the OCU was to attend aeromedical training at the RAF School of Aviation Medicine at North Luffenham. Known as 'AMTC', the school delivered a comprehensive syllabus of academic aviation medicine subjects. Type-specific aircrew survival equipment was issued during the course and, most importantly, we received training in the barometric chamber. Here, we would learn the hazards of high-level flight in the form of hypoxia training and rapid decompression drills.

A senior RAF doctor, a specialist in the art of aviation medicine, talked casually about the effect of altitude on the body before explaining how our eyes process visual contacts in the air. With the rods and cones that allow us to differentiate moving objects, we are more likely to see an aircraft approaching from the beam if it moves across our field of view. The relative movement, literally, catches our eye. In a combat jet, it is vital to see your opponent if he is close. You may wish to kill him, but you certainly do not want to bump into him as this is invariably terminal. An aircraft approaching on a collision stays in the same position relative to you and is, therefore, harder to spot. The secret, the doctor explained, is to keep your head moving in the cockpit. That way, the aircraft you want to avoid will be more visible because your head is introducing a small relative movement. At a more practical level, we learned that the effects of four pints of Ruddles ale on the gut, when combined with a rapid decompression of the simulated cabin, could be traumatic and dramatic in equal measures.

A behavioural scientist lectured us on the way our minds work in processing information. He talked about motor neurone patterns and how we allow the mind to set up little routines to complete our everyday tasks. When you brush your teeth, you probably begin at the same place in the mouth and run through a similar sequence to catch every tooth. Stop in the middle and you probably will have to start all over again because the motor neurone pattern has been disturbed.

Why is this relevant to flying a Phantom? On final approach, a pilot runs through key checks to ensure the aircraft is configured for landing; among those is the vital task of lowering the undercarriage. Interrupt the sequence of events and it is highly likely that one of those checks could be forgotten. Failing to lower the gear is embarrassing and expensive, yet it could be caused by a simple interruption. This is why checks are done at a certain range and that if ever an air traffic controller gives an instruction to change heading during this sequence, he or she will always prefix the instruction with 'interrupting checks'.

Then, it was on to the dreaded topic: hypoxia. The brain needs oxygen to function. Interrupt that supply and simple tasks become difficult. Remove the supply completely and death ensues—never a good thing, particularly when flying a 25-ton jet. Once at height, we were encouraged to remove our oxygen masks and carry out simple drills, such as counting to ten or doing simple calculations. There was clearly no difference in the pilots' performance as they had been specially selected for failing the maths tests at Biggin Hill but the deterioration was instantly visible among the navigators. The symptoms such as bluing of the fingernails were identified in the hope that, if it ever happened for real, we would spot the signs and carry out the loss of oxygen drills. It was a sobering demonstration of the risks we would face in the air.

From there, we moved on to kit-fitting; this was the first time that I felt that my dream was soon to be realised. First came my brand-new Mark 3 helmet, even more modern than the 'bonedomes' I had seen in the recruiting posters and way more tactical than the Mark 1, two-piece affair I had worn in the Varsity and Dominie. The helmet sat on the head suspended from a complex cradle of strings and supports inside. Each string was carefully adjusted to sculpt the helmet to the head. A neck cradle cinched tight to prevent the helmet being dragged from the head by the slipstream on ejection. The visor was adjusted to sit snug around the oxygen mask so that there was no annoying leakage of light around the periphery. Slowly, the paraphernalia that I would need to survive in the air was added, each piece tailored to me. The *g* suit with its intrusive laces was added to the pile along with three flying suits and, finally, the life-saving jacket that joined the other items. A personal equipment connector that provided vital services, such as radio and oxygen when I was sitting in the ejection seat, had to be specially fitted in a rig to ensure it pulled out when I stood up after a sortie. Being stuck to a Martin-Baker seat at the wrong time during an emergency situation was bad. I left carrying many thousands of pounds worth of Her Majesty's flying equipment, which was added to my 'slop chit'.

Looking back on the preparation I received before being thrust into my new 'office', it was clearly inadequate when compared to the pilots I would soon join at Coningsby. In later years, the massive leap from the sedate speeds in the Jet Provost to the high tempo of the Phantom was recognised and a phase was added at the Tactical Weapons Unit flying the Hawk. Initially, the training for navigators was on a ride-along basis occupying empty seats on pilot training sorties. Slowly, a formal syllabus was agreed and flying hours allocated to navigator training. New subjects, such as air combat familiarisation, were introduced to ease the transition. It was not an ideal preparation for a Phantom navigator, given that the Hawk T1 lacked any modern avionics, but it was a step in the right direction. Simple training on air intercepts procedures were added, taught by ex-air defence navigators at the basic stage using PC-based trainers. While the Saudis commissioned Handley Page Jetstreams fitted with air intercept radars to begin their own training process early, the RAF lagged behind.

It was all moot because, ready or not, my next stop was the Phantom Operational Conversion Unit.

Philip Keeble strikes a pose in front of a Phantom.

David Gledhill after his final flight in Typhoon T1 ZE806 at RAF Coningsby on 30 March 2010.

The Red Arrows, the inspiration for many prospective aircrew, perform a break manoeuvre.

A Slingsby T31 glider at the South Yorkshire Air Museum. Many air cadets, including David Gledhill, flew their early solo sorties in such machines.

A Rollason D62b Condor in the typical yellow livery.

A Rollason D62b Condor in which David Gledhill flew his first powered solo flight.

De Havilland DHC-1 Chipmunks of the University of Birmingham Air Squadron.

De Havilland DHC-1 Chipmunk WK518 of the Battle of Britain Memorial Flight.

The view from the back seat of a Chipmunk downwind to the grass runway at RAF Coningsby.

De Havilland DHC-1 Chipmunk WK518 of the Battle of Britain Memorial Flight, with the engine cowling raised.

Jet Provost T Mark 3A XM383 displayed at the Newark Air Museum.

Jet Provost T Mark 5As in close formation. (*Jerry Ward*)

Varsity T Mark 1 WF369 displayed at the Newark Air Museum.

A Varsity T Mark 1 captured in flight. This picture was a logbook insert in David Gledhill's logbook throughout his flying career. (*UK MOD Crown Copyright*)

Philip Keeble strikes a pose in front of a Folland Gnat at RAF Valley.

Jaguar T Mark 2A XX829 displayed at Newark Air Museum. Both the authors flew Jaguars on a number of occasions and Philip was cleared to fly solo on type.

Dominie T Mark 1 XS709 in which David Gledhill flew a number of sorties during the advanced phase of navigation training.

A Folland Gnat, XR534, displayed at Newark Air Museum, similar to those flown by No. 4 Flying Training School at RAF Valley.

Left: The 'Spook'—created by McDonnell Douglas technical artist Anthony 'Tony' Wong—was the universal symbol of the Phantom Force. Neil Beach has produced a British flavour in his inimitable style. (*Neil Beach*)

Below: A Hawker Hunter flies close formation on the camera ship. (*From the collection of Winston 'Scruph' Oliver; courtesy of the Oliver family*)

A 234 Squadron Hunter in the vertical.
(*From the collection of Winston 'Scruph' Oliver; courtesy of the Oliver family*)

A Hunter of Hawker Hunter Aviation breaks into the circuit at RAF Coningsby.

Phantom FGR2 XT895 of 228 OCU cleans up after an overshoot at RAF Coningsby. (*Terry Senior*)

A Hunter of Hawker Hunter Aviation overshoots after an approach at RAF Coningsby.

Above: The Phantom mission simulator displayed at Newark Air Museum. This simulator served at RAF Coningsby for many years.

Right: The graduation ceremony for No. 190 Air Navigation Course.

Royal Air Force Finningley
No. 6 FLYING TRAINING SCHOOL

189 NAVIGATOR COURSE
190 NAVIGATOR COURSE
56 AIR ENGINEER COURSE
56 AIR ELECTRONICS OPERATOR COURSE

Graduation Parade

FRIDAY
6th JUNE, 1975

REVIEWING OFFICER:

AIR MARSHAL SIR NEVILLE STACK, KCB, CVO, CBE, AFC, RAF
AIR OFFICER COMMANDING-IN-CHIEF, TRAINING COMMAND

A Hastings T Mark 1 that served as a navigation trainer at No. 230 OCU at RAF Scampton. David Gledhill flew a number of sorties in this airframe when undergoing lead-in training. The airframe is now on display at the Cold War Museum in Berlin.

The afterburner can of a Rolls-Royce Spey engine fitted to the RAF Phantom. In reheat, the Spey produced 20,000 lb of thrust.

A Rolls-Royce Spey engine as fitted to the RAF Phantom.

Phantom XV393 of No. 228 OCU makes a flapless approach at RAF Coningsby. (*Terry Senior*)

Phantom XT893 of No. 228 OCU departs from RAF Coningsby in full reheat. The 'aux. air doors' on the rear fuselage relieved the pressure in the engine bay at slow speeds and closed shortly after take-off. (*Terry Senior*)

Phantom XV393 of No. 228 OCU departs from RAF Coningsby. (*Terry Senior*)

Phantom XT894 of No. 228 OCU makes a normal, full-flap approach at RAF Coningsby. (*Terry Senior*)

In close formation with Phantom XV433 of No. 228 OCU. (*Andrew Lister Tomlinson*)

Phantom FGR2 XV424 shows a full weapon load of four Skyflashs and four AIM-9L Sidewinders.

This is the 7.29 express for the German border.

Compare this with the 7.29 stopping train to London Bridge.

What you are comparing, in fact, is two ways of life. One of these you know or can imagine. The other is well represented by the aircraft in the picture. It is a Phantom. Crew, one pilot, one navigator.

They are flying from RAF Brüggen, in Germany. Almost all the work the Phantoms do from here is at low level – the most demanding, most exhilarating flying there is.

At high level, say in a big jet, you have little sensation of speed. But in a Phantom at two or three hundred feet, you have no trouble in understanding that you are in a Mach 2 aeroplane. As one Phantom navigator said, "it can be quite a ride."

Speed like this leaves you no room for error. Your timing, your awareness, your control, the way you use your instruments and electronic aids – all these demand the highest professional ability.

This is why, before you join a Phantom Squadron, you qualify in some of the most intensive professional training open to anyone. It takes about as long as a degree course.

When you are with your Squadron, it will be several months before you are 'combat-ready'. There is a lot of 'intelligence reading' but you fly at least one sortie every working day.

Your squadron's task in Germany is to be able to locate vital targets behind enemy lines and then destroy them. So your year's flying programme will include high-speed navigation exercises to find simulated targets, together with live armament training using practice weapons, including bombs, guns and rockets, and in various types of attack... and your accuracy will be measured in yards and seconds.

Your 7.29 express is a precision instrument – a witness to the serious purpose of the work you do.

If you want a job where you can say that £3,000 a year in your early twenties is not the most important thing that you get out of it – find out about flying. It could be right for you.

To find out more, visit your nearest RAF Careers Information Office - address in phone book - or post this coupon to Group Captain F. Westcott, MRIM, RAF Adastral House (958RXP), London WC1X 8RU
Please send me information about flying careers

Name

Address

Date of Birth   (Age limits, 17-25)
With this coupon please enclose a separate note listing your present and/or intended educational qualifications. Minimum is 5 acceptable O-levels including English language and maths, or equivalent. If you can offer A-levels or a degree, so much the better.

RAF officer AIRCREW

Mar 1974

A recruitment poster for prospective aircrew, issued by the RAF at the height of the Cold War. (*UK MOD Crown Copyright [1974]*)

A 64 (R) Squadron Phantom taking part in an air defence exercise, taxiing along the lazy runway at RAF Coningsby. (*Linton Chilcott*)

A 64 (R) Squadron Phantom prepares for an exercise sortie at RAF Coningsby. (*Linton Chilcott*)

The authors pose together while holding Northern QRA at RAF Leuchars in 1984.

David Gledhill with his former pilot, Tony Wheeler, with the cockpit section of Phantom FGR2 XV490 at Newark Air Museum. The cockpit is owned by Mike Davey and is painted in the colour scheme it wore while serving on No. 92 Squadron. (*Mike Young*)

Phantom FGR2 XV496 of No. 92 Squadron makes an approach.

Phantom XT909 of No. 228 OCU taxies past the photographer. (*Terry Senior*)

Phantom FGR2 XV433 rolls in full reheat. (*Andrew Lister Tomlinson*)

Fully loaded Phantom FGR2 XV490 taxis onto the apron in front of the QRA shed at RAF Wattisham.

The RAF Leuchars QRA shed with a Phantom FG1 holding Readiness 10.

The RAF Wattisham QRA shed with a Phantom FGR2 holding Readiness 10.

David Gledhill's 56 Squadron 'Op Badge'.

David Gledhill's 1,000-hour patch.

Philip Keeble's 43 Squadron 'Op Badge'.

Philip Keeble's QFI patch.

A mock AIM-7 Sparrow missile in the foreground with an AIM-9 Sidewinder behind.

Phantom FGR2 XV494 fires a Skyflash semi-active air-to-air missile from the rear station. (*Geoff Lee*)

A Phantom breaks into the circuit from close formation. (*Al Sawyer*)

Phantom XT897 of No. 228 OCU makes a normal, full-flap approach at RAF Coningsby. (*Terry Senior*)

Phantom XT897 of No. 228 OCU touches down at RAF Coningsby. The intense smoke shows the ferocity of a Phantom 'arrival'. (*Terry Senior*)

A clean wing Phantom of 228 OCU deploys the brake parachute to slow the aircraft down. The tanks were removed for the air combat phase. (*Terry Senior*)

The ground crew refuel XV499 prior to a display at West Malling in 1989. (*Stuart Forth*)

The ground crew carry out after-start checks on Phantom FGR2 XV499. (*Stuart Forth*)

The navigator enters the front cockpit to carry out power-on checks. (*Stuart Forth*)

The crew of XV499. They were tragically killed shortly afterwards in an accident at the Abingdon Airshow. (*Stuart Forth*)

A Typhoon of No. 29 Squadron carries out a display practice at RAF Coningsby.

Turning finals to Runway 25 in Typhoon T1 ZE806 at RAF Coningsby.

A Typhoon F2 flies close formation on the camera ship.

10

Phantom Operational Conversion

The McDonnell Douglas F-4 Phantom II raised many emotions among those who flew it. Keebs explains:

What a beast of a plane this was, a real mean machine—a case of brute force over elegance. This was an aircraft that I thoroughly enjoyed flying; I respected it and appreciated it as a weapon of war but I never grew to really love it, like I did the Hunter. Yet come the day, if the balloon went up, of all the aircraft that I would like to have flown into war and into deadly combat, the Phantom was the one at the top of my list. It had the complete package for its day and beyond—an excellent air intercept radar, eight missiles, a Gatling gun, two reheats, and a navigator. Let us not forget the backseater without whom my life would have been a whole lot harder. The one thing that it did not have was aerodynamics. The F-4 flew a bit like the comedians Les Dawson or Eric Morecambe playing the piano, 'playing all the right notes, just not in the right order!' The F-4 had anhedral, dihedral, and even a touch of cathedral but not all in the right places. Have a look at a photograph of the Phantom and you will see something that is inelegant yet aggressive, but also has a stark splendour all of its own; there are corners and cranks in the wings and devices to help it fly right but as a US Air Force test pilot once said to me, 'This aircraft should never have been released into service flying like it does'. In a way, he was correct but he had a lot to learn about the jet as a weapons delivery platform because I think he failed to appreciate that the F-4 was one of the world's greatest fighter aircraft. You just had to learn how to treat it right. Just like a bull mastiff I once owned, it was ugly, fierce, faithful and just great to have on your side—just as long as it was fed.

No. 228 Operational Conversion Unit, shortened to the 'Phantom OCU', had a long and distinguished history before a newly promoted Pilot Officer Gledhill ever walked through the doors in 1975. Losing the 'Acting' prefix from my rank gave an air of a little more permanence, albeit I had a long way to go before being awarded the accolade of 'operational'.

The OCU was organised to support different elements of the training. No. 1 Squadron took the new student course and delivered the academic systems training during the ground school phase. Most lectures were classroom based but a key element of the training was conducted in the flight simulator and another part task trainer known as the air intercept trainer. Later, when the Tornado air intercept trainer was delivered, the AI trainer was renamed as the Phantom air intercept trainer better known as the PIT; the abbreviation was harsh but fair. No. 2 Squadron conducted the flying training and was located closer to the flight line in No. 4 Hangar at RAF Coningsby. Co-located with No. 3 Squadron, which provided the engineering support, the combined force of nearly 150 aircrew and ground crew was, by far, the largest unit on the station.

The syllabus was broken down into five phases completed consecutively. Starting with the ground school phase in No. 1 Squadron, the new crews were remote from the daily flying activity but the sound of jet engines nearby bode well. The remaining phases were conducted in a purpose-built annexe sitting alongside the hangar adjacent to, but still some way distant away from, the aircraft servicing platform, from where the Phantoms operated. Even so, the smell of AVTUR jet fuel was in the air and the noise of Rolls-Royce Speys close by finally brought home the realisation that flying was imminent. The conversion phase introduced the complexities of the Phantom's flight systems and was then followed by three flying phases. The basic radar phase taught the fundamentals of air intercepts before the art of three-dimensional manoeuvring was introduced during the air combat phase. The course culminated with the advanced radar phase, which introduced more exotic target profiles and more demanding scenarios.

As Keebs suggests, one of the strengths of the Phantom was the concept of crew cooperation. The aircraft was unashamedly analogue and computers had yet to feature in aviation design. It was simply impractical to expect one man to operate the multitude of systems given the level of technology, but, while certain things could only be achieved in one cockpit, the workload could be shared. Clearly, only the pilot could physically fly the aircraft and only the navigator could operate the radar system and programme the defensive aids equipment, but each crew member had a different workload at different stages of flight. A navigator might be at the limits of his capacity as he set up a supersonic intercept profile while a pilot may be busiest when jockeying a heavy Phantom during a ground-controlled approach in cloud. Careful monitoring from the other cockpit and carefully timed advice might prevent a simple mistake developing into a crisis. Equally, ill-timed intervention might mean the difference between a long roll out behind a target or might stretch that tenuous capacity beyond its limit with disastrous results. This art was known as crew cooperation.

There were a variety of courses available to reflect different training needs. As an *ab initio* crewman, I had little concept of flying or fighting a modern combat jet and I would have expected to share the course with similarly inexperienced aircrew, although this model was never perfect. The long course was four months in length and designed to build an air defence pilot or navigator from scratch. Nothing was assumed except a basic grounding in aviation fundamentals and the comprehensive syllabus covered every aspect starting with operational principles. A 'Short Course' was roughly half the duration and provided refresher training for experienced Phantom crews returning after completing a tour of ground duties which might have meant up to three years away from the cockpit. During my time, it also provided the means to train aircrew transferring from the Phantom ground attack squadrons who were experienced on type but had little experience of air intercept work or air combat. A 'Lightning Course' was specific to the era as many Lightning squadrons were folding during the 1970s and a large number of Lightning pilots would transition to the new aircraft to form the rump of the air defence Phantom squadrons. Although limited in their knowledge of the Phantom, they were already seasoned air defenders and most had many hours of operational flying time, although they found working with a navigator to be a strange experience. Their course focused on the Phantom systems and offered a tailored flying syllabus.

The 'Meet and Greet' on the first Sunday before the start of the course had undertones of the school dance as different characters sought to make impressions in the testosterone-laden atmosphere of a fighter unit. As always, the instructors took the chance to weigh up the new intake and put names to faces. The key player was the course mentor, an experienced instructor nominated to act as 'nanny' to the course members as they progressed. He would make sure that the training was coherent but, more importantly, intervene if anyone failed any exercises along the way. He would steer his charges through the numerous pitfalls of operational conversion, programming each event on the course. Our mentor was to be a grizzly old Rhodesian called Al Vosloo, who had been Pontius's navigator. He had flown the Javelin in the air defence role as well as the Phantom on ground attack duties and was hugely experienced although a hard taskmaster. The new pilots and navigators were invited to pair up as a student crew. Although many of the sorties would be flown with an instructor in the other cockpit, some events would be scheduled as a student crew ride to give confidence as skills developed. They would also, however, 'fly' simulator exercises together and be paired in the AI trainer sessions.

My course was a microcosm of backgrounds. The senior student was a wing commander about to take command of one of the operational squadrons but he had just finished a ground tour and had previously flown the Lightning. The course dates fitted well with his planned takeover dates so he was offered the luxury of a long course despite his experience. In the spirit of crew cooperation, it seemed obvious that the 'hairy old Lighting pilot' would be able to help a rather naive pilot officer to navigate the potential swamps that lay ahead. It proved to be a sound move and he was able to offer sage advice, even if it was slightly frustrating that his basic intercept skills were far superior to my own during the early training. As befitted his status, we became 'Crew 1'.

A course normally comprised six crews but for No. 6 Air Defence Course, we had an additional pilot. Two pilots from allied air forces—one German who had flown the F-4F, the other, an American who had flown the F-4E, both experienced Phantom air defenders—unusually, were allocated to the long course because short courses were not available to meet their arrival dates. Although they were allocated the full time and hours for a long course, it was clear that they would not need the full syllabus given their experience, and that their course content could be tailored to their needs. This fell to the course mentor to manage. It also gave them the luxury of time to assimilate the way we Brits operated. The German pilot was to join me on my first squadron and explained the differences between the British and the German forces very well. He wondered how the Brits had won the Second World War. The explanation for him was simple: 'You Brits operate in chaos all the time'. One navigator who was destined to be the unit test navigator at the Phantom maintenance unit at RAF Aldergrove in Northern Ireland required less training. While he would need extensive training on systems, he would not need to understand the mechanics of air interceptions to the same standard as those of us who would go to operational squadrons. These three individuals would move ahead of the rest of the course as they progressed and would graduate early.

My course coincided with the final operational deployment of HMS *Ark Royal*, the Fleet Air Arm's last remaining catapult-equipped carrier, which operated a squadron of F-4K Phantoms. It seemed obvious that, despite the demise of the Navy Phantom Training Flight, crews would still be needed to man the last Navy Phantom squadron, No. 892 Naval Air Squadron. Ironically, a Navy pilot and an observer, as Navy navigators were known, joined the course. Both were ex-Sea King aircrew but, rather than join the *Ark Royal*, they were posted on an exchange tour with the RAF at Leuchars in Scotland. Ironically, RAF crews from other courses and one navigator from my own course would supplement Navy aircrew, joining the ship for its final deployment.

The remainder of the course came from a variety of backgrounds, including a 'creamy' QFI. This was a first tour pilot who had been 'creamed off' to remain within the flying training system as an instructor despite a lack of operational experience and he was crewed with a former Andover transport navigator. One of the navigator instructors from Finningley had completed his tour of duty and was destined for an RAF Phantom squadron. The final element was two *ab initio* crews for which the course was designed and of which I was part.

One *ab initio* pilot would eventually fail to meet the rigorous standards and was 'chopped', leaving an imbalance. Having started with a spare pilot, we were now a pilot short. It was decided that my experienced pilot would take on another navigator who was struggling and that I would become a 'spare'. Whether that was to be a good thing or a bad thing, I was never sure. In reality, with much of the course flown with instructors in the opposite seats, it had little impact.

The ground school squadron lived in a purpose-designed building close to the officers' mess so the early days of the course began with a leisurely walk to work after a full English breakfast. Mess life still had an air of grandeur and having a

The course photograph for No. 31 (Air Defence Long) Course at 228 OCU attended by Philip Keeble. (*UK MOD Crown Copyright [1975]*)

The course photograph for No. 6 (Air Defence Long) Course at 228 OCU attended by David Gledhill. (*UK MOD Crown Copyright [1975]*)

'batman' to press my trousers, shine my shoes, and bring me a cup of coffee with my wake-up call was a welcome end to the rigours of the training regimen. I was learning to like officer status and the prospect of operational life. The waiter service in the dining room was also a nice touch for a working-class lad from Yorkshire who had joined the Air Force straight from school.

The course opened with a ground school phase lasting four weeks during which the Phantom systems were dissected in minute detail. Unlike a family car, if a Phantom developed a fault in the air, it was not possible to pull into a lay-by to check under the bonnet. Aircrew needed to understand the complexities of how systems worked, how they interacted, and, more importantly, the basic drills to recover as much functionality as possible, to allow the aircraft to be recovered as soon as practicable, in the event of an emergency. The operation of the jet engines driven by the complex fuel system was perhaps easily understood, but a myriad of secondary systems kept the Phantom flying. Dual power control systems operated the flying control surfaces with a utility system to drive the lesser systems, such as nose wheel steering, the refuelling probe, and the radar scanner. Understanding the intricacies of these systems was to become second nature because if it was hard on the ground, it was far more difficult after a failure in the air.

One of the early treats was to visit the flying squadron for a first look at a Phantom for real. It made an immediate impression on Keebs.

A general look around the F-4, I have described its 'beauty' earlier—two Rolls-Royce Spey bypass turbo-fan engines producing astounding thrust and which also powered the services of the electrics and hydraulics. Control column in the right place complete with a trigger—most important that. Primitive gunsight (LCOSS) was in the front windscreen. All seemed OK so far. It was very much a '60s–'70s unergonomic instrument panel, the switches thrown around willy-nilly and abandoned in the cockpit and labelled with American words. It was just a case of finding out what did what. It was a child of its time but compared to Russian aircraft of a similar generation, it was streets ahead. There was a round glass radar screen sat in the middle of my front instrument panel; 'I won't be needing that', I voiced at this stage, 'it must be navigators for the use of only'. I guessed wrong. This was to be a device that I grew to fear and loathe in equal measure for it was the pilot's radar repeater, it being a 'B' Scope for the air intercept radar. 'Thank you for that information but what on earth is a 'B' scope when it is working from an AI radar?' 'Oh, you'll soon find out,' came the reply, with a smirk.

Radars then—never had one, never used one, never been taught a thing about them. They might have come in handy for weather avoidance on some previous flights but to me, they were a black art form. The navigators, on the other hand, bless their little cotton socks, knew all about radars and how they worked. Put simply, it was 'ping, pong' and divide by two. Ping was the noise the pulse signal made as it went out and pong was the returning echo. Take the time interval and you can work out how far away the target object is and tell the target's height. Next lesson: note your own speed and the known sound of your ping pulse, now scrutinise the sound of the pong and from Doppler shift, so you can work out the target's speed. So now we have all that we need: a position, a height, and a speed; it is that easy. The rest of the theory is based on the FM Principle—shorthand for quite clever (or something 'magic'). 'Any questions? No? Good. Next!' 'Let's move on to flying the beast'. Not so fast for, sadly, there was much more to come.

The AI radar or airborne intercept radar was first discovered just before the war at RAF Bawdsey Manor, the very same place where my AOC's 'Formal Warning' had taken place. Radar was extremely effective during the Second World War when the AI Mark IV was fitted to Bristol Beaufighters and helped to end the Blitz. It was followed by the much-improved Mark VIII radar, which was later used to devastating effect by the Mosquito night fighters. The first radar displays were simple representations known as an A-scope showing the range and, to a degree, the direction to an echoing object. If the 'blip', as an airborne target is universally known, had a propensity to be stronger on one side or another of the datum line, a rough bearing could be determined. Early radars were fixed and could only see a response if the fighter was pointing directly at a target both in height and/or azimuth. These types of radar were just about suitable for airborne use; developments continued and, eventually, they moved into the microwave age with the equipment greatly reduced in size and weight and thus able to generate a lot more power. Despite these improvements in design, the radar detection ranges still remained limited being not much more than a few miles and therefore relied on ground controllers to position the fighter behind the target. It was not until the advent of the Mark 18 that detection ranges started to increase to around 30 miles. Eventually, along came the Mark 23 radar, as fitted to the Lightning, with its monopulse tracking system, which allowed much greater resolution giving detection ranges, in theory, up to a more useful 40 miles.

Westinghouse designed a pulse Doppler radar for the F-4, which was built under licence in the United Kingdom by Ferranti; it was known as the AN/AWG 11 for the Phantom FG1 and the AN/AWG 12 for the Phantom FGR2. The Phantom radar system was a very capable one and used the Doppler effect to determine the target's speed; this meant that it was now able to differentiate between a moving target and the static ground return clutter, giving the Phantom a lookdown and shootdown capability—a big step forward over pulse only radars. The radar generated and transmitted a pulse of high energy, electromagnetic radiation in a waveform and fired it out of an antenna. As it radiated out, it scattered; when it hit an object, a small percentage of the signal was reflected back into the receiver. Once received, the data is analysed and translated into a signal which is displayed on a screen. The 'B-Scope' display followed in the 1950s and was fitted to the F-4s; by then, the scanner could physically scan from side to side and up and down thus covering a large three-dimensional block of air space. These new radars gave a much more useful interpretation of the air picture showing azimuth, range, and elevation. The information had to be displayed in a form that could be interpreted by the crew. With a traditional 'cheese wedge' shaped radar display, the azimuth limits extend out to the maximum range of the radar originating from a zero-range point on the nose of the aircraft, with the sweep of the radar fanning out from the centre. This is fine for mapping radars where the area of interest is way ahead of the aircraft, but in air defence work, much of the finesse of an intercept occurs at short ranges inside 10 miles. With a traditional wedge display, the area of interest would be condensed into an undecipherable contraction near the zero-range point. For that reason, the baseline at short ranges was expanded out into a horizontal flat-bottomed display on a 'B Scope', expanding the scaling size made it easier to read and interpret. Understanding this unusual display was one of the early lessons. If I had kept notes or a diary, I suspect that I may well have written about this stage of the course 'Have I made a big mistake in choosing air defence as a future career?' Various training aids had been constructed to aid students learn this complex science, along with two huge mission simulators which occupied separate bays adjacent to the classroom complex, it was in here that the early classroom training was reinforced. Given that the Phantom weapons system was still classified, access both to the building and then to the simulator itself was via locked security doors and seemed dramatic after the relaxed atmosphere of the academic training machine.

I had already been a simulator instructor, although for the first fourteen years of my career, I had very little experience of them. The Chipmunk and the Jet Provost did not have much in the way of synthetic training aids, neither did the Canberra. I had been taught in an old wartime Link Trainer which was of very little help and apart from the Gnat cockpit procedures and emergencies trainer (CEPT), that was basically it. When I was posted to the Jaguar OCU as a simulator instructor and lecturer, it came as a bit of a shock to the system. What did I know about simulators, or the Jaguar for that matter? Absolutely nothing was the answer but I soon learnt. The Jaguar simulator was a relatively modern piece of kit with full mission simulation and weapon capability; it had high fidelity aerodynamic modelling, an excellent high-resolution cockpit visual system, and a multi-axis hydraulic motion platform. At RAF Lossiemouth, we had two simulators. In one, the visuals were based on the Welsh Marches and the other on the inner German border; we knew who our enemies were. The visuals were a complicated arrangement in that each large geographical area was perfectly reproduced as a three-dimensional model on a sizeable scale. The simulators sat in a substantial building, almost a small hangar, that covered an area about the size of a basketball court. Over the top of the model hung a vast array of very powerful 500-watt lamps that took an enormous amount of power, so much so that during the power shortages of the 1970s miners' strike, we were often asked to turn the simulators off so that the rest of Morayshire could go about their normal business of brewing whisky. The Lossiemouth simulator ranked about the sixth highest user of electricity in the region, including a number of medium-sized towns. A colossal bank of computers ran each simulator, also using huge amounts of power in their own right; they were similar computers to those used to run the Apollo moon shots. Overall, the

Jaguar simulator was high tech for its time and did an excellent job of training the pilots. Certainly, when I got to fly the Jaguar, I did not notice any meaningful differences between reality and simulation. If you had to do a sim tour, this was the place to be. The Phantom Sim, on the other hand, was past its best by the time I arrived as a student; it had only a very simplistic motion system and, although it once had a visual set-up, both had long been disabled and were no longer in operation. The original visual system had also used a model, which represented a small area around RAF Coningsby with a camera suspended over the landmass to capture an image that was projected on to a screen positioned in front of the pilot's cockpit. All that had long gone but it was still an adequate training aid for both the pilot and navigator in terms of cockpit drills, emergencies, and radar exercises; however, moving from this simulator to the real world of flying was a quantum jump. I probably ended up my career with having about as much sim flying/instructing time as I have proper flying, but that does not mean that I ever found that they thrilled me much for there is nothing like the real thing. As good as they are in switchery and procedures training, they are of limited use if they are not state of the art and fully in synchronisation with the current service development standard of the aircraft. With virtual reality (VR), modern visual systems have come on in leaps and bounds in recent years, as has so much other high-tech gear, and now simulators are much closer to being representative of the real world.

Dave had arrived when the visual system was still been in operation and it had been used as a simple tool to practise visual identification procedures. A model of a Hastings was mounted on a stick, which gave a rudimentary image of the target as the Phantom closed in range. The mechanics of overtaking were never quite mastered and the high closure rates against what was a stationary target made the simulation unrealistic, leading to its demise. The model survives as does the original M1 mission simulator and can still be seen at Newark Air Museum.

The first seven simulator exercises concentrated on specific aircraft systems for each mission but also allowed the embryonic Phantom crews to learn the complexities of firing up a Phantom from its dormant state. There was no ignition key to start a Phantom but the drills for doing so were contained in the flight reference cards, which extended to nearly 100 pages of close typed text; it was this document with which the crews would become intimately familiar before ever sitting in the real thing. The first half contained the normal drills for start-up, taxi, take-off, recovery, landing, and shut down. The other half contained the emergency procedures. Weapons drills were in a separate supplement.

Bold face drills, which was the nickname for the immediate action drills, were learned parrot fashion and crews had to be 100 per cent correct in recall. The pilot would carry out these initial actions, unbidden, in the event of an emergency before the navigator pulled out the FRCs and led the pilot through the extended drills. Precision was vital and errors at this stage costly.

The 'FIRE/OVHT/ENG WARNINGS IN FLIGHT' drill, transcribed from the flight reference cards, was a good example, opening with an indication that this was a serious problem:

'WARNING: If double fire warning on when carrying centreline tank, immediately jettison the centreline tank.'
   Ominous!
   The drill continued:
'ENG or FIRE and OVHT.
Engine: Confirm left or right.
[Not as obvious as it might seem!]
Throttle: Off.
RAT: Extend.
Engine Master: Off.
Bleed control: Isolate.
If warning goes out:
Fire Test: Operate.
If normal: Land ASAP.
If warning remains on or Fire Test abnormal: Check for other signs of fire.
If fire confirmed: EJECT.
If fire not confirmed: Land ASAP.'

Crews began to realise that operating a Phantom was not a risk-free lifestyle.

The initial simulator exercises were designed to teach the necessary analytical skills and the crew cooperation needed to recover a sick Phantom safely. Some exercises would lead to the fault being cleared by the simulator staff and the sortie could continue in order to maximise the training. Some drills might be so serious that they would lead to the inevitable loss of the jet and to the crew ejecting. Unsurprisingly, such disaster scenarios were held until the end of the hour-long session.

Given the complexity of air interceptions, it was impractical to expect students to absorb the lessons exclusively in the air and a training aid that offered a more forgiving learning environment was needed to bridge the gap. This was known as the air intercept trainer and students would spend much of their week either receiving formal instruction or in self-help sessions. Driven from a massive cupboard-like structure which would be misidentified by modern aviators as a computer cabinet, the trainer operated on the analogue principle with cogs and gears rather than microchips driving the output. Nowadays, the functions of the trainer could be delivered by an entry-level laptop computer, but this was cutting-edge technology in the early '70s.

The training cycle began during the ground school phase, as always, with a lecture from a staff navigator from the flying squadron who introduced the basic principles of air intercepts, such as turning circles, collision angles, and relative tracks. These were the tools that allowed a navigator to set up an intercept profile once he had detected the target on radar. This in itself was a surprisingly difficult task, which entailed manually controlling the scanner in the nose of the Phantom using a tiny thumbwheel on the navigator's hand controller. In an exercise scenario, he might have a huge volume of airspace to search, sometimes from ground level to 60,000 feet. The aim of an academic intercept was to position two aircraft flying at well in excess of 400 mph, and at different heights, at a point within missile or gun parameters to engage the target if hostile or to continue for a visual identification if the identity was unknown.

Once identified, the crew might be asked to shadow the target, which might begin to evade. All these profiles had precise parameters to follow and, although air interception was a science, it was underpinned by an art. One of the early concepts was 'TLAR', which stood for 'that looks about right'; navigators soon developed a sixth sense when an intercept was 'on rails' or, more importantly, about to go badly wrong. Given that the aim was to set two 25-ton Phantoms on a collision course, it was important to set firm ground rules, such as safe height separation. Intercepts were conducted with 2,000 feet height separation in the front sector, reducing to 1,000 feet once in behind. Errors might be dangerous.

The Phantom radar controls were replicated at a console for the student navigator and acted exactly as those in the real aircraft. A real navigator's hand controller and radar control panel were used because operating those controls, sometimes in the dead of night in the Iceland–Faeroes Gap, had to be done by feel. Critical knobs and switches were shaped allowing them to be identified by touch so realism at a basic level was important. The pilot had a simple stick and throttles on his own console and a series of buttons to select weapons functions but while the turn rates were modelled accurately, it was by no means a simulator. The aim of the trainer was to practise the exercises, repeatedly, until the profiles became second nature but only at a procedural level.

Targets were programmed by the staff navigator using rotary knobs on the instructor station to set up the fighter and target at a start point normally 50 miles apart. The Phantom was unleashed on a given vector at a specific height, which could be adjusted using the simulator controls as the intercept progressed. More advanced profiles might demand that the target change heading or height and the instructor would reprogramme the profile when needed.

A simple representation showing where the two aircraft were positioned in relation to each other could be projected on to a screen in front of the consoles. As the intercept progressed, the symbols would lurch towards each other, reinforcing the tentative air picture in the student navigator's mind. Naturally, the good guy was blue and the bad guy was red. It was, after all, the Cold War. This luxury was only offered at the early stages and could be turned off as training progressed. The navigator could be further isolated by drawing down screens to prevent that elusive 'peep' which would solidify his air picture. For much of the syllabus, information gained from the scope would be the only means to pursue the target and to adjust the intercept profile.

The navigators were expected to understand the principles of how the Phantom handled in the air, and how to react to a systems failure, so in a similar vein, the pilots were expected to be able to run a basic interception unaided.

Keebs did not adapt immediately to the theories. While in the AI trainer, I appeared to my instructor as if I understood the concepts of radar theory, but I was bemused most of the time. I think that the staff instructors took pity on pilots, for some of us really did not understand much of what was going on. I found the initial phase of an intercept made sense by using the 1 in 60 rule and using simple mathematical trigonometry; 10 degrees right at 60 miles represented a 10-mile-wide displacement, thus it follows that 20 degrees right at 30 miles is still 10 miles displaced, 9 degrees right at 20 miles is 3 miles displaced, and so on. At long range, the 'B' scope display seemed logical but at short ranges, the scaling was most peculiar with the widened-out baseline. To enable its use at short range the scaling was artificially fashioned to perform some complicated algorithm where a target 'appeared' to move out and away from the nose as the scale expanded. This last bit was all totally lost on me; for me, it all turned to worms as you approached the final stages as the target closed inside 10 miles—instead of coming closer to the nose, it would actually appear to drift outwards towards the edge of the scope. It is difficult to describe any further without going into a lot of technical twaddle, so I will not. Suffice to say, it was confusing. Maybe Dave will elucidate it all for us. Yet beware of the diagrams; you have been warned.

Running an accurate intercept was critical in finding the target as a crew, so there was only one thing for it—when it came for my turn to perform an intercept, I watched what my navigator did and copied him. Not the best method I agree, but it gave an appearance of knowing what was going on, even if it was not the most precise method in the world. Nonetheless, even slow learners eventually learn, and by the time we had flown a couple of live sorties in the air and I could see what happened in the real world, it all began to make sense. The penny had dropped. Some two plus years later, when I was back on the Phantom OCU as a pilot instructor (PI), teaching this stuff to baby navigators, I came with more than a degree of empathy. I resent anyone who says that it was a case of 'the blind leading the blind' as I spent much time in the back seat with a student pilot in the front that, I might even dare to say, I became quite good at working and understanding the radar, but modesty prevents me from saying so.

Some years later, Dave was involved in the formulation of the requirement for a new means to introduce the concept of air intercepts. With the advent of personal computers in the 1980s, a new system known as the micro AI trainer (MAIT) was developed by the RAF Training Branch at nearby RAF Newton. A software programme running on an early PC allowed the radar display to be replicated. A computer screen fitted with a simple computer joystick and throttle offered a simple rendition of the Phantom radar scope and the associated symbology allowing the ground school instructors to introduce the concept of the 'B Scope' a few weeks earlier. More importantly, it allowed students to run simple intercepts in their spare time making the transition less painful. Even later, it would be introduced during basic navigator training at Finningley, easing the transition yet more.

With the simulator phase out of the way, for the time being, climbing into a Phantom and starting it up with a modicum of understanding of what to do if the dreaded telelight panel flashed up an emergency, it was time to make the short move to the flight line to join our QFIs for 'Convex'.

Now, this was more like it, decided Keebs. The chance to get the mighty Phantom into the skies and boy did it do so with some 'get-up-and-go'. The Jaguar had reheats but not like this; this was something else. These engines were forceful to say the least—a right kick in the backside when selected. The culmination of all that ground training was to actually get to fly this awesome aircraft airborne.

Originally designed in the mid-1950s and built as a carrier-based interceptor/ air superiority fighter for the US Navy, the Phantom first entered British service with the Royal Navy's Fleet Air Arm in the form of the F-4K (FG1) replacing the Sea Vixen. Luckily for the RAF, the refit of HMS Eagle was cancelled and the twenty aircraft that had been allocated to her were purloined by the RAF; with some modifications and upgrades, it became the F-4M (FGR2). Both types were fitted with British made avionics and, of course, with more powerful Rolls-Royce Spey engines, each producing a whopping 20,515 lb of reheated thrust. The RAF inherited the remaining FG1s at a later date and, although they were retrofitted with the SUU-23 gun and a gunsight, they remained, basically, in the FG1 navalised configuration. The Phantom replaced most of the RAF Lightnings because it had a much longer range, far better radar, superior weapons fit, and, last but certainly not least, a navigator. It was a superb fighter for the interception of Soviet aircraft, or anyone else for that matter. However, the Phantom was capable of more than just air defence. In the early days, in addition to being able to carry eight air-to-air missiles and an external gun pod, it carried a huge array of weaponry in the strike/attack role. During the Cold War, 'strike' denoted a nuclear capability whereas 'attack' meant conventional weapons. It could also be fitted with an external reconnaissance pod and so, eventually, replaced the strike and recce Canberras in RAF Germany. This was truly a multi-role combat aircraft and remained supreme for nearly thirty years of service. The order for 118 airframes proved to be a splendid purchase and it became one of the most iconic aircraft in aviation history. It celebrated its sixtieth anniversary in May 2018.

Back to the flying; convex 2 (CV2) was the pilot's first sortie, CV1 being for the navigator students. I had once flown a passenger trip in a Lightning F6 out in Singapore many moons ago, so I knew roughly what to expect but when those twin reheats kicked in, I was taken aback with the sheer ferocity of their power. In what seemed like a mere flash of time, we were airborne, raising the 'gear' (American-speak for the undercarriage) and climbing like a dingbat for the heavens. 'Oh yes, this will do very nicely, thank you', I thought.

It is worth saying just a bit about the flying behaviour of the Phantom because it was unlike any aircraft that I had flown before or since. There was one golden rule and that was, 'buffet means boots'. Without going too much into the peculiarities of the Phantom's aerodynamics, suffice it to say that at the higher angles of attack, i.e. above 19 units/degrees of AOA, a phenomenon known as aileron reversal occurred. When the aircraft approached the stalling speed, the aileron/spoiler combination plus the unusual aerodynamic form of the wings produced adverse aileron yaw. At this point, the control inputs would reverse in desired purpose and in the case of the Phantom could lead to an incipient spin if the pilot continued to mishandle the controls, and trust me in the Phantom that was not a nice experience. The aircraft would warn of an impending departure from controlled flight first by wing rock, which as the name suggests is a rapid and uncommanded oscillation of the wings and then, without further notice, there would follow a nose slice where the nose slashed in the opposite direction to the demanded input. If allowed to continue, it would develop into a full spin where it was only the deployment of the brake parachute that would recover it. I once discovered those initial consequences with an American test pilot in the front seat when I explained that nose slice would occur if he took the aircraft beyond the stall. He did not believe me and wanted to see it for himself, which he did. It took him greatly by surprise, even though he had been briefed specifically on the trait; it made my eyes water too. To summarise, as the Phantom approached high AOA (the stall) and felt the pre-stall buffet, the pilot would roll using the secondary effect of yaw by using lots of rudder and not the ailerons, thus avoiding all those nasty adverse aileron shenanigans. This prompted the term, 'buffet means boots'.

Convex 2 was an hour and a half of blasting around the sky doing aerobatics, stalls, and max. rate turns before returning to the circuit. The Phantom had one or two other idiosyncrasies, as if its peculiar aerodynamics was not enough. The first was that at low speed with a low nose attitude, high rates of descent could build up very quickly during the final approach turn. To offset this danger, the crew had to monitor the vertical speed indicator extremely carefully around the finals. I experienced this quirk one gloomy evening when in the back seat of a twin-sticker checking out a very experienced wing commander in the night circuit. We allowed the rate of descent to build up because of the lack of visual cues and got closer to the ground than we would have liked. Descending rapidly, I took over, selected maximum dry power, and we recovered the situation back into a climb. This demonstrated another Phantom anomaly in that afterburner could not be selected using the back-seat throttles, which could only operate from idle to max Mil. Power. This meant that the front seater had to be the one to select and deselect burner, which could be a challenge for an unwary QFI. The incident alarmed us both despite the fact that we were both old hands on the jet.

That brings me nicely on to my next point. The Rolls-Royce Spey engines were extremely powerful jet engines but were bypass turbofans and thus took a long time to spool up from low RPM before reaching peak thrust. Once at full power, they were great but until then, the delay could be fraught with tension. With these compounding problems at work, the Phantom could bite extremely hard. Having been shown the problems, a new pilot should have been fully aware of the difficulties and have been ready for them. I say 'should have' but there is an old saying in the RAF that 'complacency kills', and it was easy to be caught out in the F-4 as I related in *Patrolling the Cold War Skies*. Another early lesson was that when at high speed during aerobatic manoeuvres (or in air combat), if you buried the nose down, it was an absolute swine to bring the nose back up above the horizon and to re-establish a positive rate of climb—been there, done that, got the T-shirt, as I suspect have most former Phantom pilots. The Phantom earned its nickname 'The Rhino' not just for its shape but for the fact that when it put its head down and charged, there was no stopping it. So, on the first trip, there were many unusual aspects to learn on how to tame the beast.

Convex 3 was next, which included general handling (GH) and high-speed runs. This is where the old 'Toom' really came into its own in accelerating impressively and going very fast. This was more like it; crack in those burners, watch the engine reheat nozzle gauges do their thing, and see the Mach meter whistle through the sound barrier, eventually registering some impressive Mach numbers, but boy did it use the fuel up quickly—only fifty minutes this trip, a whole forty minutes shorter than the last sortie. With time only for one circuit; what a way to burn fuel. In my case, I enjoyed this aspect a tad too much and was forever after heavy on the throttles, always landing with less fuel than my wingmen.

The subsequent sortie, Convex 4, included more GH followed by nine circuits. This trip exposed another peccadillo of the jet, namely its single-engined performance. Handling the Phantom in this configuration was by no means as bad or as dangerous as the asymmetric Canberra but it still had the potential to be just as disastrous if not managed correctly. During a practice single-engine overshoot, when close to the ground, waiting for the single remaining Spey engine to reach full power was a nervous time. A safety margin known as the 'engine out allowance' (EOA) was applied to the minimum approach height, which ensured that an overshoot was initiated at a suitable height to avoid unforeseen contact with the ground. With increased sink rate and the time lag of the engine winding up, this was a real risk and not to be underestimated. When coming in to land on one engine, a decision was made early to either overshoot or commit to a landing and, once that decision was made, it was black or white—there could be no grey areas. Someone must have previously come across this buttock-clenching dead space, waiting for the engine to respond, and have frightened themselves enough to mention it to others. It would have been too easy to ignore such phenomena and allow others to make the same mistake, so such honesty was commendable.

Convex 5 was my first 'solo', albeit with a staff navigator—brave chap—and was a repeat of the earlier exercises. Two trips followed introducing instrument flying, then a further 'solo' trip was programmed, this time with my own crew navigator (a fellow student) and according to my logbook, we did a practice diversion to RAF Honington and five circuits. That does not sound very rock and roll to me but I expect I showed him my prowess at aerobatics and smooth landings. Actually, smooth landings were not the recommended way to land in a Phantom as this was an aircraft designed to 'arrive' on an aircraft carrier and was built to take the most extreme punishment. The aim was to pop the chute out as soon as the wheels touched down, or a mite earlier for that matter, and to thump it in. Roll out with the brake chute in tow and jettison the bundle of washing at the far end of the runway. Having said that, the odd landing made your teeth rattle but the old bird could take it. There was a smidgeon of truth that the final landing checks were 'gear, flaps, hyd pressures and gum shield'.

The three close formation sorties that ensued seemed to go much as expected each lasting about one hour and thirty minutes so obviously not much use of reheat. There was one specific exercise that will remain forever burned in my memory. The low-level acceleration to supersonic speeds during the day was memorable— but at night, it was truly eye-watering. Setting up the exercise correctly was vital; it began off the Norfolk coast at 1,000 feet in the dark in relatively good weather with a horizon sufficient to be able to see the lights of the towns and villages along the coastline; now, we were prepared for the challenge. Once pointing away from the coastline and at least 15 miles out to sea, the burners were selected and the aircraft would accelerate rapidly through the Mach within a short period of time. It does not sound too bad, but it was. Mere words cannot do justice to the sheer horror of this exercise and it was one that I abhorred, even more so when I became an instructor and had to sit in the back seat while some inexperienced pilot performed the manoeuvre upon my own person. The problems occurred as the aircraft approached the sound barrier, where there would be a large pressure change over the airframe as the supersonic shock wave moved backwards, thus adversely affecting the pressure instruments. This effect was known as 'transonic jump' and caused the altimeter to unwind spuriously by about 500 feet. The vertical speed indicator would show a steep rate of descent seemingly towards the pitch-black sea—luckily, the horizon gyro unit (HGU) showed the outside world still as straight and level. In that one instrument alone, you gave your complete 100 per cent trust. Conversely, as you popped the airbrakes out and slowed down to subsonic speeds, the pressure wave moved forwards and the instruments would move in the opposite direction, now showing an apparent ascent. Here is the second danger for it would be all too easy to think that you were in a steep climb and push the stick forward, thus ending up in the North Sea, which understandably would be a very nasty way to conclude the evening.

The human body was also complicit in all this sensory trickery as the vestibular system, the semicircular canals in the ears, which acts as the bodies balance organs and would be thrown into disarray without their normal visual references from the eyes, and therefore leading to severe vertigo. Staying safe and alive depended on believing just one gyroscopic instrument. Now can you see why we were nervous? Rightly so. Why did we do it? That is a very good question; this exercise was all part of the learning experience to develop handling skills that would be needed in the days ahead, once on a front-line squadron where this discipline would be used for real over the sea at night trying to find, or avoid the enemy.

A friend who joined the RAF at the same time as myself went on to fly the Lightning at RAF Coltishall where they demonstrated a similar exercise, only the instrument errors on the Lightning were such that the altimeter actually registered a height below sea level. It was a phenomenon so distressing that the chap chopped himself by withdrawing from flying because he was unable to cope; being unable to trust his senses, he was left lacking in confidence. At some time in their careers, most military pilots suffered sensory illusions to some degree or another. During early instrument flying training, an exercise to induce the leans was flown with each new pilot to demonstrate the problem. I suffered a bad case of the leans one dusky evening when approaching the airfield at RAF Leuchars—a cloud bank at the edge of a frontal system slanted downwards at an angle to the ground and not parallel to the horizon; as I came off instruments and looked ahead for the runway, my eyes told my brain that I was not wings level as I expected. It might have persuaded me to respond incorrectly had I trusted my senses rather than check the instruments. It was a bizarre and disturbing experience and extremely forceful in nature. As I sat in the coffee bar unwinding and pondering this event, other pilots came into the crew room and reported the exact same phenomena on their own approach. That I was not alone in the experience was of some comfort to me, nevertheless, it was a most weird and disconcerting episode. Other pilots have suffered far worse experiences.

Shortly after my daunting night trip came my first instrument rating test on the Phantom. An instrument rating is the licence to fly in bad weather and dictates how close to the ground a pilot can fly during an instrument approach to an airfield before taking over visually. For new pilots on the F-4, a White Rating allowed a radar descent into an airfield on a precision approach down to 400 feet in cloud, with visibilities down to 1,500 meters runway visual range. As skills developed, a Green Rating allowed a minimum descent height of 200 feet in visibilities down to 600 metres RVR. This equated to 450 metres as observed by the Met Man. The final accolade possible was to be awarded a Master Green Rating, which was only given to the most experienced pilots on type and demanded the very highest skills in instrument flying—only surpassed by the instrument rating examiners (IRE) for whom the firmaments were the limit. Many a time, these instrument limitations have been broken in the name of expediency, even to the point of people collecting bits of local shrubbery in the undercarriage.

Finally, with a final four-ship formation, the pilot conversion on to type was done and dusted. It had taken less than a month. It had been short and sweet, albeit hard work, but at least it had been most enjoyable. The Phantom radar conversion was also hard work but not very enjoyable, other than the joy of flying the jet itself. Ah well, I had made my bed so I might as well lie in, and as things turned out in the long run, I was glad that I did.

Dave recalls that for the navigators, Convex was a much more leisurely affair consisting of only four sorties, one of which was flown at night, to allow us to assimilate the airborne use of the equipment in the back cockpit. The spare time as the pilots plied their trade was spent either consolidating the lessons learned in the AI trainer through self-help sessions or by digging into the reams of order books and technical manuals.

I flew my first trip in a Phantom in XV472 on 26 March 1976 with the boss of the OCU in the front seat and was beginning to believe that I would only ever fly with senior officers. The sortie passed in a blur, almost as quickly as the

Lincolnshire fields whizzing past below as I adapted to the rigours of high-speed flight. Often flown as a singleton, unusually, a second Phantom accompanied us and I experienced true 'battle' formation for the first time as the wingman flew a wider formation than I had been used to at Finningley. Line abreast, the other Phantom mirrored our moves. Shortly, we split for individual exercises and as I fired up the radar for real, I searched for my first airborne contact. It was some time into the sortie before I made the elusive detection but suffice to say that the synthetic depiction in the simulators on the ground was much different from the performance of the radar in the air, particularly in pulse Doppler mode. The profile mirrored that of one of the early pilot exercises but adapted to meet a navigator's needs. After a 'high-speed run', a euphemistic term for flying supersonic, the pilot demonstrated flight at the extremes of the envelope including high *g* turns, slow speed handling, and rapid climbs and descents. I was able to use the radar to paint the coastline and to home on the recovery point at Skegness. Remarkably, the thousands of caravans on the coastline acted as a perfect radar reflector and could be seen from way out in the North Sea. I am sure most caravan owners have no idea that they have acted as a beacon for returning airmen for so many years. It was also a delight to have an inertial navigation system that provided an instant readout of position and a course to steer to any selected waypoint. My academic navigation training suddenly seemed redundant.

By the end of the sortie, I was experiencing a feeling which was to be prevalent for the majority of my first year. As a pilot, I had never felt ill in the air but in the cramped confines of the back seat of a Phantom, trussed up in a bulky immersion suit and strapped in the ejection seat wearing a life jacket and parachute harness, the conditions were claustrophobic. Add to the fact that there was no control over the cabin conditioning in the back cockpit, plus the fact that the cockpit rail sloped downwards giving a false horizon, and the result was predictable. People suffer travel sickness in a car but if the car was to roll inverted or slam around a corner on two wheels, the effect would be heightened. In the back of a Phantom, air sickness was an occupational hazard yet some navigators were, mercifully, unaffected. Those who did learned to work through the debilitating discomfort or face 'the chop'. One colleague suffered air sickness throughout his career and was ill on most sorties. How he continued to function effectively will remain a mystery as I am sure I would not have had the fortitude had my affliction carried on beyond the six months I suffered. Staggering from the cockpit after a short seventy minutes, it was a relief to be back on the ground but the feeling of elation was profound.

Convex 6 followed quite quickly in which the increasingly confident student crew launched into the wild blue yonder in one of Her Majesty's expensive combat aeroplanes. With a vast two hours and twenty minutes Phantom time by the end of the sortie, I could almost complete my pre-sortie cockpit checks without the aid of the voluminous checklist that was tucked into my immersion suit pocket. Fortuitously, the sortie passed without incident and apart from the pre-take-off and recovery checks, my cards remained stowed.

There was a short gap for the navigators as the pilots delved deeper into handling. With very limited experience, night flying arrived remarkably quickly. If firing up a Phantom in daylight was a trial, doing the same at night was truly a challenge. Fortuitously, the apron where XT899 was positioned was well lit. The first task for a navigator on arrival at the aircraft was to apply external power to allow the systems to be brought online. This meant climbing first into the back seat and checking that essential switches were turned off. It was ill-advised to radiate the ground crew with radar waves if the radar had inadvertently been left on. At that point, I walked gingerly along the ramp that stretched along the side of the fuselage into the front cockpit wearing the full panoply of flight gear. The ramp was designed properly to channel the airflow into the engines at supersonic speeds but for most flights, it performed a far more mundane role, as a walkway, during the start procedure. Convex 15 was a low-key event with minimal sortie content and gave the opportunity to fly around a pre-planned navigation route using the inertial navigation system, taking a look at the radar in all its modes and finishing with, in my case, a practice diversion to Binbrook. After a final crew ride known as Convex 12, my short conversion to the Phantom was over. I had amassed just short of five hours and, when I next climbed into the cockpit, was expected to use the Phantom in the role for which it was intended.

Having endured the rigours of the conversion phase, the pilots had a relative holiday during the basic radar phase as the emphasis switched to the navigators. This was where the transition to using an aircraft as an operational weapons system began. There was no margin for error with two jets closing on a collision course at combined speeds approaching 1,000 miles per hour. At those speeds, the time from turn in at 50 miles to the merge was measured in seconds not hours, and if the intercept was not executed correctly, the fighter would roll out many miles behind its prey.

The division of responsibilities was easy in the Phantom. Although the pilot had a repeater display, the navigator had the main display in the back cockpit, operated the radar controls and planned and executed the intercept using verbal commands. Once visual with the target, the pilot took over, engaging the target with the most appropriate weapon while the navigator guarded the 'six o'clock' looking for other threats that might engage the aircraft while the pilot was busy. On a bright blue day, the transition to the visual attack might come quite early but the crews trained for the dark, dank night, meaning the navigator might have to control the intercept on radar to the point where he locked on for a firing, firmly established in the rear hemisphere. This might mean that neither crew member had ever seen the target.

To intercept another aircraft, a number of fundamental principles were in play. The aim was to achieve a roll out position about 2 miles behind the target after completing a 'final turn'. By adjusting the long-range approach using changes in heading, the navigator could put the Phantom on to an ideal approach path.

The first parameter was the track crossing angle (TCA), which was the angle between the fighter's heading and the target heading. As an example, a '90 TCA' meant that the angle between the two headings was 90 degrees. For academic purposes, the syllabus included 90, 120, 150, and 180 intercepts. All intercepts were assessed against the collision angle because the angle off the nose from which a target would approach differed on different TCAs. If the target held a collision approach, it would track along a steady bearing with reference to the fighter and they would pass at the exact same spot at the merge; hence the term 'collision approach'. As an example, a 90 collision would run down the radar scope at 42 degrees off the nose, but each TCA had a different collision angle. Clearly, a 180 collision would fly straight towards the fighter at 0 degrees angle off straight down the extended centreline drawn out from the fighter's nose.

The next fundamental was the concept of a 'tight' approach or a 'slack' approach. A 'tight attack' would position the target outside the collision angle and, if the navigator did nothing to adjust the approach, the target would pass behind the fighter, leaving a long turn to achieve the correct roll out. Conversely, a 'slack attack' would approach inside the collision angle and cross well ahead of the fighter resulting in a roll out in excess of the desired range, again if the approach was not adjusted.

For a 180 approach, the ideal lateral displacement depended on the fighter's height. At low level, a 5-mile displacement was used, increasing to 8 miles at medium level and 15 miles at a high level. This reflected the loss in performance in the upper air and the need for a wider turning circle. Based on a fighter speed of Mach 0.9 and a target speed of Mach 0.8 (giving the fighter an overtake advantage), 'keys' were calculated to determine where a target would appear on the radar scope if the fighter was following an ideal approach path. A simple table that navigators learned by heart was the core of flying a successful intercept. This seemingly unintelligible block of figures could be adapted for any airborne situation. Other vital terms were 'hot' and 'cold'. A 'hot' target depicted with a positive value would cross the nose and was closing whereas a cold target depicted by a negative value had already crossed the nose and was opening. Often, this translated into one coming towards or one going away.

TCA	Collision	30 nm	25 nm	20 nm	15 nm	10 nm	Turn Key	Crosses nose
60	55	50	49	48	45	40	-10 at 2.5	3 NM
90	42	37	36	34	32	26	0 at 4	4 NM
120	28	21	19	17	14	6	-10 at 6	8 NM
150	14	4	2	-1	-7	-18	-25 at 9	22 NM
180	0	-16	-20	-24	-32	N/A	-40 at 12	N/A

These values could be plotted as a 'blip track' which showed, in effect, a time-lapse image of how the blip would track down the radar scope if it followed an ideal approach. If the contact was at a point off the ideal 'blip track', a 30-degree heading change would be held until the blip resumed the ideal plus or minus 30 degrees. At that point, a turn back would place the blip on the ideal approach.

When all else failed, the navigator resorted to short range procedures. These might also be employed if the target was detected at extremely short range, if the target had evaded negating the efforts to set up a precise approach, or in the unlikely event that the navigator had made serious errors in his calculations of the intercept geometry, perish the thought. There were two procedures that could recover a poor approach to the target. A line was drawn mentally on the radar scope from zero range at 45 degrees off the centreline to the left of the nose, out to a point on the nose at 6 miles, and back to 45 degrees off on the right at zero range. A second procedure used a line drawn from 45 degrees off at zero range on the left out to 45 degrees off at 4 miles on the left, to a similar point at 45 degrees off at 4 miles on the right, and back to 45 degrees off at zero range on the right. The concept was simple. If the target hit these last-ditch lines on the radar scope, a hard turn towards was initiated and a blind turn at 3 g would achieve a 2-mile roll out. It was not pretty but it was undoubtedly effective. Lightning pilots used these procedures as the norm. Sorry, I could not resist it.

While I have described the intercept procedures in simple terms, the basic interceptions manual went to thirty pages of theory, underpinned with graphs and calculations and guaranteed to solve the worst case of insomnia. Even so, it merely scratched the surface of the subject and real-world intercepts relied on many other tweaks and adjustments to succeed. Most importantly, at this stage, it assumed a non-evading target which real-world targets seemed, unsportingly, to forget.

One of the enduring myths is that the navigator had no control over the aircraft. While that was true in the physical sense and while many of the OCU Phantoms were fitted with dual flight controls, control was exercised using voice commands. One of the tenets of crew cooperation was that once the navigator called 'Judy' to the fighter controller (the codeword meaning I have control of the intercept), the pilot would follow his commands implicitly. Only if the safety of the aircraft was in jeopardy would he override the voice commands. Many pilots followed the voice commands out of idle curiosity, although they were, naturally, too modest to admit this fact.

The commands were not random but followed a strict methodology so that the position of the aircraft could be adjusted in three dimensions. The heading could be adjusted using compass information, either in numbers of degrees or a turn on to a heading. Left or right was expressed in nautical terms—port and starboard, for example, 'starboard 30'. Alternatively, the navigator might initiate a turn that would continue until he called a roll out. 'Come port, I'll roll you out'. This might be used if a target began to make an orbit and there was no way of knowing how long the turn might last. Although, at this early stage of training, the target and fighter speeds were fixed, once established in behind a target, speed was used to

The OCU basic interceptions guide. (*UK MOD Crown Copyright [1983]*)

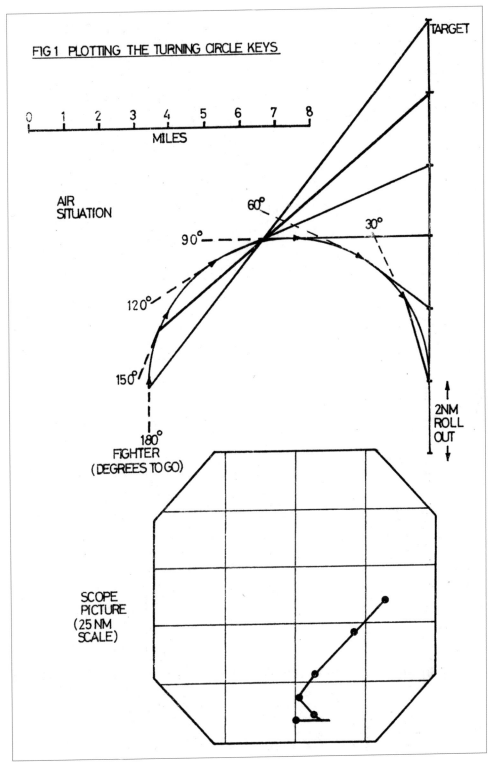

The turn keys for a head-on stern attack, showing how the blip would track down the radar scope. (*UK MOD Crown Copyright [1983]*)

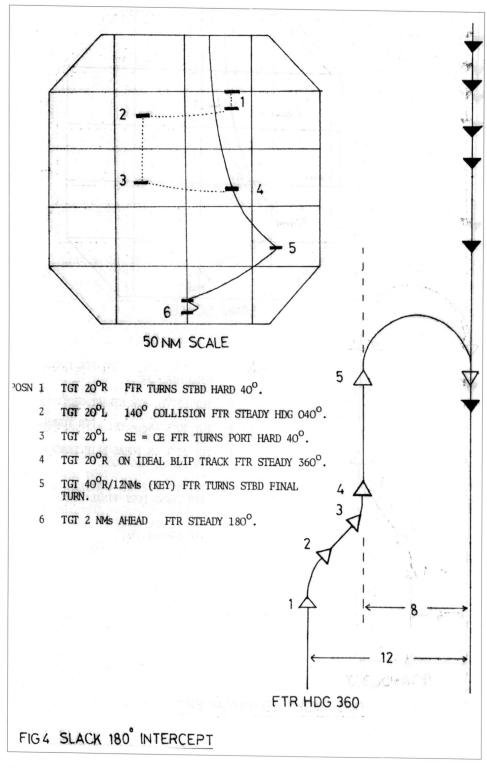

50 NM SCALE

POSN 1   TGT 20°R   FTR TURNS STBD HARD 40°.

2   TGT 20°L   140° COLLISION FTR STEADY HDG 040°.

3   TGT 20°L   SE = CE FTR TURNS PORT HARD 40°.

4   TGT 20°R   ON IDEAL BLIP TRACK FTR STEADY 360°.

5   TGT 40°R/12NMs (KEY) FTR TURNS STBD FINAL TURN.

6   TGT 2 NMs AHEAD   FTR STEADY 180°.

FTR HDG 360

FIG 4 SLACK 180° INTERCEPT

A graphic showing how to adjust the long-range approach and how the blip would react on the radar scope. (*UK MOD Crown Copyright [1983]*) close in range by asking for a speed to fly. At long range, this was done in chunks of 50 knots using the commands 'more speed' or 'speed back'. The most important fact was that an intercept was a three-dimensional manoeuvre and thinking in three dimensions was vital. Height was the most vital parameter because it brought the Phantom into close proximity with a moving object—the target or a fixed object, namely the sea or the ground. The navigator would normally ask for specific height, say 'descend to 8,000 feet' but not always. Once again, the command 'go down' or 'go up' would begin a fixed rate climb or descent until the call of 'level'. Once below 5,000 feet, height became even more important as the risk of hitting the ground increased. If the descent was overland, the concept of safety altitude came into play as the height of the terrain became increasingly relevant. Even though the pilot was physically controlling the jet, avoiding the ground or the sea was a crew responsibility. Height checks in the descent were regular and increased markedly as the ground approached. Checks were initiated from both cockpits with each check confirmed from the other. Errors could occur in setting the correct pressure setting on the altimeters so making sure you were both using the same datum was vital. Height was the parameter that could kill.

To control the final turn, another series of commands came into play. The turning circles on which the intercept geometry was based assumed the Phantom would fly a 'Rate 1 Turn' at 45 degrees angle of bank at 1 g. In order to finesse a 2-mile roll out, the turn rate might need to be increased in order to lead the target or lag the target. Pulling lead closed the range and lagging increased the range by shortening or lengthening the flight path. The call 'harder' or 'ease' achieved this.

Equipped with these basic commands, a navigator could control the aircraft with precision. This was voice control long before technology companies even thought of the concept.

Visual identification procedures or 'visidents' would become a staple of the trade and even in good weather, using the radar allowed a much more controlled approach into the vicinity of the target. The operational procedure, however, assumed a target flying at night, without lights or in cloud. The approach began from the 2-mile roll out point and at medium level was made from below. Commands became much more precise, more dynamic and more critical. To control a radar contact inside 1,000 yards, when it may begin to drift rapidly towards the edge of the scope, absolute precision was demanded of both men. Setting an 8-degree approach path and approaching from zero azimuth or directly astern, the navigator controlled the closure towards the target. With a computer game, such control has no consequence. In a Phantom on a dark night at 1,000 feet over the North Sea, that 'skating blip' represented 25 tons of airframe flying at 400 knots plus. Crews learned precision rapidly. Navigators asked for, and pilots delivered, accuracies of 1 degree in heading and 5 knots in speed. The height would be held with rock steady accuracy because staying alive depended on it. The final stabilised position was directly line astern, about 300 yards from the target looking up at about 20 degrees of elevation. The pilot could only go closer if he was visual with the target and, worryingly, it was possible to get to that point without being able to see the object of your attention. It might be that the only thing visible was the cockpit lights of a darkened jet flying low over the sea or a star suddenly extinguished by the bulk of the target's airframe.

The astute will have recognised that approaching a target flying at an extremely low level from below might not be the most risk-free solution so the profile was adjusted below 5,000 feet to approach from above. Descending down the 5-degree line in to 500 yards, the target would disappear below the nose making it impossible to identify visually. For that reason, an offset was thrown in, jinking out to stabilise at 300 yards in the target's four or eight o'clock, looking down from about 10 degrees above the target.

Students would practise this procedure endlessly, in the AI trainer, the simulator, and the aeroplane until the procedures were ingrained and the profiles memorised.

Sitting in close formation was not the most comfortable position yet crews might be asked to shadow a Russian Bear for many minutes. A more adaptable method was needed; this was known as shadowing. The procedure was flown about 1–2 miles behind the target and the aim was to follow in trail reacting to any evasion. If the radar was locked up, the exercise was simple. The Sidewinder steering dot on the display gave an indication when the target turned or changed height. It was relatively simple for either crew member to interpret the movements, to 'fly the dot' and stay in position. Doing so, however, meant that the crew concentrated exclusively on that one target to the detriment of anything else in the immediate area. If the Bear was flying in formation with another Bear, it might be nice to know what both aircraft were getting up to. It was not unknown for Soviet crews to push RAF crews to the limits of safe flight. On the OCU course, however, the procedure was flown in search mode adding pressure on the navigator who needed to track the target manually using the navigator's hand controller as well as giving commands to the pilot. The cues when the target evaded were also less apparent, relying on movement of the blip on the scope rather than the lively steering dot. Operationally, the pilot could quite easily fly the profile using the steering dot assisted only when the target became less compliant.

With a target flying the same heading as the Phantom, the 'blip' would sit quite happily at zero azimuth, on the nose, at 1 mile. Once the heading, height, or speed changed, action was needed. If the heading changed, the blip would begin to drift away from the centreline. If the target's height changed the first thing a navigator might notice was that the blip disappeared. Rolling the thumbwheel in either direction would re-establish radar contact and the fighter's height could be adjusted to follow. If the target increased speed, the blip would increase in range, or conversely rush down the radar scope. Once a change was seen, the navigator fine-tuned the parameters to return to equilibrium. If it was, for example, a routine heading change, a simple alteration of heading would fix the problem. If the changes were random, constant adjustment might be needed. Some days, it was a luxury to simply look out of the canopy and be able to shadow visually.

There were two basic attack profiles that would be taught on the OCU. An 'Attack-Reattack' was a head-on profile designed to put the aircraft in the optimum position, in the forward hemisphere, ready to launch a Sparrow, and later a Skyflash missile. The navigator would position the Phantom on a high-aspect, collision course, 2,000 feet below the target, aiming for a point in space along its extended flight path. The range at which the radar was locked up would vary with height. For a Sparrow to guide, it had to receive a guidance signal transmitted by the main AN/AWG 12 radar, reflected back from the target and received by the tiny antenna in the nose of the missile. The Sparrow was tuned to this frequency before launch and would guide along the beam to its target. This was known as semi-active guidance. At medium level, a typical Sparrow firing was at 10–12 miles, long before the crew could see the target. At a low level, it would be much closer, maybe only 5–6 miles away. Once the pilot had launched the missile, a breakaway manoeuvre away from the target's flight path put the target towards the edge of the radar coverage. This had two effects. It gave the Phantom room to manoeuvre in behind by increasing the lateral separation, but it also collapsed a hostile fighter's weapons envelope, making it harder to target the inbound Phantom. At a defined range, a hard turn towards the target was initiated and the Phantom manoeuvred into the stern hemisphere for a follow-up Sidewinder shot. This gave the maximum probability of achieving a kill in the event of a Sparrow missile failure. In some cases, for example, a supersonic target, it was likely that the Phantom would roll out too far behind and outside parameters for a follow-up shot. In this case, two Sparrows may be committed in the head sector to increase the probability of kill, albeit at the expense of additional weapons use.

The second profile known as a 'stern attack' discounted a head-on shot, opting instead to position directly into the target's stern hemisphere. There was a higher likelihood that the fighter would be seen as it made its approach from the beam but the displaced attack was easier to control and required less performance to achieve success. The stern attack was the preferred profile for intercepting Soviet intruders or wayward civilian aircraft. By the end of the basic radar phase, the new crews would be able to fly each profile in their sleep.

Each sortie followed a defined pattern, starting with a briefing during which the domestics for the sortie such as diversions and fuel recovery states were given. A mission briefing from the staff navigator would discuss the intercept profiles and, during an OCU training sortie, this would be in some depth. Mandatory safety rules were always briefed as were the criteria to achieve a DCO (duty carried out). After the air work, the mission ended with a thorough debriefing, during which every aspect of the mission was analysed carefully to ensure all lessons had been captured. The first part of the debrief was held in the debriefing room, but the final event was for the staff navigator to assess the radar film. The KD41 camera fitted over the radar scope in the back cockpit and filmed the radar display capturing the images on old-style cine film on celluloid. The cassette from the camera was delivered to the Station Photographic Section after landing and arrived back at the squadron after about forty-five minutes. Loaded on to a rattling cine projector, the flickering images captured the detail of the intercepts, albeit lacking any sound from the cockpit. It was one of the instructor skills to determine why mistakes had

Above: Preparing for a sortie on 228 OCU.

Below: A Phantom captured over Lincolnshire by the strike camera from a second Phantom. (*From the collection of Winston 'Scruph' Oliver; courtesy of the Oliver family; UK MOD Crown Copyright [1971]*)

been made using notes taken in the air and combining those with a good deal of information from the staff pilot who had watched the intercepts in the air.

It was at this stage that pilot and navigator banter was developed and honed. It was tradition to deride the contribution of the man in the other cockpit as often as possible yet, hopefully, in a witty manner. After an emergency in the air, one student pilot was heard to say 'I think.' The staff navigator uttered the immortal words: 'You just wiggle your arms and legs in an appealing fashion and leave me to do the thinking.'

As an experienced pilot already, using the Phantom in this way was new to Keebs: the basic radar phase of the course was the introduction to using the radar while airborne to practise intercepts, from now on, as the pilot, it would all be captain time, with either a staff navigator or a fellow course student in the backseat. We took off in pairs with each aircraft taking it in turns—one run as the target and the next as the fighter. There was a lot to take in to begin with as not only was it important to understand the mechanics of the intercepts but there was a whole new world of air defence procedures and terminology.

The ground-controlled interception (GCI) sites for RAF Coningsby were at RAF Boulmer, RAF Neatishead, or RAF Staxton Wold; they oversaw the operating areas we flew in. The controllers were responsible for the airspace making sure that we did not come close to other traffic, that we stayed in our allotted area, and they controlled the intercept set-ups to our pre-briefed parameters. The level of control for the inbound attack varied from 'Alpha' control, where the intercept was completely organised from the ground, to 'Delta' control where only an initial bearing and a distance to the target was given, such as 'Bogey bears 060 range 45'—the rest is all yours, sport.

There was a plethora of new buzzwords and codewords to learn, some of which are listed in the glossary. I had visited the Buchan GCI site on the east coast of Scotland while holding with the Hunter Tactical Weapons Unit at RAF Lossiemouth and at that time it had been of passing interest. Now the pressure was on to understand how, as a crew, I could progress through the syllabus. The thing about any crewed aircraft is being able to work together as a team, the better you understood one another and cooperated together, the more effective you became but that was easier said than done. Although my fellow navigator students were a great bunch, I could not say the same for all the staff navigators who sporadically seemed to have some sort of point to make, becoming quite obstructive and obstreperous at times. Having once been an unenthusiastic instructor myself, I understood that they would rather be serving on a Phantom squadron in Germany, flying operationally, rather than baby-sitting a bunch of newbies. That said, later, when I found myself in the same situation as a F-4 instructor, there was a professional responsibility to do the best that you could for your student even if you might not be sending one another a Christmas card that year.

Let us look at an early air defence intercept sortie from a pilot's perspective. Time to get airborne once more, enjoying the mighty thrust of the Phantom afterburners, level off at medium level, check in with GCI with a weather check, weapons checks complete, radar checked out OK, and ready for vectors for the first split. The first sortie would be a case of pure radar handling, seeing the different modes and getting the best out of the radar picture, changing scales, height search pattern, scan display, radar gain, etc. The pilot had a repeater screen in the front and, apart from a few exceptions, not a lot of control over the radar itself, but we did own the only trigger in the aircraft. Over the next few splits, ideal set-ups would be set up by the GCI and then later with diverse set-ups. There would be no more perfect 180 by 8 miles or 0 miles but displacements that would be random to make sure that the intercept approach had to be adjusted to get into the ideal position. Once in that correct position, it was time to learn how to get from passing on opposite tracks to turning in behind the target. When the target reached a known azimuth, the turn was called for and adjusted accordingly so that the target crossed the nose on the 90 degrees with 4 miles to go, ensuring a 2-mile roll out in its six o'clock position, or not.

Initially, it was the navigator's job to control the intercept with the pilot monitoring the parameters of height, speed, and airspace; while doing that, it was important to have situational awareness ready for the next phase of the intercept. Then it was time for the student pilot to have a go at an intercept, perhaps with not quite so much finesse.

In quieter moments both crew members monitored the airmanship issues such as position in relation to airways, distance from base, fuel required for recovery and so on. At all times good crew cooperation dictated that we should both have an idea of what was occurring in the other cockpit, to help when possible.

In the next phase of the intercept, the instructions from the controller might be either to engage or to identify, normally nominated at turn in. It was the culmination of all the hard work to ensure that the fighter was in a position to comply with instructions; however, this might change during an intercept as, for example, late intelligence might override a 'Mission to Identify' into one of 'Mission to Engage'—with a missile shot.

Following naturally on from the intercepts phase came the combat phase. Although the Phantom did not really possess the reputation as a pure 'dogfighter', it was more than capable in the visual arena if flown and operated well. It was the strength of the weapon system that was the key, and knowing how to employ that system that would keep a Phantom crew alive operationally.

Keebs recalls really enjoying the air combat phase of the course. Up to now, it had been a case of enduring the radar phase but now we could unleash the Phantom to do what it did best—fight—and in doing that, it was more than capable. It was not the best turning and burning machine in the Western arsenal but if used astutely and appropriately, it could hold its own against most other jets. I will not start with the basics as I covered some of those with the TWU course so we shall get into the good stuff. The trick was to find the opposition's weak spots. Could he fly as fast or as high as me? Could he turn as well as me? What was his aircraft like to fly at low speed? Could he accelerate like a bat out of hell? What was his zoom capability? Was he single-seat? Were we well matched? Were his weapons' capabilities or radar performance equal to mine? Did he have any defensive countermeasures, such as flares or chaff? Did he prefer to fight in the vertical or would he drag it down to base height perhaps in a 'death spiral'? Would he shoot and run, or did he prefer a close-quarter fight? Hopefully, he would avoid going into a rolling scissors because that would expose my weaknesses in the same way as I would try to discover his, and so it went on. It was a three-dimensional game of chess in a way but one that would have deadly consequences if it ever came for real. There were academic books listing other air forces and their aircraft with all the performance figures. They were kept in the security vault and were there for study; however, it was not until you actually flew against a different type of aircraft that you could get a handle on which were the winning tactics and which were not. Much more of this would come later on the squadron especially when dissimilar air combat training (DACT) was introduced, but the basic OCU combat lessons as flown against another Phantom gave a very good grounding.

Entering a fight, there were a number of other points that the Phantom crew needed to assess rapidly during the opening moves—importantly, what aircraft were we fighting and how many? Was it a single bomber or two fighters? Would they react defensively or become aggressive? Did we have an advantage, or were we in a neutral engagement, or crucially were we at a disadvantage? The first situation was good and was to be capitalised upon. The second was not too bad and it was worth a tentative manoeuvre to see how things went. The third was very bad and it was time to get out of there. Time to plug in the burners, contrive a minimum separation pass, blow through at Warp Factor five, preferably at base height, and (for real) enter cloud. If the opposition turned and chased then it was a case of watch him closely, keep running with your tail between your legs and your sphincter going 'half a crown, sixpence'. Should he approach within missile range then hard turn towards keeping energy levels high, meet him head-on, shoot him in the face, and blast through, hoping that home base is not too far away and is in the right direction. If not, repeat all of the above and try again, this time pointing in the right direction. There were more questions to answer but that is a good start to be going on with one *versus* one, in the smallest nutshell that I could find.

Two *versus* one was a different kettle of fish. This was all about coordinated tactics with one fighter being 'engaged' and keeping the enemy tied up and predicable while the other fighter remained 'free', manoeuvring to a point where he had a distinct advantage to shoot. If there was no immediate success then the two roles of free and engaged fighters could switch between aircraft in order to try to achieve a kill. If the shot opportunity was lost, the process continued until the kill was achieved. One *versus* two was a nasty case of shoot first, see what is left, and mop up the pieces—or run away bravely.

Throughout the fight, airmanship was paramount. There were safety bubbles drawn around the opponent into which thou shalt not pass. Also, there were inevitable airspace restrictions, base height was sacrosanct, 'g' limits to observe, or aircraft configurations that could severely limit and affect the combat profiles; in addition to all this, there were cloud, sun, and contrails to consider, plus direction and distance to base—all these played a part. Of course, and most importantly, it was essential to keep your combat fuel in reserve; did I have enough fuel to enter the fight, engage, and see if I could win, then still disengage successfully and make it back to base with enough fighting gas in the tanks in case I got bounced? There were so many questions and so little time in which to decide.

Most air combat trips lasted about thirty minutes. Blast up to height, set up a visual split about 5 miles apart, turn in towards one another, both crews called 'Tally Ho', and the games began. A call of 'No Tally' (meaning no visual contact) from both aircraft meant the fight would be stopped—a 'No Tally' from one combatant followed by a 'Continue' from the other aircraft was a radio call that you did not want to hear; that meant that he could see you even if you could not see him. This call was, more often, than not, followed by a call of 'Fox 2, knock it off', as the missile kill was taken, totally unobserved.

After three or four combat splits, we would quickly be down to 'Joker', or minimum fuel, meaning the end of the exercise. Time to level out, check instruments, orientate position, get back into formation, and make a mad dash for home for the debrief. Mistakes had been made but most importantly what lessons were there were to be learned? After a cup of tea and a re-brief for the next exercise, it was time to do it all again. Flying two or three combat trips in a day meant you had been through a physical and mental wringer but a couple of beers in the bar at cease work would soon ease the aches and pains. Occasionally, the debrief/finger poking would spill over into our social time, such was the enthusiasm and competitive nature for the 'sport of kings'.

If the air combat phase challenged the pilots, for an *ab initio* navigator, it was truly mind-blowing. The basic radar phase had been relatively sedate, but during the air combat phase, from the outset, the target would be deliberately aggressive. Gone was the sedentary compliance and not only did the target evade during the run in but the moment he sighted the fighter he would manoeuvre aggressively to negate the attack. Predictable intercepts against compliant targets were a thing of the past and the air combat scenario was more reminiscent of the real world. From first sight, both aircraft would begin to manoeuvre in the vertical plane, which was where the Phantom fought best. In a three-dimensional, gyrating world, up and down became relative terms and the first skill was to begin to see the opponent relative to your own aircraft not the ground. This concept was known as 'gyros out'.

New terms described the basic fighter manoeuvres, or BFMs, with 'high yo-yo', 'low yo-yo', and 'lag pursuit roll' added to the growing lexicon. These were the means by which the Phantom was operated to its limits. Drawing circles on a piece of paper on the ground was easy but air combat manoeuvres are flown in three dimensions. Learning how a Phantom would react when operated at its maximum angle of attack or the limit of its performance was about to begin. Sticks with small fighters attached to the end became essential training tools as the tiny fighters were used to demonstrate 3D manoeuvres in the debriefing room.

The navigator might be the only crew member with sight of the 'bogey' as the hostile aircraft was known and, if so, had to be able to control the aircraft in the 3D world. The aim was to get the pilot sighted once again following the merge as, once in visual contact, he could fly the aircraft more efficiently. Keeping sight of the opponent was critical so navigators had to control events by verbal commands in the interim. 'Roll Left', 'Roll Right', 'Pull', 'Push', 'Buster', and 'Gate' became the means to re-position an opponent in the dynamic environment until the pilot regained visual contact. The first exercises began with the student pilot in an offensive position in the rear quadrant pulling his nose on to the target. This was known as an offensive perch. Once established 'in the saddle', the defender would counter the attack using the basic manoeuvres to negate the attack. In full afterburner and at the limits of performance, the attack would progress to a natural conclusion. This might be a kill, an overshoot into a rolling melee known as a rolling scissors, or into a stalemate. The air combat leader would allow the exercise to continue until the learning point had been made. The event was then repeated with the student pilot in the defensive position trying, desperately, to negate the missile or guns shot, mostly ineffectively given the gulf in experience levels. Each BFM was then practised to build up an arsenal of responses and to recognise which technique was most appropriate.

The sorties progressed before culminating in one *versus* one splits arriving at the merge from a radar attack and finally, two Phantoms *versus* a single aggressor flown by a staff crew. This taught the navigators to control a second Phantom into a fight and the pilots to coordinate an offensive formation either as leader or wingman. Properly coordinated, a pair should always defeat a single opponent, but this was not always the case and a call of 'Fox 2' against one of the pair was recognised as a serious error, meaning the free and engaged tactics had failed. The air combat phase was hectic, covering all the disciplines in seven one *versus* one sorties and only two two *versus* one. The learning curve was steep but enormous fun.

The air combat phase ended on a less glamorous but equally demanding note with a night formation ride for the student pilots. The night formation exercise CV13 was indeed unlucky for some, noted Keebs—unlucky for the staff QFI that sat in the back seat for one, and myself for another. The navigators avoided this part of the course and very wisely so in my opinion (a fact strongly endorsed by Dave). In fact, most staff PIs tried to be away on leave or call in sick if they could. Night formation was more than a trifle hairy because all that training that had come previously had been achieved in daylight, but now it was bleeding dark—as dark as the darkest hole on a dark night during a power cut. It was virtually impossible to judge, to any exact degree of certainty, just how close you really were to one another because the Phantom external lighting left an awful lot to be desired. With only a few dim navigation lights, we prayed for a moonlit night—'a bomber's moon' as it was known during the war but this time for the benefit of us fighters. There was little hope of a good moon during the cloudy autumn nights in the UK and actually when the moon did pop out from behind the clouds, it emphasised just how stupid flying in close formation at night really was.

So then here we go then into CV13. Airborne in a thirty-second stream, into radar trail and close up on the leader to within a few hundred yards. When 'visual' with the flashing anti-collision lights, turn the radar off and close up into wide echelon position. Turn both aircraft's anti-collision lights off and all other lights to minimum, then move into a chummy echelon. Let the sheer horror of it all dissipate and allow your breathing to settle down, once settled, a few climbing and descending turns before it was back to base for a 'pairs' radar approach before overshooting, climbing back up to height, swapping places, and repeating the whole performance again. Once everyone was sufficiently scared, it was a tick in the box and we went to the bar, job done. Meanwhile, the navigators were at home watching Cilla Black presenting *Blind Date*, or perhaps *The Clothes Show*, along with their Babycham and cashew nuts. From the navigator's perspective, returning to reality, as the QFIs stole the back seat flying time, the navigators manned the ops desk and acted as duty officer flying. Admittedly, there was little enthusiasm to take part in the mating ritual, especially when only a single student pilot was scheduled and a spare back seat sortie was on offer. Under such circumstances, night flying could be classified as a minor emergency. On reflection, this was a phase happily left to the pilots.

The final phase of the course, the advanced radar phase, was almost universally popular, not least because it signalled that the end was near but also because failures at this stage were less common after the rigours of the previous phases. More advanced target profiles were introduced that challenged both crew members equally. Targets became less compliant and evasion was introduced. Starting with an unknown heading, by the time the navigator had established the parameters and begun an intercept, they had changed, meaning that the original geometry was wrong. As a consequence, the navigator had to replan the whole intercept again. Welcome to the realities of an evading target. Suddenly, the basic radar profiles seemed positively attractive.

Limited multi-target work was introduced to increase the tactical challenge. Other targets approached at a high level, above 50,000 feet, requiring an alternative attack profile or supersonic speeds that reduced reaction times and made it far harder to achieve a re-attack. Some elements, such as electronic jamming and air-to-air refuelling, would not be introduced until the operational work-up on the squadron, but the intercepts during the advanced phase were much more operationally relevant. For the pilots, the challenges of handling the Phantom at a high speed and at a high level introduced new problems. For the navigators, the profiles were more demanding and needed greater mental agility and sharper reactions. In later years, overland profiles were added which increased the difficulties many times over.

One final sortie would consolidate the training in the form of the 'End of Course War'. Launched from a simulated ground alert by the exercise controller, crews headed out to a combat air patrol in the Wash. A variety of targets, including, for the first time, other types, such as Vulcans and Canberras, flew against the CAP, to be intercepted by the students. The staff crews acted as targets and positively relished the chance to be devious and unpredictable. The student crews returned after relatively short times in the air clutching radar film which would prove, or disprove, the simulated kills.

Keebs recalled his final trip was trying to catch a staff crew batting along at very low altitude at 550+ knots, trying very hard not to be caught. It was a case of plug in the burners, feel the kick in your back as they lit and accelerate to over Mach 1, trying to avoid overflying any ships that lay along the flight path and, all the while, trying to decipher what was a ground return and what was an aircraft on a very cluttered radar scope.

With graduation confirmed, postings day was a cause for celebration. For Dave in 1976, the air defence Phantom force was building up and postings were as diverse as Suffolk, Coningsby, Leuchars in Scotland and Wildenrath in Germany. An added incentive was that some crews were nominated to join 892 Naval Air Squadron of the Fleet Air Arm for the final cruise of the catapult-equipped HMS *Ark Royal*, flying the Phantom from the deck. In those delightfully un-PC days, copious amounts of beer were consumed and an initiation ceremony, or two, was mandatory.

For Keebs in 1981, with eighty-two hours F-4 under his belt, it was time to pack his bags and head north once again to Bonny Scotland for his first fighter tour on the historic 43(F) Squadron, a.k.a. the 'Fighting Cocks'. For Dave, it had been a shorter trip to Sunny Suffolk to join 56 (Fighter) Squadron, aka the 'Firebirds', at RAF Wattisham for his first operational tour with a mere forty-nine hours and fifteen minutes, of which only one hour and fifteen minutes had been at night. The operational work-up beckoned.

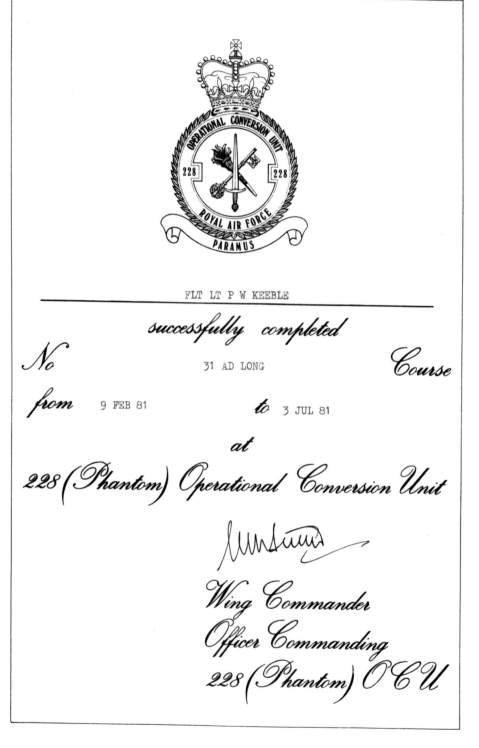

FLT LT P W KEEBLE

successfully completed

No   31 AD LONG   *Course*

from   9 FEB 81   *to*   3 JUL 81

at

228 (Phantom) Operational Conversion Unit

Wing Commander
Officer Commanding
228 (Phantom) OCU

Philip Keeble's OCU course graduation certificate.

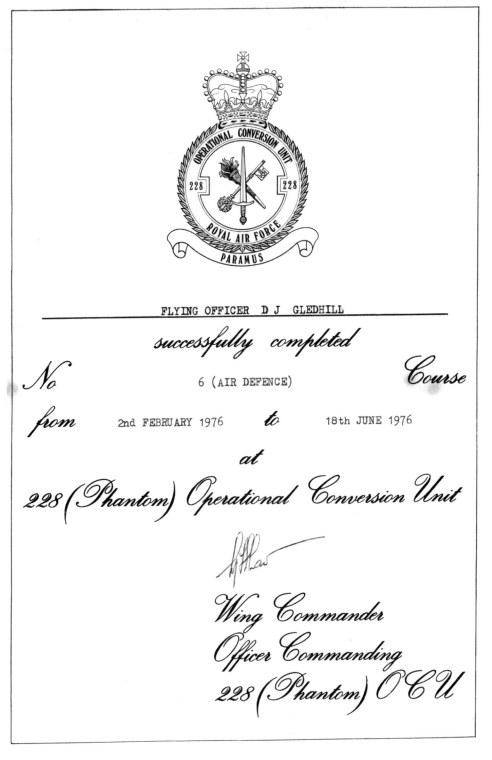

FLYING OFFICER D J GLEDHILL

successfully completed

No   6 (AIR DEFENCE)   *Course*

from   2nd FEBRUARY 1976   *to*   18th JUNE 1976

at

228 (Phantom) Operational Conversion Unit

Wing Commander
Officer Commanding
228 (Phantom) OCU

David Gledhill's OCU course graduation certificate.

11

Air Defence Squadron Operational Workup

Philip Keeble

July 1981, 43(F) Squadron, RAF Leuchars, Fife, Scotland
On arrival, the family moved into married quarters, the kids enrolled at the local school, the boxes were unpacked, and I reported for duty on Monday morning for early met brief. So far it seemed straightforward enough. I had arrived on my first fighter squadron at the age of thirty-four. It was not my first squadron but it was my first fighter squadron and the RAF's finest fighter unit. It was a thrill and privilege to become a serving member on the iconic 'Fighting Cocks'. Originally, I had been destined for a Phantom squadron in Germany but that was changed because 43(F) Squadron asked for someone with experience to be posted in because of the dilution of experienced pilots on the squadron at that time. I was the only pilot on the squadron other than the boss and the flight commanders who had flown other aircraft types and had served previously on an operational squadron, despite its lack of experience the squadron was amazing because it compensated with its enthusiasm and professional training regime.

A lot of that of course stemmed from the brilliant boss, Wing Commander Harry Drew, who made it apparent that a good boss can make a squadron and a poor one break it, but I guess that is the same the whole world over. He was a great leader, a blunt and straight-talking man, and one whom I would have followed through thick and thin. At my arrival interview, he mentioned that I would not be doing any station duty officer duties at RAF Leuchars and I warmed to him instantly, but he went on to explain that he would find plenty of other things to keep me busy. He was true to his word. He also hated paperwork, so he was a man after my own heart. My navigator, Rob, was detailed to be his official administration man and letter writer so I always knew where to find him when we were not flying because he would be ploughing through the boss's in-tray. As a crew, Rob and I hit it off straight away and we flew a lot together. On 43 (F) Squadron we did not fly as constituted crews, unlike the recce force where each crew was assigned to specific Russian targets, here we mixed and matched pilots and navigators as and when necessary, but I guess about a third of my sorties were with Rob. Later, he went on to a glorious career in the RAF, for which I take no credit. My last navigator on 43(F) Squadron was Steve Haslam, 'Haz', one of life's characters, of whom I will tell more later. Fighter squadrons were jam-packed with characters; this was still true then, and today, as it was in the Battle of Britain. Most aircrew were larger than life and had equally large egos to match. If I were to say that it was one way of surviving, I would not be far from the truth. Introverts, and there were a few, sometimes had a hard time on a fighter squadron. For me, it was certainly very different from my earlier reconnaissance squadron where we had to be self-contained as an autonomous crew operating around the globe, taking instructions via signals from our operating authority *en route*. A fighter squadron could sometimes look a bit like a pack to outsiders. Here, we were a tight-knit community on 43 (F) whereas I had been on 39 (PR) Squadron for eighteen months before I finally met all the squadron members.

Before I move on to the flying, there were 101 things to absorb, besides operating a Phantom. There was the squadron history for starters. Now, this may seem a little tame but a perusal of the squadron photo albums showed the horrendous loss of life that occurred on a daily basis during the First World War. Young boys, barely trained, would pitch up in the morning and be dead by teatime. Many would not see out their first week on the squadron. It was a sobering experience to look at all those innocent faces and think of the loved ones they left behind. In those days, if you saw it through your first month of the war, then you were doing well and, probably, had a good chance of surviving. It was a steep learning curve and I was just grateful and glad that times had changed. Then there were the squadron songs to learn; first the generic fighter squadron's favourite, 'The Flag', which had been popularised by the Germans during the Second World War. It seems odd I know but, nevertheless, it entered into the squadron's songbook. There was a little ditty that naturally took liberties with the reputation of our sister squadron, 111(F) Squadron or the 'Tremblers'. Finally, there was our signature song 'Forty-Three are in the bar tonight'. Of course, we needed a squadron drink, and in our case, it was a 'Fighting Cocktail', which was in the squadron's colours of black and white. It consisted of the coffee liqueur Kahlúa and Baileys Irish Cream, poured carefully so as to produce a distinct colour stratum. It was drunk in a single shot known as a 'yam sing' and was truly vile. Only a good, strong pint of British ale could truly take away the taste. The 'Op Pot' was an endurance test that would await all that passed the squadron conversion phase and was the ritual to mark the milestone once they had earned their 'Op Patch'.

The Phantom FG1s of the Leuchars Wing differed from the FGR2s operated by the OCU and the other front-line F-4 squadrons. The FG1 was a fine ship and a slightly sportier model than the FGR2; it handled slightly better as well (but that is a relative term). The FG1 was the original British version of the F-4 and had remained 'navalised' in that it still had its carrier-friendly folding wing mechanism, an extendable nose wheel, a slightly different bleed air duct system, plus in addition a slightly smaller radar and nose cone, a slotted tailplane, and a primitive navigation system, powered by a hamster on a wheel. Unfortunately, the RAF had not bought enough hamsters and the earlier animals had stayed on the sinking ship when the Navy retired their FG1s. What the FG1 did not have, unlike the FGR2, was a high-frequency radio which gave long-range communication or the inertial navigation and attack system (INAS). Now these two assets would have made a huge difference to the two squadrons stationed at RAF Leuchars whose primary role was to mount QRA, patrolling the northern airspace in the Iceland–Faeroes Gap. It would have been useful, firstly, to know where you were in that vast, frozen, oceanic world and, secondly, to be able to speak to someone in authority and tell them what was going on. In the event, we relied on the tanker or the airborne early warning (AEW) aircraft to relay messages for us, but that was not always possible. Being 'temporarily unsure of one's position' up in the Gap was a common occurrence. I can understand giving the jets with INAS to the RAFG squadrons as it was always handy to know which side of the Iron Curtain border you were on—you should read Dave's book *Phantom in the Cold War* for a full description of RAF Germany Phantom operations. I can also understand the logistics of having the same aircraft type, namely the FGR2s at RAF Coningsby, because that is where the OCU trained the crews for the variant that served the majority of the squadrons, but having the FGR2s at RAF Wattisham, where they were able to better cope with limited navigation kit and radios, operating along the East Coast areas seemed irrational. Explain that logic to me if you can. Not having the correct equipment on Northern QRA meant that life could be a bit exciting sometimes when chasing Russians; fuel reserves became a bit of a problem at times as our sister squadron 'Tremblers' found out on one occasion to their cost. After an oversight, a crew was forced to jettison their external fuel tanks and weapons in order to make it back to dry land—all eight missiles, down into the bottom of the ocean. Since the demise of the traditional aircraft carriers, one of the major roles that had been assigned to 43 (F) Squadron was to keep the Royal Navy safe and happy in supporting their operations. We were known as a Tactical Air Support for Maritime Operations (TASMO) squadron. In effect, that meant that the Navy could call upon us to offer them air cover and support whenever and wherever needed, often hundreds of miles out to sea.

The squadron convex had to be tackled before I could even consider myself operational; first came a two-stick ride with the squadron QFI in the 'T' bird for my arrival check. It concentrated on the handling differences between the two marks of Phantom, the FGR2 and the FG1, a look at the local flying area and a practice diversion to our closest civilian airfields. Once checked out as safe, the rest of the convex could begin in earnest. On 43 (F) Squadron, the 'T' bird was always flown in 'Alpha fit', which meant that the external fuel tanks were removed. Uncluttered, the aircraft was relatively light and sprightly, unlike flying in 'Charlie fit' with two external fuel tanks under the wings. The main fit for QRA was known as 'Delta fit' with three external tanks; two under the wings and a large tank on the centreline station gave extra fuel. Add to that for QRA there was the little matter of eight missiles loaded on board, all this meant that this was now a true heavyweight jet. Happily, the thrust was more than up to the job of getting us airborne under almost all circumstances.

Other convexes followed, including one flown with an experienced navigator looking at the local procedures with a little radar handling and a practice diversion to Edinburgh thrown in. The next eighteen sorties were very much a recap of the advanced radar phase that I had just completed on the OCU, but on steroids. There was a lot more of everything; more targets, more fighters, more evasion. Within these sorties, if fuel permitted, we visited the northern diversions in the Scottish islands. The main options were Stornoway on Lewis and Harris, Kirkwall in the Orkneys, and Lerwick in the Shetlands. It also gave us a chance to talk to and visit the military radar units at RAF Buchan and RAF Benbecula. There was a NATO radar site in the Faeroes call sign 'Polestar', whose job it was to fill in the radar gaps between Iceland, the UK, and Norway. Adding to the overall coverage were the venerable Avro Shackletons AEW, from 8 Squadron at RAF Lossiemouth, which were planned to be replaced by the airborne early warning version of the Hawker Siddeley Nimrod, the AEW3, in the 1980s. The 'Shacks', call sign 'Anyface', were modified with radars taken from the Fleet Air Arm's Fairey Gannets and pressed into service. With the demise of the Nimrod project and the somewhat delayed arrival of the Boeing E-3D Sentry in the early 1990s, the Shacks continued and proved to be an admirable stopgap in doing a sterling job with their team of talented fighter controllers on board. Without a doubt, they were an important asset to the UK Air Defence Ground Environment at the time, although the E-3D when it arrived provided a quantum improvement in performance.

Some twenty trips and twenty-five hours flying time later came my first ever AAR sortie behind a Victor tanker from RAF Marham. It was time for the white-knuckle ride of a lifetime. Since the Second World War, there had been a number of different techniques used to pass fuel from one aircraft to another while airborne. The system used by the RAF, and incidentally the US Navy, is called the 'probe and drogue' method; this is where the tanker streams a reinforced hose from a drum fitted in a pod on the wings, or attached in the rear of the fuselage. Connected to the end of the hose is a drogue, or basket, inside of which is a coupling union into which the receiving aircraft drives its nozzle and, after making a firm contact between the two, the fuel flows. It is not as easy as it sounds. If practised on a nice calm day and, if the pilot could actually see what was occurring, then it might have been easy but it was not. If a butterfly flapped its wings in the Caribbean, the basket would sway from side to side over the Arctic Ocean like a Costa Rican rumba dancer. If a fairy sneezed in Finland, the basket would bob up and down like a Finnish ski jumper. If someone opened a window in Perth, Australia, then you might as well pack up and go home for the basket would act like a whirling dervish. The rubber hosepipe was about 80 feet in length and semi-flexible and was subjected to the vagaries of turbulence from the natural instability of the surrounding air and from the vortices from the tanker aircraft itself. This tanking madness called for cool nerves and a steady hand. Luckily, I had those very qualities, or so I thought until I came to my first encounter with the basket. The sortie was flown in a single-stick aircraft with an experienced navigator in the backseat rather than in the two-sticker with the squadron QFI. I do not know why, but perhaps Dave will offer some thoughts later. Maybe QFIs were not expendable. The Phantom refuelling probe was in a housing a fair way back on the fuselage, somewhere behind the rear cockpit; when extended, it was only just abeam the pilot's head. It was not actually possible to look ahead at the tanker, to pick up the formation references, and still see the basket and nozzle at the same time. For that reason, the *experts* had come up with a cunning plan whereby the navigator, who could see perfectly clearly what was happening, would become a talking remote controller. When the pilot had achieved a safe and steady formation position on the tanker, avoiding getting entangled in the hose, the navigator would start a running commentary for the pilot to follow his instructions:

'Forward two feet; steady'.

'Up one foot; steady'.

'Down a tadge'.

'Left one foot'.

'Forward'.

'You've missed at seven o'clock'.

This I could tell, because in my peripheral vision I could just sneak a glance during the final seconds of the contact and see what was happening. The navigators would then accuse us of peeping, which was the reason why we missed.

'You lunged'.

'No, I didn't, let's try again' ... and again ... until on one lucky prod:

'You're in'.

Hopefully, it was a positive connection because the next action was to push forward with just a dash of power to allow the drum mechanism to wind in a few feet to unlock the valves within the pipes and allow the pumps to up to wind up full pressure. At that point would come the welcome call from the tanker of 'fuel flows'. Refuelling from a Victor wing hose would deliver fuel at about 1,220 lb a minute whereas if it was from the hose drum unit (HDU) in the fuselage, it would be at about three times that rate. As I had already found with many skills acquired during my training, the more you practised, the more you improved, and the more you became confident in your newly learnt talents. Tanking was a key skill and one that would be called upon throughout my subsequent years in the fighter force. I tanked from a variety of other types, including the VC-10, the Tristar, the Hercules, the KC10, and my personal favourite, the Vulcan. I will leave the nightmare of refuelling from a USAF KC-135 until later.

The second AAR method used by the USAF was totally different and instead of the 'probe and drogue' they used a 'flying boom' where the tanker had a dedicated operator whose job it was to manually fly the boom, projecting out from below the tanker, into a receiver unit on top of the fighter/bomber. It was said to be more efficient and safer, there were pros and cons for both methods which I will not go into here for there are excellent books on the subject. Suffice it to say that the US Navy did not like the USAF method and used one very similar to the RAF.

During my first AAR trip over the North Sea I was either using radio calls, or using the 'comms out' technique known as 'silent procedures', that is operating by using the traffic light system on the refuelling pod. The thing about this sortie was to remember that there was no pressure. We had plenty of fuel aboard our Phantom and we could take our time and be nice and steady. There would be many occasions in the years ahead when we would not enjoy that luxury and the lessons learnt during those early sorties would have to be ingrained and become second nature. I have seen experienced pilots make a complete hash of it and ram into the basket so fast that the sheer force broke up the metal spokes, causing debris to go down the starboard engine intake triggering an engine failure. There was a weak link built into the system between the basket and the nozzle, which was intended to break if someone was too energetic causing the crew to return to base with their 'trophy' drogue still attached to the end of their nozzle; that is if they actually had enough fuel to get home.

At first, tanker convex sorties were scheduled when the weather was nice but it would not always be that way. Tanking in turbulence was not a sport but more like a gladiatorial jousting contest. Finally, along would come the opportunity to do it all in the dark. Night tanking is much like any previous night formation only much more dangerous. This time it would be a much larger object that we could hit; one in the form of a Handley Page Victor K2 weighing in at some 200,000 lb of which 109,000 lb was fuel. Our much smaller McDonnell Douglas F-4 Phantom weighed in at about a quarter of that, even when full of fuel. My cockpit would be the first to feel the full impact if I got it wrong. Sadly, in the 1970s, a Victor tanker was lost when a Buccaneer pilot pulled up when breaking contact shearing off the Victor's tailplane. Aerial refuelling was a bread and butter exercise in staying airborne longer. No one said that it was going to be easy.

One of the other principle skills to be learned on the squadron was how to cope with jamming, i.e. the means to deceive the fighter's radar thus denying it vital information, and electronic countermeasures (ECM) to overcome this. I know Dave will cover this in more depth. From a pilot's perspective, it was a dark art but one that the enemy seemed to be very keen on There were many different forms of aerial radar jamming, the first going back to the Second World War was releasing 'chaff', also called 'Window', (bundles of radar reflective aluminium strips) designed to overwhelm the German radars. Communications jamming, in which radio frequencies are blotted out with noise, or spoofing, where misleading messages are transmitted to bamboozle or hoodwink the listener. This was used for real by the Soviets during exercises in the Cold War. The Phantom radar had been designed with clever circuitry that could allow the fighter to home in on the source of the jamming. For this part of my squadron work-up a Canberra aircraft, fitted out as a jammer, operated against us in an exercise known as 'Exercise Profit'. Both crews were carefully briefed on safety aspects but even then, it was risky. I remember a crew in a Phantom suffering a mid-air collision with a Canberra one night, so the boundaries were tightly adhered to. After my op check I was involved in two sorties referred to as 'Opex 2 Bravo', one of which involved two Phantoms against four Canberras and another with four Phantoms against two Canberras, these were exciting sorties but as long as everyone stuck to the plan and obeyed the rules, the sorties were perfectly safe, in theory.

It was now into September and I had been on the squadron for a little over a month. The pace of flying was moving rapidly. I was checked out for air combat with the QWIP; that was shortly followed by a couple of air combat sorties with an experienced navigator, in this case, a USAF weapons system operator (or WSO as the USAF called their back-seaters) who was serving on an exchange tour. It was during one of these trips that I was introduced to the infamous 'Mexican Dust-Off', a head-to-head pass inside the legal minimum separation distance and designed to scare the living daylights out of the opposition. I also discovered that the collective noun for a group of Rhinos was a 'crash', seeming all too appropriate.

Soon came the day when I was expected to show my newly developed prowess on my final sortie, the 'Op Check', flown with the squadron QWIN; we were scrambled from ground alert against a Vulcan bomber. The target was cleared for heavy evasion and various target profiles and assorted scenarios were thrown up against us. An hour of the sortie was in daylight and the last half an hour in the dark, after which I am glad to report that I passed and was declared 'Operational'. The past eight weeks had been a haze, with fifty-five hours of high-pressure flying with nearly half of my trips flown at night in the wee small hours when the rest of the world was peacefully asleep. As a result of my previous experience, I had been given a somewhat expedited operational convex. There was a shortage of operational pilots and I was needed on the front line. At long last, I was an operational fighter pilot on a truly great fighter squadron. Life was good. Naturally, the learning did not stop there. One memorable sortie was when we were flying a night attack on RAF Binbrook in Lincolnshire, simulating a pair of hostile intruders. We were intercepted by a pair of Lightnings scrambled as part of their station evaluation. If I were to say that the ensuing intercept and subsequent encounter got a little electrifying, I would not be exaggerating one little bit. It was an eye-opener as to what went on when no one was looking. There would be plenty more of that.

Before I got anywhere near the 'Q' shed, there was finally the little matter of drinking the 'Op Pot', typically scheduled on a Friday in the crew room at cease work. The squadron assembled and the call went out, 'Bring out the Op Pot', which in the case of 43 Squadron was a yard of ale. Other units had their own versions but they all had the same purpose—to deliver a large amount of beer to the poor unfortunate recipient which had to be consumed in one go. It was a rite of passage marking an important stage in one's life, yet it was also of a sort of welcome to the club. The pot should have contained a large amount of beer but, in my case, some wag thought that it might be amusing to see it drunk in milk. Milk it was then, and down it went to a loud cheer. On reflection, I thought that beer might have been easier rather than 2.5 pints of cold, full-fat milk but a couple of weeks later, I had the opportunity to find out when I was 'requested' to try it again only this time properly, which I duly did.

With the job done, I could now take my rightful place in guarding the UK skies from those pesky Russians. Northern 'Q' was the pinnacle of the fighter force in the UK and was its main peacetime role. It was at the cutting edge of the Cold War, right bang in the front line where west met east. I had now been in the RAF for exactly sixteen years, done two Canberra tours, one tour as a flying instructor, and one on a ground tour. Add to that a whole heap of flying courses on a variety of jets including two OCUs, the Tactical Weapons Unit, and the Central Flying School course at RAF Little Rissington, and here I was, now operational on 43(F) Squadron flying the Phantom; I was as proud as punch, as was my right.

A couple of shifts went by with no Soviet activity but then on the night of 6 December 1981 at about 11 p.m., just as I was climbing into my bunk for the night, the hooter went off without any warning. My training kicked in: out of bed, into my immersion suit, boots on, run for the jet, harness and life jacket ready at the foot of the steps, climb ladder, the engineers had the ground power on, into the cockpit, strap-in, pins out, start the right engine, canopy closed, hydraulics and generators both looking OK, start the left, temperatures and pressures OK, Rob my navigator's ready, navigation system online, disconnect external power, Noddy caps removed from the missiles, and we were ready to go. Checking in with the master controller on the telebrief, we got the scramble message, which actually sounded more relaxed than it was:

'Leuchars this is Buchan, alert one Phantom.'

'Buchan, this is Leuchars. Q1.'

'Q1 vector 340 make angels 30. Scramble, scramble, scramble, acknowledge.'

'Q1 acknowledged. Scrambling.'

Doors open, wave chocks away, and dismiss the ground crew, brakes off, power on, and fast taxi the short distance to the runway. Air traffic control are alert and give us instant clearance for take-off. Final checks, seat pins out, canopy locked, pitot heaters on, flaps at take-off, pre-take-off checks complete and up to full power while still on the move. Engines look good in Mil Power. Into reheat, port engine good ... starboard burner failed to light.

'Rob, I'm happy to go with just the one if you are?'

'Affirmative. Let's go.'

Starboard burner back into max dry.

'We'll sort that out later.'

We were off in a cacophony of noise and a single plume of flame complete with its beautiful reheat 'shock diamonds' on the port and a cold, dark nozzle on the other. Fully loaded in 'Delta fit' with three external tanks and eight missiles we were very heavy but the power was more than sufficient to make it safely down the runway and blast off into the dark sky. Leaving the airfield and the surrounding Fife countryside to continue sleeping peaceably once more while we were off hunting the Soviets—wow, what a buzz. It was my first live launch and my heart did not stop racing for some considerable time. We checked in with Buchan and confirmed the details; we headed north to see what we could find. A Victor tanker had launched from Marham shortly after us and would follow up sometime. It would be a useful asset later.

Unbeknown to us, our sister squadron 'Tremblers' were holding their pre-Christmas party in the old control tower just a few yards away from the Q shed. When they heard the hooter sound, they poured out on to the tower balcony with stopwatches already running to view the show and time the event. We had ten minutes in which to be airborne; the Q2 crew sat in their jet waiting to replace us if needed. There was no way on this earth that I was going to let that happen. 'Tremblers' were taking more than a passing interest in the turn of events with my one and only reheat and fully expected an aborted take, which would mean we would not meet our scramble time. Happily, their early Christmas present became a great disappointment as I disappeared over the North Sea and headed north to find Santa. Reluctantly, they withdrew indoors to finish the beer. I did not get my Christmas present that day for the Russians on hearing of my release from the traps had decided to beat a hasty withdrawal back to their Motherland rather than face 'Killer Keeble'. It was a wise decision on their part but a great disappointment for Rob and me. My logbook reads '2:15 Night. Nil Int.'

Although I was no longer a QRA virgin, I still needed to see an actual Soviet aircraft. There were a number of fruitless scrambles in the coming months and it was not until 27 July that I finally got to intercept a pair of Bison Bravos from the Soviet Air Force serving with their OCU and on a training flight. They were a beautiful sight to behold, shiny yet dangerous at the same time; they acted friendly enough and gave us a wave. On that same launch, we were refuelled by an American KC-135, which was sent up to support us. To say that was tricky is a massive understatement so I will try to tell it as it really was—it was bloody difficult, and I cannot think of many other tasks that were as demanding, nor required such focused concentration, or such extreme motor skills. The USAF KC-135 used a boom refuelling system but was modified in order to support the RAF, it still had its flying boom but attached to the end was a short length of rubber hose used to adapt it to a probe and drogue system with a small basket. The only good thing about the KC-135 system was that the hose did not bounce around very much at all, in fact, quite the opposite—it was an almost semi-rigid pipe that in itself led to difficulties. In order to get the fuel to flow, the receiving aircraft had to connect with the basket and then push firmly forwards so that the hose formed a 'S' shape bend. This does not sound too bad, but if there was not enough force exerted by the thrust of the engines then the tensional forces in the 'S' curve were powerful enough, trying to unkink the hose, to force the aircraft backwards, expelling you from the basket if you were lucky, or snapping the probe off if you were not. Now that we understand the basics of the problem, all we have to do is connect, push, and hold, that is fine at medium to low level, but transiting up towards the Arctic Circle we are cruising at a high level to save fuel and where the thrust tapers off.

Picture the scene—I am cruising along needing some fuel and I am in a heavy jet at about my maximum altitude when up pops a friendly KC-135 offering to fill me to full courtesy of Uncle Sam. I gladly accept and roll in behind the tanker and proceed to joust with the basket. On entering, I suffer the indignity of not having enough power to hold the counter-push of the hose, despite using full dry thrust. As a result, I am spat out of the basket and have to try again. OK, this time, we will have to use a little throttle magic. With one in dry and one in minimum burner I now have enough power plus now a bit of asymmetric thrust, causing unwanted yaw, but hey I am an ex-Canberra man and this is nothing I cannot cope with. Pushing back into the basket using minimum burner on one and varying the dry throttle on the other I finesse my position and we stay in. Fuel flows. Not so fast, Philip, for soon my navigator, Colin, informs me that, 'we are actually using more fuel than we are taking on board'. 'This cannot be a good thing,' I think I knowing where this is going to end up. If I keep this going, we will end up in the Arctic Ocean. OK, it is time for a chat with the tanker driver; it took just one brevity word: 'Toboggan.' With that, the tanker gently eased off some of his power and descended allowing me the luxury of cancelling the one burner back into dry power, staying connected the whole while. Colin chips in again, this time with good news. 'Phil, Fuel increases.' Phew—I know I make it all sound so easy and simple but that is because I was a flying instructor and that was my job; I think that if I told you about the sweating, grunting, and swearing, plus the skill and the anxiety, you would not believe me and say that I was exaggerating, so I will not. By the end of our downward excursion, we are now into the thicker but bumpier clouds and it was a relief to disconnect, climb back up to height, say thanks and farewell to our American friend and get on with the job of finding those two Soviet Bisons. I am assuming that with all the shenanigans, the KC-135 had enough fuel to get back to his base in East Anglia or West Montana, or from wherever he had come. Not that I am ungrateful but give me a Victor tanker every time.

I had plenty more amusement with other tankers around the world over the coming years. Chatting to Haz, my subsequent navigator, he commented, 'I don't know what the QFI's taught the young pilots about 135s but a lot could not do it and so we would ask the tanker just to slow down instead.' That would be Convex 118, 'Climbing and Descending whilst Tanking' in the QFI's handbook. Perhaps best left to the navigators, this sortie should was left out of the Convex.

Air combat debriefing was a challenging reconstruction exercise but was undergoing radical changes with the advent of the computer age. The ACMI in Sardinia was an electronic system that recorded the aircraft's data while they flew in simulated air combat; that information could then be used to reproduce the engagements for later debriefing. This was *Star Wars* and *Top Gun* rolled into one, only 1,000 times more realistic. The ACMI installation was hosted by the Italian Air Force airfield at Decimomannu airfield, near to the city of Cagliari. The range itself was sited off the west coast of the island. I will not go into any great detail of how it was all set up and if you want a fuller description then try Dave's book *Phantom in Focus*. In short, each aircraft carried a transmitter that broadcasted its flight and weapons parameters to a series of hi-tech, static buoys positioned around the range. The buoys received and transmitted the information of each aircraft back to the central computer at Decimomannu in real time, enabling the range safety officer to assess every weapon shot and validate whether it was a 'kill' or 'no kill'. A 'kill' meant that the 'dead guy' had to leave the fight and wait for another scenario to be set up. The tiny coffin shape that appeared around the aircraft symbol, on the display, was quite graphic. The information was stored on massive computers back at base, correlated and loaded into a projector unit in the big screen theatre for viewing and analysis. The combatants would assemble for a post-sortie debrief where every fight could be rerun and every tactic, manoeuvre, and shot scrutinised and assessed for effectiveness. From that, lessons could be learned and incorporated into future sorties.

In the baking hot of August 1982, Sardinia was a sweltering 35+ degrees Celsius; that was mega hot for flying. This was not exactly the weather for violent exercise, although there were exceptions to that rule and this was one of them. Flying fifteen sorties in a fortnight, none longer than forty-five minutes and most about thirty-five, was an extreme use of aviation fuel but this was the ultimate training in non-lethal combat flying that there was. It was tremendous value, giving us an edge that would make all the difference in a real scenario. If it could save just one crew and their aircraft, then that would make it all worthwhile come a war.

During the detachment we began with Phantom *v.* Phantom, one *v.* one; then two *v.* one, followed by two *v.* two. Dissimilar air combat (DACT) came next against a variety of opponents, including the USAF F-5 Aggressors and the USAF F-15s. The two *v.* two, and the one *v.* one *v.* one scenarios were particularly challenging. The former required a good deal of coordination while the latter pitted each singleton against the other two players—every man for himself. The final monster scenarios of two *v.* two *v.* two were without a doubt the pinnacle, and with the F-5s and F-15s in the melee, it was as complicated as a 'Mad Woman's Knitting', as we used to say. It was just a cloud of fighters and egos competing for the honour of winning. In fact, just surviving was a bonus. After two weeks of intense air combat in this state-of-the-art, high-tech combat facility, drinking tonic water by day and cheap red plonk at night, I felt guilty about taking my pay home at the end of that month, meagre as it was. This was probably the best work-up for the Cold War that I could possibly imagine for its time. Even that high-tech stuff has been superseded by the podded RAIDS system (Rangeless Airborne Instrumented Distribution System), which is even more sophisticated using modern data link technology, giving greater geographical flexibility.

Live weapons training of air-to-air firing of the SUU-23 cannon was undertaken at RAF Akrotiri on the Mediterranean island of Cyprus. To fire the gun you needed a number of things to come together. Firstly, extensive airspace that is devoid of all other extraneous aircraft. Secondly, no one can be floating about on the sea below and thirdly, good weather. To combine all three in the UK is pretty difficult to achieve at almost any time of the year, which is why every fighter squadron detached to Cyprus for their annual armament practice camp (APC). My first one came in November 1982 when 43 Squadron flew out, heading for IAF Brindisi in Italy on the first leg. We had set off at some unearthly hour of the morning so as to arrive in Cyprus in daylight and in time for a cold Carlsberg; off we trudged across France before the croissants were even cooked and into Italy where we came within range of the Italian air traffic controllers. Now I do not have a particularly good opinion of air traffic services anywhere south of the 46th parallel, with one or two notable exceptions, and sure enough, true to form, five aircraft were all too much for Italian Air Traffic Control to handle and our formation was soon split to the five winds on different frequencies and vectored for different approaches. Eventually, we landed safely (a loose term used here), refuelled, and set off on the second leg. It was a relief at the end of a long day to speak to the controllers at RAF Akrotiri and be professionally organised into safe landings. The next few weeks were a hive of activity with an abundance of lectures interrupted by flying plus a chance to enjoy the late Mediterranean sun. There was a lot to learn about air-to-air such as muzzle velocity, time of flight, gravity drop, harmonisation, dispersion, angle off, and how the gunsight computer (the LCOSS) worked. We learned how it was used and by what method it was directed, which in the case of the Phantom was by the radar. To have an accurate range to the target was indeed a luxury not afforded to me by the Hunter system.

After a dual cine sortie with the QWIP came four practice cine trips with my navigator and then I was ready to call the big moment: live shooting. 'In Hot.' 'Clear Hot,' replied the tug pilot. The Phantom gun was a 20-mm M61A1 Vulcan cannon—in other words, a six-barrel, rotary Gatling gun capable of firing 6,000 rounds in a minute, not that we carried that much ammunition. In fact, the maximum load was 1,200 rounds, which does not take long to expend, so the first rule was 'short bursts' only. In fact, the shorter the better; the intention was to fire about ten rounds on each pass. Nothing prepared you for the first run: checks done, late arm made, track the target, in range, pipper on, squeeze the trigger, and what was that barrage of noise going off underneath me? That dear boy was the sound the gun made as the hydraulics spun the six-gun barrels, each one violently expelling its plug of lead towards the target. You could even see the black swarm of deadly bullets heading off towards the flag. It was such a shame that they all missed—all 100 of them.

I was ready for the next pass. I was cool, I knew what to expect but, nevertheless, this was not a sound that I was ever going to forget. It was a combination of a violent howl and an explosive roar and you had to be in among it to appreciate its full ferocity and lethality. It sent shivers up my spine. The next pass was about fifty rounds with about three hits, but at least I was slowly getting better and better. Over the next ten trips, all went well and I was declared as 'NATO ACE Qualified', which did not stand for ace in the traditional sense but rather Allied Command Europe. These were great detachments—live firing in the ranges off the Episkopi coast during the day and live gatherings in the Akrotiri mess bar in the evening, with Kokinelli, kebabs, and/or a meze thrown in at the weekends. What more could you ask for?

Missile practice camps (MPCs) were held at the less glamorous tropical resort of RAF Valley on Anglesey in North Wales. It was a bitterly cold winter of 1983 and my navigator, Haz, and I were detailed to fire a BAe Systems Skyflash missile. Sorties were mounted from the Strike Command Air-to-Air Missile Establishment (STCAAME) situated on the airfield at Valley. Haz was one of the most laid-back and laconic individuals that I ever came across in the service. As an example, when sitting on QRA, unless the hooter sounded, he would not move from his armchair except to pee, smoke, or sleep. Often, we thought that he might have 'fallen off his perch' for all the movement he made but even he woke up and paid attention for our missile firing. I had been within a couple of seconds of firing an AIM-9L Sidewinder once but that had been called off, so this was my first time too. Not only that but it was a particularly tricky set up as we were using the radar in a fairly non-standard way. All eyes would be upon us, along with data downloads, a cine-chase aircraft, radar films, and goodness knows what else to examine the information in minute detail. Every second of this event in firing this highly expensive and secret missile would be captured; no pressure then. We flew down to Valley as a small detachment, each one of us having been briefed on our own profile that we were to fly. We had been briefed and re-briefed and we knew exactly what to do yet still we were apprehensive for there was plenty to go wrong. Needless to say that all went well but nothing prepared us for the gigantic 'whoosh' as the rocket motor fired and this 'telegraph pole of deadliness' sprung forth from the loins of the Phantom, disappearing at Mach 3 towards the poor unfortunate target, leaving behind a long trail of smoke and two adrenaline-charged crew members bemused and in awe of what had just occurred. Data later revealed that it had been a totally successful mission so we retired to the bar to celebrate with a beer or two. It would be sometime later in the Falkland Islands when I was not far off firing my second live missile but, providentially, I did not have to, and that is another story.

Not all my operational work-up was adrenaline-charged mayhem, as I was soon dispatched back to RAF Coningsby to complete the instrument rating examiner's (IRE) course. If tanking off a KC-135 was interesting and exciting, the IRE course was at the opposite end of the 'thrilling and stimulating scale'. I confess I was not a volunteer, as usual—but the boss said 'Go', so go I did—back down to Coningsby to 228 OCU from whence I had not long departed. My preparation was just one trip on the squadron in the backseat of a twin-stick FG1 with the then squadron instrument examiner to show me the horrors of how little instrumentation there was that was actually of use in the back seat. At Coningsby, a further nine trips followed in both the front and back seats of the FGR2, culminating in a back-seat ride when I was awarded a 'Master Green' instrument rating. After the final instrument rating examiners test, I reflected on the fact that I had endured sixteen hours staring at primitive instrument dials and had learned to work the radar and the awful inertial navigation attack system. It almost made me wish that I was back tanking from a KC-135. The ground school delved into the minutia of how the gyros on a heading gyro unit worked and how to work out the pressure error of the altimeters at 15,000 feet and Mach 0.9. We were required to deliver lectures to the staff and the other course members, which in my case was the riveting topic of 'RAF *en route* charts'. For those of you who are not familiar with such an august publication, they are made of green paper and have lots of straight lines and numbers on them. End of lecture. Disappointedly, I passed the course and had to return to 43(F) as the new squadron IRE. My gloom was further added to when I was pulled off QRA to do a pilot's instrument rating renewal one Friday afternoon just as the Soviets came around the North Cape. While I renewed Pete Kelly's rating, I missed intercepting four Soviet Bears. I decided that the pilot who replaced me as Q1 would be failing his instrument rating when it was next due.

There would be one last skill to learn on the squadron that was not a discipline at which air defenders were well-practised. The FG1 Phantom had been modified to carry the gun sometime after its introduction into service sixty years ago. In the aftermath of the Falklands conflict the SUU-23 found a new role for us air defenders in the form of air-to-ground gunnery. Although the Phantom's armament we carried was principally designed for air-to-air, it was obvious that the gun could be used for the secondary purpose of strafe if the Argentinians decided to invade the Falkland Islands again. Before deploying down south, we were required to have fired the Phantom's gun at the nearest certified piece of land, which for me meant going back to my old stomping ground at Tain Range. I have already described the Hunter air-to-ground capability but the big difference now was that I had a radar for ranging and did not have to use the TLAR method ('That Looks About Right'), which made opening and closing fire a whole lot easier. Having a six-barrel Gatling gun at the other end of my trigger finger meant that I could blast that little piece of Scottish real estate to kingdom come, which in turn meant that I could use it against any Argentinian gun-boats that dared to try to invade our sovereign islands. February 1983 saw me getting ready to move my little pink body and fifteen items of luggage down to Stanley Airfield via RAF Brize Norton, Oxfordshire. After a refamiliarisation on the FGR2 at RAF Wattisham with my navigator, Haz, I was all set to go. However, once more, the RAF thought that I would be better utilised elsewhere—so a few days before I departed, I was rerouted swiftly to 228 OCU at RAF Coningsby to be a Phantom QFI. I had mixed feelings about that. My wife was delighted, yet I was not too sure but there was nothing that I could do about it. 'To serve is to obey', as someone once said and so, on 10 June, I flew my last sortie on 43 (F) Squadron, leading a four-ship of FG1s on a two *v*. two sortie, said my farewells, and just five days later, on 15 June, I was learning how to teach young 'Biggles' from the back seat of an FGR2.

I was not a happy bunny leaving the front line, but there was a small consolation that I will leave for later.

David Gledhill

Keebs has described perfectly the elements of training that, necessarily, were deferred to the squadrons and I explained my own work-up in detail in *Phantom in Focus: A Navigator's Eye on Britain's Cold War Warrior*. A work-up at Wattisham where I served on my first squadron—naturally, the RAF's finest fighter unit (there may be a theme here)—was much the same as that at Coningsby or Leuchars. I will not reiterate other than to pick up on some elements from a back-seater's perspective. There were many skills over which the navigator had little influence; display flying and air-to-air gunnery come to mind. Learning the intricacies of the electronic protection measures of the AN/AWG 11/12 radar, however, was undoubtedly a navigator art. Highly classified during the Cold War, the anti-jamming functions of the radar were complex but effective and would have meant a crew could still launch a Sparrow or Skyflash missile in all but the densest electronic battlefield. Whether that would be possible fell to the back-seater, his manual dexterity, and how much of his operational work-up he absorbed.

Electronic warfare was an intrinsic element of Soviet military doctrine and every fighting formation had an EW troop embedded within it. If war had broken out along the inner German border, Phantom crews from RAF Wildenrath would have been at the forefront of the electronic battle and would have needed the skills to fight the electronic war. Most Soviet aircraft right down to the fighter-bombers, which would spearhead an attack, were equipped with self-defence jamming pods, which could jam the Phantom radar. More complex electronic support aircraft could disrupt communications channels and jam air defence ground radars. Specialist electronic combat aircraft—such as the Tu-16 Badger, the Su-24 Fencer, and the Mil-17 Hip helicopter—would operate in formation with the attackers but could also stand-off, providing cover jamming or laying chaff corridors.

The navigator had a range of protection measures built into the radar which he manipulated using the radar control panel. Although the topic was introduced on the OCU, the bulk of the training was left to the weapons instructors on the squadrons as the training had to be conducted against a specially modified jamming aircraft known as the Canberra T17 flown by 360 Squadron. These skills had to be learned quickly, and certainly before becoming combat ready, as any operational sortie might pit a crew against a jammer from the outset.

Electronic jamming came in many forms of which 'noise jamming' was the simplest. Using Keebs' 'ping pong' theory, when the radar signal was detected by the electronic warfare officer (EWO) in the Canberra, it was analysed and modified before being 'ponged'. When it arrived back at the scanner in the nose of the Phantom, it was processed by the radar receiver but the electronic noise that had been applied prevented the signal being processed correctly and a 'spoke' appeared on the radar display. Even relatively low-power jammers could obliterate a target return if the electronic trickery was correctly applied, rendering the display unusable. The fact was that this denied the Phantom navigator a key parameter that he needed to conduct an intercept, namely target range.

The basic attack profile in jamming conditions was known as a 'search stern'— in other words, a displaced, stern hemisphere attack operating the radar in search mode, or unlocked. By 'lagging' the jamming spoke around the final turn, the navigator engineered an intercept on the Canberra, albeit lacking the finesse of a full procedure. The first task was to identify the target's height by climbing to co-altitude. Already, the squeamish will realise that this was not a fun profile, particularly in the dark, as common sense tells you not to fly at the same height as another aircraft coming directly towards you. Once this vital information had been determined, the navigator positioned the Phantom a set distance above or below the target. Using simple trigonometry, he could, continually, calculate the range using the 'One In Sixty Rule' and by refining the spoke on the radar using the navigator's hand controller and controls on the radar control panel, he could eventually engineer an intercept to position the Phantom some 2 miles behind, an ideal position to engage a jammer with a Sidewinder missile at medium level.

Pulse radars could be seduced using techniques designed to prevent the radar locking on, known as range gate stealing. Even more confusing were random false targets that could be transmitted by the jammer appearing as ghost formations on the radar.

The main operating mode of the AN/AWG 12 was pulse Doppler (PD); this mode was inherently more resistant to jamming due to its high power and, just as importantly, to chaff because of the fact that it used velocity principles. Even so, it could still be jammed and the immense power of the F-15 radar caused mutual interference almost as effective as a Soviet jammer. PD used a velocity gate to lock on to a target once it had established the target speed. If it could not lock, the semi-active guidance signal that the Sparrow and Skyflash needed to track to the target could not be directed effectively. Velocity gate pull off (VGPO) allowed the opposing EWO to seduce the gate and either break lock or send deceptive responses designed to confuse. Each countermeasure was intended to make the navigator's job more difficult.

The navigator could select a range of protection measures using the radar control panel giving automatic or manual modes, which could override the jamming. One mode known as 'Man Track 1' was relatively simple. After squeezing the lock trigger, the radar began to track a hypothetical target from the point in space nominated by the navigator, using an estimated target speed set by the manual velocity knob. A synthetic target ran down the scope at the nominated speed and, by locking the radar to the jamming strobe, a marker gave an indication of potential range, allowing a semi-active missile to be released.

Alternative electronic counter-countermeasures were available and also selected via the radar control panel. Unfathomable abbreviations such as 'RSOJ', 'J', 'Aux J', 'Man Track 1', and 'Man Track 2' described each. Some were automatic but most required skilful radar set handling from the navigator and the procedures had to be learned and practised, first in the simulator and then in the air. Many were used so infrequently that it was doubtful if much success would have been achieved during the opening exchanges of a conflict. Somehow, the mental intricacies of the electronic battle were never quite as much fun as the sport of air combat.

Both Sparrow and Skyflash missiles were able to 'home on jam' because unsophisticated jamming acted as a beacon, improving the probability of achieving a kill. By employing the manual modes to put the Phantom in the correct piece of sky, the navigator could rely on the radar missiles to tackle the terminal phase of the intercept.

Although initially not equipped to counter infrared decoys known as flares, the Sidewinder was adapted in service to recognise the signature of a decoy and to reject it, homing instead on the original tracking point, which was either the hot jet pipe or the heated aerodynamic surfaces. Even without this protection, ill-timed flares or poorly dispensed flares might deploy in a line giving a ladder effect. By firing up the line of flares, the last flare was always the target. This also normally applied to false targets generated by more sophisticated electronic jammers where the target was normally at the front of the line of targets.

Fighting the electronic battle was the final stage of a new Phantom navigator's training and, once finished, operational status followed quickly.

Tanking was undoubtedly a pilot skill and Keebs has given a fascinating insight earlier; however, from the back seat, we were able to watch and compare notes given that we would fly with every pilot on the squadron and could even provide assistance to the receptive. The key to good technique came from two fundamentals. The first was smooth formation flying and the second was an awareness of the refuelling hose and basket. A good approach stemmed from a good waiting position, which was about 6 feet behind the basket and slightly low. At that point, a pilot would take his formation references on the huge airframe above and fly in close formation. As he closed, he would manoeuvre in relation to the tanker not the basket, resulting, hopefully, in a smooth connection. The natural line of the hose in the airflow dictated all. The approach was along the line of the trailing hose and was achieved by tracking the E2B standby compass up the line of the hose. The navigator would patter away using a commentary similar to the old game show *The Golden Shot*, with commands to go up a foot, right a foot, and so on. Aiming for the two o'clock position on the rim of the basket, it would adjust its position in the airflow as the Phantom approached, rising gently into contact as the jet closed with a couple of knots overtake. Listening to the commentary, the pilot could adjust his approach to make precise contact. The probe slotted into a mechanical receptacle and tiny jaws closed around the probe tip, making a solid connection that had to be physically broken through rearwards pressure. Once in contact, the Phantom could move in or out, providing the pilot followed the line of the hose, monitoring the position using coloured bands on the hose. Too far away or too close and the fuel flow stopped. An amount of leeway was acceptable providing the receiver stayed in contact. Too far left or right or up or down would place undue pressure on the probe tip. Only extreme errors would be dangerous but if the pilot disconnected with an unnatural kink in the hose, there was a strong risk that the probe would be snapped off. An out of line disconnect resulted in the hose whipping back to its natural position in the airflow and woe betide a Phantom that got in its way. For that reason, being low and right was bad because with the probe on the right, the basket would whip high and left and bang on the canopy. That was an experience to be avoided.

There were three main types of techniques that I experienced. The first was the 'stalk the basket from below' merchant who seemed to have an inherent mistrust of the tanker above. The stalker would sit low in the waiting position and rapidly rise to the point of contact often quite late in the manoeuvre. This was by far the hardest to predict from the back as the basket would naturally rise at the final approach, meaning that the two adjacent worlds had to come into a miraculous alignment at the final push. The second was the 'jostle and lunge' merchant; these seemed to be the ex-Lightning pilots used to taking a sneak peek just prior to contact. After a relatively normal approach, there would be a rapid blur within inches of the basket and a seemingly ill-fated approach would end in a frantic coupling. Again, these were rare. The final type was the most successful and by far the most common. A good wait position sitting slightly high on the natural trail line would quickly trap the basket in the airflow around the nose once we started to close and ensure it behaved more respectably at the latter stages. As the probe arrived in the vicinity of the basket, a natural rise of a few inches lifted the basket towards the tip and it would slot neatly down the centre into the mechanical jaws. The technique was basically simple but departures from the norm were frequent and varied, particularly in more turbulent air. Some days, it was simply impossible to know for certain that the basket would behave and success was never guaranteed.

The first dual rides were sometimes flown with an experienced rear-seat qualified pilot in the back, although I found this odd as they were ill-equipped for the unfamiliar role and the different perspective. Far more efficient was for the checking pilot to be alongside in another Phantom and a sage (and wary) navigator in the 'boot'. Once the skills were learned, it was like riding a bike and even after lengthy absences, crews slotted back into the routines easily and quickly. Many needed help from the back but, equally, some pilots could tank without assistance.

Keebs described the thrill of air-to-air gunnery but for my part, the activity was routine and repetitive. As we arrived in the area selected by the tug pilot for firing, he would set up on a tow and I would position the Phantom using the radar to arrive at a start point. On my call of 'commence', the Canberra would enter a turn and the Phantom pilot would take over visually and begin to track the banner with the gunsight. At that point, a parrot could have fulfilled the role. As the target tracked closer in range and passed range markers etched on to the scope in grease pencil, I began a commentary: 'Release, ready, fire, break,' all delivered in a predictable cadence. If the release point, when 'Biggles' uncaged the LCOSS, was accurate, the rest fell into line, assuming he could track the target like a God. The breakout manoeuvre was swift, violent, and sick-making, particularly after ten brandy sours in the mess bar the night before. Suffice to say, it was not the most mentally taxing role and had little operational relevance as the pattern was purely academic as it was flown at operationally unrepresentative speeds.

As Keebs has already suggested, the training led, inevitably, to one event and that was presentation of the 'Op Badge'. Worn on the right arm by fighter crews, the squadron crest denoted operational status and was only worn by combat ready crews. Of course, the formal recognition was an entry in my flying logbook stating simply '24 Feb 77, Phantom FGR2, Navigator, Operational Air Defence'. It had taken three years and five months from walking through the gates at RAF Henlow to reaching my goal but success was sweet.

The event was held at happy hour in the mess bar and was a raucous affair involving the downing of the 'Op Pot'. In the case of 56 Squadron, it was a 2-pint tankard presented by a former squadron member and brought out on this special occasion. It was not necessarily a tankard as 92 Squadron preferred a 'Yard of Ale' but it was always big and it was (nearly) always filled with foaming ale. Like Keebs, one teetotal pilot earned my dying admiration as he drank his pot filled with milk. Nowadays, such rituals are frowned upon but it was a rite of passage.

Operational work-up in the UK was markedly different from the same process in RAF Germany where the role was to provide air defence coverage, overland at low level. Originally, with a few exceptions, only experienced air defenders were posted to Germany because of the rigours of the role. The work-up was radically different and arriving with over 1,000 Phantom hours under my belt, I was still one of the less experienced members of the squadron. After three high and medium level intercept sorties, more to understand the challenges of operating with the NATO command and control centres, it was down to low level for a familiarisation. My baptism was swift because in the first month I flew on the major NATO exercise Coldfire, was introduced to operating over the North German Plain at low level and began a short air combat phase against other squadron crews. This was to prepare for one of the first detachments of the F-15As from Bitburg Air Base, which followed the next month. Very quickly, my hours built with a mix of supersonic intercepts flown over Germany at a high level and, when the weather allowed, low-level intercepts in the low-flying areas. The focus on medium level work was unusual but there was a logic in play. One of the mandatory requirements before being able to hold QRA, known as Battle Flight in RAF Germany, was to be 'phase 3 qualified'. A core skill was the visual identification profile, which allowed us to close in behind a target at any height over Germany. The 'phase 3' tag was due to the fact that the target was flying without lights and, therefore, invisible until the final stages of the profile.

Screaming along at 400 knots behind a darkened Phantom at 1,500 feet above the North German Plain is not an experience for the faint-hearted.

With the 'phase 3 tick in the box', I was very soon sitting Battle Flight waiting, patiently, for the 'Red' hordes to cross the inner German border (IGB). The reality was that most 'Alpha' scrambles, the term used for a live scramble, were to intercept stray light aircraft that had flown too close to the IGB. Very few Soviet aircraft strayed westwards, nor did we feel the need to drift into East German airspace. One of the early lessons was to understand, intimately, the airspace structures and to avoid the air defence interception zone (ADIZ) religiously. One of the most important terms to understand was 'Brass Monkey', which meant that an unauthorised aircraft had entered the ADIZ. On hearing the call transmitted on 'Guard', anyone within 100 miles of the ADIZ would turn west and ensure that they did not become a statistic of the Cold War and penetrate the IGB. Only air defence aircraft under positive radar control entered the ADIZ.

Declared limited combat ready, I was soon taking part in station exercises, part of the inevitable work-up towards the NATO TACEVAL (tactical evaluation), which drove everything. My early months included a mix of flying and I was spare firer for a practice missile firing at Valley plus a raft of affiliation sorties against Buccaneers, Harriers, Jaguars, and the occasional ECM Canberra.

By far, the majority of sorties were flown at an extremely low level, placing a huge strain on the pilot due to the proximity of the ground. If you flew at 500 feet, you were probably too high to survive. In the back, the radar was less effective at low level, suffering from electronic noise, which affected the quality of the detection, which was already reduced due to the short radar horizon. The academic techniques that had been taught on the OCU simply did not work at low level and a whole new method of doing intercepts was spawned. At the first sniff of a lock, Buccaneers and Jaguars would evade aggressively and probably not be seen again so a new technique was needed. Staying in pulse Doppler search mode, crews became adept at estimating range without ever locking up. The good news is the scanner stayed pretty much level as that was where the targets would be. It was a different world to UK air defence.

My first Battle Flight scramble came just three months into my tour and we were launched into the ADIZ. I recounted the story in *Phantom in the Cold War* but, suffice to say, we very nearly became a statistic of the Cold War game of 'cat and mouse' when the Soviet forces tried to lure us across the IGB. Life in Germany would not be straightforward and chivalry was certainly dead.

The 'Op Check' in Germany was extremely demanding and, whether pilot or navigator, you were expected to lead a four-ship of Phantoms to a low-level radar combat air patrol and to attack an incoming formation. It was alien to be coordinating four aircraft on CAP from the back cockpit as the basic fighting formation in the UK was a pair. Hitherto, I had concentrated on my own entry into the fight but now had to consider every aircraft in the vicinity. It was, however, a vital skill if low-level operations were to be effective. Our limited forces had to be massed and outnumbering the enemy who may be reluctant to fight back was fundamental. The new skills stood me in good stead once the improved Tornado weapon system entered service.

I was declared operational and, immediately, given a brand new first tour pilot to take through convex. It was a baptism of fire for both of us as I now had to spend much time worrying about what was going on in the other cockpit as well as my own. The journey was over and I had been declared operational in both the UK and Germany but the real journey was only starting. Next would come supervisory roles such as authoriser, air combat leader, and deputy flight commander. Specialist roles such as the squadron NBC officer and electronic warfare officer would also follow. Eventually, I would command a flight on the OCU and become the deputy commander of the largest Tornado F3 unit in the RAF, responsible for training all the crews beginning their own journeys to operational status. My own unit as OC 1435 Flight in the Falklands would be the pinnacle. The real journey had just begun.

A 43 Squadron Phantom FG1 flying clean wing with a SUU-23 gun.

A Bear Delta. (*UK MOD Crown Copyright [1980]; courtesy David Shaw*)

A Bear Foxtrot opens the bomb bay prior to deploying a sonobuoy. (*UK MOD Crown Copyright [1982]; courtesy David Shaw*)

A sonobuoy deployed from a Bear Foxtrot. (*UK MOD Crown Copyright [1982]; courtesy David Shaw*)

A Badger. (*UK MOD Crown Copyright [1982]; courtesy David Shaw*)

A Bison Bravo captured by Philip Keeble on a QRA sortie. (*UK MOD Crown Copyright [1982]*)

David Gledhill poses for his arrival photograph on 56 (F) Squadron with the squadron weapons instructor, Mike Bruce. (*UK MOD Crown Copyright [1976]*)

A photograph of a 56 Squadron Phantom, XV475, signed by original members of the squadron. (*UK MOD Crown Copyright [1977]*)

A Canberra T Mark 17 captured by David Gledhill during a practice Southern QRA sortie in 1977. (*UK MOD Crown Copyright [1977]*)

A Soviet Illyushin Il-38 May taken by David Gledhill off the coast of Cyprus. The May was *en route* from its base on the Black Sea to monitor the American 6th Fleet off Lebanon.

Philip Keeble's 1,000 hours Phantom certificate.

David Gledhill's 1,000 hours Phantom certificate.

Philip Keeble's flying helmet.

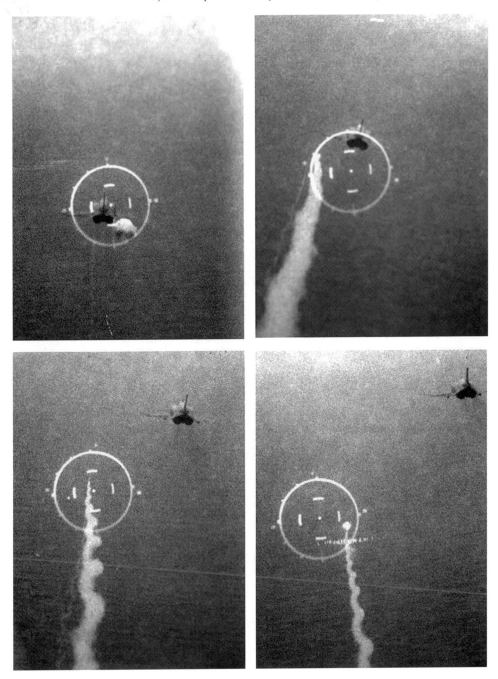

A Sidewinder missile is fired from a Phantom during a missile practice camp at RAF Valley. (*UK MOD Crown Copyright; courtesy Kevin McGee*)

David Gledhill and his pilot, Sqn Ldr John Davies, in front of a 56 Squadron Phantom. David is wearing the US-style torso harness with which the original Martin Baker ejection seat was fitted.

12

Life as an Instructor

Philip Keeble

No. 228 OCU/64 (Reserve) Squadron, RAF Coningsby, Lincolnshire, June 1983

> *'Some are born great, some achieve greatness, and some have greatness thrust upon them'.*

William Shakespeare

Obviously, the Bard of Avon had never heard of the RAF postings desk, or he might have added, 'and some are dragged into greatness, kicking, and screaming'.

Here, I was back in the QFI world, a flying instructor once again. Responsibility rather than greatness had been thrust upon me and I did not want it. I would much rather have been in the vanguard, flying operationally, rather than being in the rearguard teaching others; there was no point bitching about it. It had not worked before and it would not work now, so I had better get on and make the most of it, I guess. It seemed to me that the tours that I most enjoyed were cut short for me to go off and do something that I did not enjoy as much, and yet strangely those tours surprisingly lasted full term and longer. Some say that the MOD had perfected the 'fun detector', a fiendish device that searched everyone's fun levels and, if they reached a certain peak, they would arrange a posting to somewhere that would dampen down that enjoyment. True or not, it was certainly my experience.

Instructional tours were generally three years long; however, subject to change. I was not to know this at the time but I was about to serve for many years at

RAF Coningsby with nearly four years on 228 OCU, during which time I would amass 1,324 hours on the Phantom, followed by eighteen months on the Tornado simulator before moving on to the Tornado F2/F3 flight line as a QFI and picking up 1,098 flying hours on the Tornado. Once I had finished my RAF service, I became a Civil Service Tornado simulator instructor and spent two more years at Coningsby before moving on elsewhere. To be honest, life was not as bad as all that, as besides being a training unit for the conversion of crews on to the Phantom, 228 OCU also had a 'Reserve' role as 64(R) Shadow Squadron within Strike Command and NATO. These hidden extra resources would give the RAF additional aircraft and crews to call upon if the war came, then 228 OCU would take its place on the front line as 64(F) Squadron along with all the rest of the operational squadrons. However, while waiting for that fateful day, we would continue to exercise and practise almost as much as a normal squadron, while still training new crews for the remainder. Sometimes, the two roles clashed but, generally, it seemed to work out extremely well. We sent a steady stream of pilots and navigators off to the squadrons while keeping ourselves current and conversant with UK/NATO operations and procedures. Every instructor on the unit was an ex-front-line operational crew member and knew their stuff. In fact, 64(R) was by far the most experienced outfit in the Air Defence force.

Before I was able to climb into the cockpit on my new outfit, there was the little matter of arrival interviews, the first of which was with the station commander. I have had many interviews with senior officers over the years and none of them, to my recollection, has had a positive outcome but my arrival interview at RAF Coningsby might have turned out differently but for the fact that I failed to spot an opportunity when it was offered, one that I have lived to regret ever since. The Staish's words came as a surprise. 'I'd like you to join the Battle of Britain Memorial Flight, Flight Lieutenant Keeble,' he said. Wow, what trust. He obviously had not read my personal file. The Battle of Britain Flight (BBMF) was a lodger unit at RAF Coningsby, its Spitfires, Hurricanes, and Lancaster flown by pilots from the Phantom OCU. Now you would think that I would have bitten his hand off to be given this once in a lifetime golden opportunity to fly a Second World War fighter—you would think—but I came up with some lame excuse, saying that I had three small children who needed their father to be around, pathetic idiot that I am. Do my kids appreciate what I did for them that day? What do you think? 'Whatever', seems to sum it up. A couple of years later, when the kids were older and more independent, I realised that as a DTS (Dad's taxi service), I might actually be able to join BBMF and fly the Spitfire. 'Sorry, Phil, there are no vacancies for the foreseeable future,' was the response.

Please, if you ever meet me, I advise you not to mention this episode in my presence or even, 'Why did the Red Arrows never take you, Phil?' unless you have bought me a few beers first. Some nights, I actually manage to sleep and awake without *Tears on my Pillow*, which happens to be the title of my next book, soon to be followed by *Senior Officers and How to Evade Them*; these literary efforts are well worth pre-ordering.

Phantoms and Tornado F3s of Nos 64 and 65 Squadrons. (*UK MOD Crown Copyright [1986]*)

The instructor crews of 228 OCU on a training detachment to Cyprus in the mid-1980s. (*UK MOD Crown Copyright*)

My second interview was with my new boss of the OCU and was, mostly, the usual welcome pep talk but he did catch my attention with some unexpected news as he explained that, 'if I thought that I had got out of going to the Falklands by coming to Coningsby, that I should think again'. At least, that experience was delayed a little and until the day arrived, I had a new job to learn. First came the backseat work-up phase of four trips, then an acceptance ride with the CFS agent. The CFS agent was a very experienced Phantom flying instructor who operated under licence of the Central Flying School of the RAF, but was also one of the OCU QFIs. As an 'A1' instructor, he was a veritable god in the community and the font of all knowledge on the aircraft. With his blessing, I received clearance to instruct from 'the pit'. Next came the formation check ride and the backseat night acceptance, which as I have mentioned before, is not for the faint-hearted; from the back seat, where little was visible of the real world, it was an absolute nightmare.

The air defence workup followed next, with my first trip flown with an experienced navigator called Dave Gledhill. I wonder what happened to him? He checked me out on the latest night visual identification procedures (VIDs) using night vision goggles (NVGs), which had fairly recently been added to our air defence capabilities. Although fairly basic by modern standards, they were a quantum jump forward in operating in the dark and made night-time identification of a target a whole lot easier. Once fitted to the helmet, you could see the anti-collision lights of airliners flashing in the dark from dozens of miles away. If I was to say over 40 miles, I do not think that I would be exaggerating by much, if at all. I had had limited experience of them previously but they had certainly made QRA at Leuchars a whole lot easier. Speaking of which, within a month of arriving at the OCU, I was back up at Leuchars holding QRA in a Phantom FG1 for my old squadron so as to relieve the local crews to attend the summer ball. Guess who my navigator was for that? Yep, good old DG. Yet once more our fate was destined to be intertwined and now, here, we are writing a book in collaboration; Kismet or Karma? I do not know which. On my return to Coningsby, I continued my staff work-up and after night visual identifications came more intercept work. I flew the next work-up sortie with the station commander, who at that time was a navigator, before flying an advanced radar sortie with Dave on 'SWU AD20', an advanced radar profile but with the emphasis on teaching a new student how to cope in the air. Two more sorties followed before it was into another two *v.* two dissimilar air combat against the Lightnings from Binbrook. A three-day Exercise Priory intervened before it was my turn to teach young pilots and navigators all that I knew about being a member of a combat crew. Teaching in a Phantom was pretty much like teaching in any other aircraft, in other words—never, ever trust a student—and by remembering that golden rule you might just stay alive. Students are pesky little critters who appear to be capable of flying safely at all times until they prove that they cannot. Be ready for that occasion with your hand about 3 cm away from the control column is my advice, otherwise it can be a salutary lesson in complacency.

Switching from front to back seat was quite refreshing, and, whisper it quietly, I quite liked working the radar and pretending to be a 'fightergator'. Navigation for me was simply using the Tacan, which was all we really had in an FG1. The inertial navigation system (INAS) defeated me completely and it normally said that either I was approaching Moscow or maybe even Cairo. I do not believe that, Oslo or Lisbon? Maybe. Even I could not get that lost, for that you need a real professional, otherwise known as a member of the 'Union of the Half-Wing Master Race' (the UHWMR) and not a nice union to fall foul of.

It was from here that the structure for the next thirteen years of my life began. I would be in at first light for the early met brief but take note that it was just QFIs and their pilot students. A couple of convex sorties teaching them to fly followed before saying 'good morning' to the navigators as they pitched up around mid-morning. Next would come an intercept sortie with me and a navigator student in one aircraft and a pilot student and staff navigator in the other for radar intercept training. Then I would say goodbye to the navigators as they set off home to catch the children's TV program, *The Magic Roundabout*. After a quick cup of tea for us QFIs, it was a night trip and thus filling up what was about a forty-five–sixty-hour working week. The pressure was relentless; day in day out, year in year out, and I do not embellish by much. What sort of job is that for a man to be doing, flying the Phantom day and night when he could be in a nice, cosy, office job somewhere? A jolly good one, I would say. There were times when you could be landing from a combat sortie before the manager of Woolworths in Horncastle had even opened up the doors to let the navigators in to buy their Pick and Mix sweeties.

(Dave feels compelled to add a minor recollection here in that while Keebs was racking up the flying hours and occupying the navigator's seats, Dave amassed a paltry eight–fifteen hours in an average month and what had seemed a relentless march towards 2,000 hours on the Phantom stalled instantly. Dave became adept at putting together the 'QFI's benefit flying programme' and filling out spare moments acting as duty authoriser and duty officer flying in the tower. Not wishing to allow facts to embellish a pilot's recollection, I agree that the pressure was, indeed, relentless, and I digress.)

Looking through my logbooks, I do see rather a lot of 'Convex 14' sorties (changed from Convex 13) which was the night formation ride. I bet that if you looked in the logbook of a mere PI or a QWI as opposed to a QFI, there would be a large discrepancy in the figures, namely about fifty to zero. The other back seat qualified pilots were also supposed to teach this sortie, but I can safely say that I cannot remember a single PI or QWI ever volunteering, or even being around when the slots became available. I stand ready to be corrected.

The silver lining among all this endeavour and industry was the operational flying, which we conducted as 64(R) Squadron; as we spent a lot of our time instructing relatively academic profiles, we were only declared as 'Lim Op.' (LCR) to NATO. Equally, new crews lacked the experience of the squadron and they too were declared 'Lim Op.', once they passed their work-up. In our case, we had completed squadron tours but merely lacked current practice given that instructional flying was somewhat a priority. To remain LCR, we still undertook annual tactical checks and staff continuation training, as and when the programme allowed, but we could not hone our skills 24/7 as much as we had done on the squadrons as we had another purpose—to train the crews of the future. It was a compromise but we tried to fit both in as best we could. Regular exercises, such as tanking and affiliation, were arranged with a variety of other units and I refuelled from both the Hercules and the newly re-roled Vulcans of 50 Squadron. We would operate against almost anything that had wings, including the Hercules and the Nimrod, but more especially against the low and fast targets, such as the Harriers and the Jaguars. The South Atlantic conflict was fresh in everyone's consciousness and we, as a reserve squadron, were expected to take our place on the roster down in the Falklands exactly the same as everyone else. No. 64(R) Squadron took part in most of the Strike Command and NATO exercises and were involved in station Minevals, Maxevals, and Taceval exercises just like any other unit. Both aircrew and ground crew slept in hardened shelters with the aircrew shelter being known as the pilot's briefing facility (PBF), flying from the new hardened aircraft shelters (HAS). As an aside, it is not true that navigators were not allowed in the PBF, or that they slept outside, despite the pilot's requests.

One of the less attractive training exercises was using the aircrew respirator Mark 5 (AR5), which was the nuclear biological and chemical (NBC) protection equipment designed to keep us alive during a chemical weapons exchange. A certain Flight Lieutenant Gledhill was nominated to bring the equipment into service on 64(R) Squadron, much to the reluctance of the staff crews. We used the kit both in the simulator and in the swimming pool, practising our drills, learning how to operate and survive in a hostile environment. Dave describes the equipment in some detail in his book, *Phantom in the Cold War*. These were fiendish bits of paraphernalia designed to protect you wherever and whenever there was an NBC hazard, it seemed to me on exercises that the jeopardy was present most of the time. They were the stuff of claustrophobic nightmares.

There was also the little matter of keeping our hand in at air-to-air gunnery where we deployed on our annual trip to RAF Akrotiri to keep qualified. On top of all that, if we got behind with the student training task, such as when the weather was bad in the UK, we took our little pink bodies and our jets off to Cyprus to fly in the beautiful clear skies; unfortunately, we also had to take our trainees with us as justification, but that seemed a small price to pay for what was a win-win option.

Having been told in no uncertain terms by the boss during my arrival interview that I was earmarked for a deployment, true to his word, I was dispatched along with an instructor navigator to the Falkland Islands, arriving in February 1983 for a four-month spell on 23 (Fighter) Squadron. My deployment to RAF Stanley was a pleasant interlude. Summer in the Falklands was pretty much like summer in Wales, only with a bit more snow. In the Southern Hemisphere, there being no other land mass between the Falklands and the South Pole, there was nothing to break up the weather patterns and, furthermore, there is no warming influence from the Gulf Stream to ameliorate the cold waters swirling up from the south. It can be a bleak place, yet, at the same time, a most enchanting and unspoilt place. The islands are remote, or they were then, and are wild and unblemished, apart from the military presence. The people are warm and friendly and so, for a two-week visit, it is a great place to go on holiday and not too bad if you have got family down there with you. That said, it was very different for us living two to a cabin (telephone box-sized), within a shipping container, in semi-squalid conditions. This was not my idea of fun, yet we were not down there for fun; we were down there to defend the rights of the Falkland islanders to remain part of the United Kingdom and not to be overrun, or overruled, by the Argentinians. There was a job to be done and if it meant killing to maintain the peace of the islands then so be it—note the irony. There was a simple fact of life for the Argentinian military; if you do not want to get shot, then stay away.

The flying was truly superb, probably the best that I had ever experienced. There were few limits and rules—just 'do not cock up and do not get hurt'. It was my kind of place in that I had to do what I had to do to get the job done and if I did so somewhat exuberantly, no one would mind. Sure enough, no one did. We flew affiliation sorties against the Harriers at heights considered to be at an ultra-low level over this beautiful countryside with a sparse population who did not complain because they did not mind and were happy to see us. We flew attacks against Royal Navy ships and Army missile installations at low level and conducted air-to-air refuelling on most sorties. There was the excitement of landing on to a very short runway with five arrestor cables stretched across to ensure that you did not go off the end. It was like landing on an aircraft carrier deck, only without the up and down movements of the boat. All sorties were flown as a pair with both aircraft fully loaded with eight missiles, a gun, and two external fuel tanks. This was the place to be. With QRA every other day and regular live launches, it was a bit like being back at Leuchars holding Northern 'Q', only this time without the Russians. If you needed something to get the job done, there was a terrific 'can do' spirit among the units on the base, even among the other services. Stanley was definitely a tri-service place where I could swap a pair of flying gloves for most things in the Army stores and thus, I ended up with a full set of decent olive-green kit for my days off. The RAF-issued cold/wet weather clothing was rubbish and was just what it said on the tin—cold and wet. Apart from the separation from the family, I loved it. I was flying day and night, locked and loaded on active QRA. It was just what I wanted. I was back on a fighter squadron, this time 23 (Fighter) Squadron, The Red Eagles, with its squadron drink chilli vodka. Why do they do it? It was foul stuff. Four months later, the deployment was over and it was back on the Hercules for the long return slog to Ascension Island and thence onwards home to see what mail and tasks had accumulated while I had been gone. If you want to read more on the subject, may I refer you to Dave's excellent book, *Fighters over the Falklands*, also published by Fonthill Media.

After a month's leave, it was back to the normality of everyday life in the UK. Nothing had changed much, except me; I think that now I was readier for the 'normal' and had got whatever it was out of my system, for a while anyway. We had plenty of detachments to other NATO bases to train with their crews and to collect the local wine to show our appreciation for their local culture. All that just about kept me stabilised. I would spend another four years flying the Phantom with the OCU—four action-packed, busy, rewarding, and happy years before my posting on to the Tornado F3.

David Gledhill

I arrived back on the OCU in 1982 after completing two operational tours, at a time of transition. Up to that time, the unit had been manned by the old guard, a core of instructors who, put politely, were set in their ways. Most had learned their air defence skills during the ground attack days when techniques were more rudimentary and, while they had many years of experience on the Phantom and, in some cases, the Javelin and Sea Vixen, most had little true operational air defence experience. Again, many were exceptional instructors but lacked operational credibility and tended towards the old Hunter mentality of 'if I can do it, why can't you?'

After an enlightening discussion with my poster prior to my return from Germany, it was apparent that the intention was to break up the *status quo* and to reduce the average age of the OCU staff by a significant factor. The 'Coningsby Mafia' (as the clique had been known) was being dismantled.

New instructors underwent a staff work-up on arrival that in my case was little short of useless. The transition to instructor is a subtle but momentous change and, for me, it was a new role despite my squadron convex roles. On an operational squadron, with a few minor exceptions, the emphasis is on one's own performance. Developing personal skills and executing them to the limit of perfection is the ambition, and extensive debriefings help this goal. As an instructor, your own performance has to be a given and the emphasis shifts to what is going on in the other cockpit. In the highly scripted scenarios defined by the OCU syllabus, certain actions would lead to predictable results. If that failed to occur, the reason was normally apparent. It was vital to recognise if your own performance was lacking and to ensure that a student was not criticised or disadvantaged in that event.

When looking at output standards, it was important to recognise that operational flying often put crews at the extremes of the envelope. A weak navigator passed on to the squadron as a training risk added pressure to an overstretched training system. Indeed, a poor navigator could be detrimental to mission effectiveness and add to the workload of a stretched pilot. A weak pilot, however, might lose control of the aircraft and, crucially, risk not only his own life but the life of his back-seater. For that reason, standards were high and if there was any doubt, there was no doubt. The 'chop rate' was brutal at times despite the huge cost to the taxpayer of training a Phantom crew.

There were two major elements of the instructor work-up. The first phase was to refresh the knowledge of the intercept profiles. There was a 'school solution' in executing each profile and this was made clear to the students in the brief that introduced each phase. It was important not to bring squadron tricks and nuances to the OCU. Those could be practised during staff continuation sorties. A '90' attack had to be flown in a precise way and standardisation was vital to ensure students received the same guidance from every instructor. Reverting to OCU methods caused few issues but imagine my dismay when the work-up consisted of merely a few sorties running basic intercepts. I was confident in my abilities as I had amassed 1,500 hours on the Phantom by then. I was, however, inexperienced in the means to pass on my skills. That grounding was sadly lacking and achieved more by photosynthesis than by instruction. Within weeks, I was cleared to instruct but my development as an instructor began through experience.

The air combat leader work-up came some months later after a period of consolidation and was vastly better as, by then, the 'Young Guard' had taken charge of that phase and a shake-up had occurred. The mechanics of basic fighter manoeuvres were rehearsed to allow navigators to recognise and correct inaccurate and ineffective flying and poor tactics in the other cockpit. The intricacies of single circle and two circle fights and when to employ them; also, the concept of 'God's *g*' and its effect in a three-dimensional world were reinforced. Crew coordination was vital and I was not delighted to be allocated the lecture as my first instructional role. It is an abstract concept to pass on but a failure of crew coordination guaranteed a mission failure or, in some cases, worse. The skills of setting up air combat splits and, most importantly, the ability to record events in the air and reconstruct engagements when back on the ground was practised at some length. Air combat was a challenge at the best of times, but when a student pilot was unpredictable in the air, it took every ounce of skill to reinforce a learning objective. Again, I lost track of the number of calls of 'go hard port' followed by the jet leaping off in the direction of 'the other port'. The ensuing rap of my bonedome on the canopy could be painful. Even so, by this stage, I was feeling much more confident in my ability to instruct. There was no finer moment than if my student pilot rolled out in the staff pilot's 'Six' and I called a 'terminate'.

Later on, I would become responsible for the staff work-up programme and I set about establishing a cadre of 'instructors of instructors' who could develop the essential skills needed to teach. The emphasis shifted from 'doing' to 'teaching' with, hopefully, a positive influence on the quality of instructor. It also gave a welcome opportunity to adopt the 'student Bloggs' role and to screw up intercepts on purpose. This was the least challenging role of my instructional career.

The majority of formal instruction was conducted in the AI trainer where the staff navigator could monitor the activity in each cockpit closely on a one-to-one basis. Alone in the cockpit in the air, and lacking the luxury of audio recording, it could be difficult to analyse the students' actions other than from hastily scribbled notes. There was no escape from scrutiny in the shirt-sleeve environment in the trainer and any mistake was readily apparent. The methodology was simple. The first event was to demonstrate the new profile yourself. If you could not execute a perfect—well, passable—intercept, you had no right to be instructing. The remainder of the session was devoted to the student navigator conducting endless repeats of the profile until the instructor was confident that it would be repeated in the air. It was a well-known phenomenon that 50 per cent of one's mental capacity was left behind on the ground. Most students, and to be frank most instructors, carried 'cheat sheets' on the kneeboard, which recorded vital *aide-memoires*, such as the turnkeys. When the memory deserted you in the cockpit, a quick glance would give the essential stimulus. With the navigator sorted and a pass guaranteed, the student pilot was expected to run at least one intercept without assistance, more if time permitted.

This methodology extended into the air with the first intercept conducted as a crew. For subsequent runs, the pilot instructor would expect the student navigator to shoulder more of the workload and to demonstrate sound airmanship. The staff navigator would find the target and perhaps lock up and allow the student pilot to demonstrate his prowess at finessing a 2-mile roll out.

One of the highlights of an instructor's tour was to be given the role of course mentor. This was a pivotal role and required attention to detail of the highest order. At the simplest level, the mentor programmed the course activity. Each phase began with a phase brief in the classroom to establish the fundamentals. The cycle of AI trainer followed by simulator followed by flying had to be followed for each event in sequence. To fail to do so short-changed the student crew. Interspersed were academic lectures on topics as diverse as aircraft recognition, intelligence matters, and air-to-air weapons.

Following the progress of each student was vital to ensure that slow progress was identified early. Some students responded better to different instructional styles. The brash retread might need a 'stick' approach whereas the young, under-confident *ab initio* pilot might need the 'carrot' approach. No matter the ability, failure was a tense time. If a student failed an event, immediate action was needed. If that was extra simulator or AI trainer work, it was much easier as resources were more freely available. I lost track of the number of out-of-hours sessions I ran with my charges to ease them through a sticky patch. Flying was much more difficult. At £10,000 per hour, flexibility was limited. A student was allowed a single failure per phase after which a refly was scheduled. A further failure resulted in the student being placed on review. If he showed promise, a consolidation package was agreed normally with a nominated staff crew to conduct the training. The test was not whether he could pass the trip but rather if could he become operational. Any failure during this stage was instant suspension. While this might seem harsh, the pressure and level of complexity of events would continue to accelerate so failure to grasp the basics might indicate an inability to absorb future training. Some distinguished experts stumbled occasionally yet went on to become outstanding operators and instructors, but the weak link was often readily evident. Recourses to the following course were extremely rare on the OCU, unlike at earlier stages of training, and were only approved, *in extremis*, by Group Headquarters.

Captaincy, to which Keebs has already alluded, was a thorny issue. Unlike some other forces, such as the Nimrod force, which had embraced navigator captains, the RAF Phantom force remained stubbornly reluctant. The Royal Navy had forged a path and senior navigators had been nominated as captain many years earlier. Some traits may have contributed to this reluctance. Firstly, the boss of the Phantom OCU and, subsequently, the Tornado F3 OCU was not only a pilot but the job specification demanded that he be a qualified flying instructor. This set a tone despite the fact that the majority of the syllabus was tactical in nature, rather than academic flying training. Indeed, the conversion element where the QFI was king lasted only four weeks out of a four-month course.

There are two elements to flying a military mission. The first occurs before flight and is known as authorisation. This is a supervisory function and ensures that the sortie is planned in accordance with military regulations and conducted in a safe and professional manner. The authoriser is responsible for ensuring that the crew are qualified and current, that the plan complies with appropriate flying orders and that the aim and objectives of the sortie are relevant. He checks that clearances, say for low flying, have been sought. Finally, he ensures that any relevant warnings are briefed and that the crew is aware of restrictions that might affect the sortie, such as the recovery state and fuel on the ground. The sortie might be self-authorised by the senior member of the crew, either pilot or navigator, or if there is no authoriser within the crew, a duty authoriser is always available on the ground when flying is underway. This ensures that the planning of each sortie is carefully scrutinised.

The first friction point comes when a young pilot with perhaps five hours on the Phantom acts as captain of the aeroplane yet his navigator and authoriser is sitting only 6 feet behind and monitoring his every move as his instructor. The role of authoriser in this case extends into the air and any failure to comply with, or moves to exceed the authorisation, would feature strongly in the debrief and write up and probably lead to suspension from training.

'No stick, no vote' is the oft-quoted mantra, mostly by those unfamiliar with life in a two-seat fast jet. Happily, I was never put to the test but the mantra is, assuredly, untrue. Had I said 'don't do that' and been ignored, retribution would have been swift and decisive. Add to that, I lost track of the number of times I heard a QFI brief a new student about to embark on his first 'solo' that, although he might be the captain of the aircraft, he would be wise to heed sage advice from the back cockpit should it be offered in an emergency situation.

On an operational squadron, invariably, the pilot with 'hands on' was the favoured crewman to act as captain. This was not always the case say, for example, if the sortie was a check ride or an early conversion sortie. While later in the life of the Tornado F3, navigators and weapons instructors became commanders of the OCU, the reluctance to embrace navigator captains remained on the Phantom force.

I was to have a notable event during my time as an instructor. A friend who had undergone navigator training with me at Finningley had since re-mustered from Nimrod navigator to fast jet pilot and was posted to Phantoms. I was lucky enough to fly his first 'solo' on type in his new guise. Such transitions were rare but it was a unique event for former navigator colleagues to fly together in the same aircraft. He went on to fly on a squadron and even to take passengers flying. I hope it is true that he scared a few 'first timers' by wearing his navigator's brevet for the sortie.

Although being an instructor could be frustrating and most, given the chance, would have taken a posting back to a squadron in a heartbeat, seeing students' progress on to front-line squadrons and, eventually, become operational was a truly rewarding experience. With the throughput of trainees, at one time, I probably knew over 75 per cent of front-line Phantom aircrew. I hope I had a small part to play in some of their undoubted successes. Many remain firm friends today.

Phantom FGR2 XT905 of 228 OCU at RAF Coningsby. (*Terry Senior*)

13

Training a Fighter Pilot Today

What of the present and what of the future? Some things change very little and some things change a lot. The basic concepts of flying have not changed much at all and the ground training has evolved from 'chalk and talk' on a blackboard, through whiteboards and marker pens, to overhead projectors, to interactive software packages using state-of-the-art graphics. Computer science makes for a tremendous training aid when it comes to learning and helps to understand complicated subjects far easier. Hardware, on the other hand, does tend to be more revolutionary. New aircraft are much more sophisticated and complicated than their predecessors and, for that reason, the pilots that fly in them must evolve. The Typhoon was a quantum leap forward over the Tornado and the Phantom before that. The Hawk T2 is technologically light years away from the Hawk T1 and its predecessor the Gnat. An operational pilot today needs to be able to manipulate the computers allowing them to do what they do best in flying the aircraft, thus leaving the pilot to get on with the myriad of operational tasks asked of them.

In ten years' time, where will it all be? Will we actually have any manned aircraft at all or will war be conducted by drones flown from a computer console tucked away somewhere nice and safe? Those days are already with us and such air vehicles are flown from control rooms at Nellis Air Force Base and RAF Waddington allowing unmanned aircraft to be placed in harm's way more readily than the manned equivalent. Will manned aircraft continue on forever? Maybe, maybe not.

I have very limited experience of the Typhoon only having seen the simulation at BAe Systems Warton and having sat in the EAP development cockpit. On the other hand, Dave has actually flown in a Typhoon and so I will leave that side of things for him to tell. I will cover in brief what leads up to the Typhoon. First comes elementary flying training in an aircraft, such as the existing Grob G115, also known as the Tutor T1 and now replaced by the Grob 120TP Prefect T1. The Grob is a light, fixed-wing aircraft built in Germany, and currently, it provides the mount for Nos 3 and 6 Flying Training Schools at RAF Cranwell and RAF Barkston Heath, plus the air experience flights and university air squadrons. The Grob is of carbon composite construction, a two-seater trainer with an all up weight of 990 kg (2,183 lb). It carries 143 litres of fuel (about 38 gallons), which, if my maths is right, gives it a range of 610 nautical miles. It has an air-cooled piston engine with a maximum speed of 185 knots, a cruising speed of 125 knots, and a service ceiling of 10,000 feet. There have been some avionic modifications since its arrival into RAF service, adding a Garmin GPS system, digital engine instruments, and an updated instrument panel.

The next stage sees the Beechcraft T-6C Texan II, the next generation of primary trainer, replacing the Short Tucano T1. The Texan is a single-engined turboprop tandem trainer built in the USA. The flying training has been phased from RAF Linton-on-Ouse in Yorkshire, transferring to RAF Valley in Wales along with their Texans. As contracts and plans change, this strategy may also change. This Texan has a lot more going for it with an all up weight of 2,948 kg (6,500 lb). Its Pratt and Whitney engine pushes out 1,100 shaft horsepower, achieving 315 knots, cruising at 280 knots with a range of 900 nautical miles and a service ceiling of just over 30,000 feet. These figures are very similar to that of the Tucano but the avionics are in a whole different class.

Finally comes the fast jet stuff with the BAe Systems Hawk T2 with its Rolls-Royce Adour turbofan, giving 6,500 lb of thrust, a top speed of 555 knots, and a maximum altitude of 42,000 feet. Already in service with No. 4FTS, the Hawk is used to train future pilots for the front line. The list of extras of the Hawk T2 are extensive, among which is a glass cockpit, a head-up display, hands-on-throttle-and-stick (HOTAS) controls, an integrated inertial navigation system supported by the global positioning system (IN/GPS), a synthetic radar, and seven wing stations for weapons and fuel tanks. Stationed at RAF Valley, it will make the airspace over North Wales very busy, although perhaps not as busy as in the '60s. The three new aircraft will do the same job as those I have flown but in a more modern and effective way in preparing pilots to fly the Typhoon and the F-35 Lightning II. The skill sets and the standards to successfully perform these tasks will become more stringent as the bar is raised to match the reduced demand in the number of pilots. It will be exciting days for those whose aim is the stars.

From a navigator's perspective, life has already changed. With the end of navigator training at RAF Cranwell and with the demise of the Tornado GR4, navigators will serve only on a limited number of large aircraft and not in a true navigational role. The term 'weapon system operator' had already been coined and the traditional navigator brevet with its prominent 'N' was replaced by a similar single wing brevet with a Queen's crown. Navigator training stopped in November 2011 but, with the recognition that the role is still important for large aircraft such as Poseidon, it has since resumed, albeit in the guise of the weapon systems operator.

Having been involved in the development of Typhoon in the electronic warfare specialisation, the thrust of the design was to improve the 'man-machine interface' to the point where software replaced manpower. Functions were automated and streamlined such that decisions were taken by integrated systems and presented as fact to the pilot. More processing means less decision making allowing the pilot to concentrate on applying tactical solutions. Why undertake mental gymnastics to decide on an attack profile when a computer can ease the workload? Why analyse which surface-to-air missile is tracking you if a software programme can give the answer? The key is whether this is done correctly and effectively. A well-integrated digital cockpit is perfectly viable for a single person unlike the analogue equivalents during the early days of the Cold War. The mechanics of flying a Typhoon are radically different. The airframe is unstable so without a computer, it cannot fly. With the complex fly-by-wire system, handling is carefree and the pilot is given the best performance based on his or her demands. If the airframe cannot execute the manoeuvre, the computer says no. When it works, it is flawless. When it does not work, the pilot reverts to having to analyse why. Happily, the latter is increasingly rare and one person really can operate a number of integrated systems alone, although data overload is a constant worry.

As I revealed in my book *Operational Test: Honing the Edge*, a key to operational effectiveness is to evaluate each operational function extensively. The system must be able to be flown effectively by a new first tour pilot. If not, it is not fit for purpose and more redesign and further testing is needed until it can. If a pilot may face an air-to-air missile of a specific type on the future battlefield, the system must be tested against that threat and be proved to work. The training to make sure the new pilot can fly the nominated profiles effectively must follow.

Training a future pilot has already changed and will never go back to the type of training Keebs and I saw in the height of the Cold War. The world has moved on.

Looking back at how cockpits developed is a fascinating exercise. From our experiences, starting with homebuilt designs, progressing through the analogue cockpits of the training fleet such as the Jet Provost, the Gnat, the Varsity, and the Dominie that we have described, little changed even with the advent of the Phantom. They were still analogue designs and computers held little sway. The modern digital cockpits of the Hawk T2 and Typhoon are barely recognisable as descendants. Even so, there can be little doubt that their predecessors hold many happy, and unhappy memories for legions of aircrew who rose to the challenge to finally make it to the front line.

A Rollason D62b Condor cockpit.

Opposite page: A Jet Provost T Mark 3 cockpit.

A Jet Provost T Mark 4 cockpit.

A Jet Provost T Mark 5 cockpit. David Gledhill flew this aircraft, XW 302, during training.

Cockpit of a Folland Gnat with modern avionics additions at the Farnborough International Air Show 2014. G-MOUR flies with the Gnat Display Team. (*Paul Heasman*)

The navigator's station in a Varsity T Mark 1.

The navigator's station in a Dominie T Mark 1. The Ecko 190 radar is mounted centrally with the four dials of the Decca navigation system to the right and above. (*Jeff Jefford*)

The front cockpit of the Phantom.

The back cockpit of the Phantom.

Epilogue

Philip Keeble

That, dear readers, is how to train a Cold War Phantom crew from both a pilot's and a navigator's perspective; I hope that it gives you a taste of how it was carried out. It took dedication and hard work to reach the front line on an RAF squadron and once there, the pressure did not let up, it never would. There were a number of occasions in the past when we were brought to a heightened alert status because something was kicking off and there will similar occasions in the future.

For us operational crews such as Dave and myself, it was a 'gripping' time, if that is the right word, as Mikhail Gorbachev said in February 1986: 'Never, perhaps, in the post war decades was the situation in the world as explosive and hence, more difficult and unfavourable, as in the first half of the 1980s'. He should know as he had his finger on the nuclear button. Nothing in the Cold War came as close to an all-out nuclear war than in November 1983 when the Soviets responded dramatically to the NATO Exercise 'Able Archer 83'. The scenario was a simulated nuclear attack from NATO upon the USSR but the hierarchy thought that it was a real attack, heightened by senior political involvement in the West. When the exercise escalated from DEFCON 5 to DEFCON 1, Soviet generals prepared to initiate a pre-emptive strike. Fortunately for the world, that outcome was avoided but it was a close thing. It is an incident well worth reading about and is recounted in Dave's book *Phantom in the Cold War*, which describes the actions of the 'man who saved the world'.

There were close shaves along the way right up to the end of the Cold War in 1991. However, peace is fragile and young men and women will always be required to take their place on the front line, until kingdom come. It is a great job.

It is a demanding job. It is a rewarding job. It is a thrilling job. I am glad that I did it and I know that those who follow will think so too.

'*Per ardua ad astra*' (roughly meaning 'through adversity to the stars') was the motto of the Royal Flying Corps and is still the motto of the RAF, the Royal Australian Air Force, the Royal Canadian Air Force, and the Royal New Zealand Air Force; it was also the motto of the Indian Air Force, the South African Air Force, and other Commonwealth air forces until their independence. As an aviation motto, it dates back to the formation of the RFC in 1912; it possibly has its roots in Virgil's *Aeneid*. The phrase itself and is said by authoritative academics to have no definitive translation; it is thus 'dog Latin', which sounds just perfect for the Royal Air Force.

In an earlier chapter, I quoted from the John Gillespie Magee Jr. poem 'High Flight', and now I would like to indulge myself by quoting a few lines from another one of his poems, this time from his 'Per Ardua':

> *They that have climbed the white mists of the morning;*
> *They that have soared, before the world's awake.*
> *To herald up their foeman to them, scorning*
> *The thin dawn's rest their weary folk might take;*
> *Some that have left other mouths to tell the story*
> *Of high, blue battle, quite young limbs that bled.*
> *How they thundered up the clouds to glory.*
> *Or fallen to an English field stained red ...*

This poem was written as a tribute to those who died in the Battle of Britain but it is also a fitting epitaph and tribute to the many aircrews who have died for their country over the past 100 years and more, the poet captures the essence of operational flying—getting airborne in the morning mist and thundering up into the clouds before the world is awake to face the enemy. So much of it has not changed in those intervening forty years since the Battle of Britain, and so this book gives us great pleasure to continue 'to tell the story of the high blue battle' and is dedicated to all the fallen.

I shall close with a couple of compositions, written anonymously. Much is absolutely true, especially in the first which describes flying over the sea at night and 'last trips'. I do not necessarily agree with the remark made about the 'person in the other seat.'

Essay on Pilots

Pilots are people who drive aeroplanes for other people who can't fly. Passengers are people who say they fly, but really just ride. Fighter pilots are steely-eyed, weapons systems managers who kill bad people and break things. However, they can also be very charming and personable. The average fighter pilot, despite sometimes having a swaggering exterior, is very much capable of such feelings as love, affection, intimacy and caring. (However, these feelings don't necessarily involve anyone else). Both optimists and pessimists contribute to society. The optimist invented the aeroplane; the pessimist, the parachute. Death is just nature's way of telling you to watch your airspeed and height. As a pilot only two bad things can happen to you (and one of them will):

a. One day you will walk out to the aircraft, knowing it is your last flight.

b. One day you will walk out to the aircraft, not knowing it is your last flight.

There are rules and there are laws. The rules are made by men who think that they know how to fly your aeroplane better than you. The laws (of physics) were made by God. You can, and sometimes should, suspend the rules, but you can never suspend the laws.

About rules:

a. The rules are a good place to hide if you don't have a better idea, or the talent to execute it.

b. If you deviate from a rule, it must be a flawless performance.

(e.g., if you fly under a bridge, do not hit the bridge).

Before each flight, make sure that your bladder is empty and your fuel tanks are full. He who demands everything that his aircraft can give him is a pilot but he who demands one iota more is a fool. There are certain aircraft sounds that can only be heard at night and over the sea. Most of them are scary. I've flown in both aircraft seats. Can someone tell me why the other one is always occupied by an idiot?

You have to make up your mind about growing up and becoming a pilot. You can do one or the other, not both.

Anon.

Finally, this is a copy of a letter that I found recently; it is how one boy aged ten years old sees the art of flying. I think that it sums up how a lot of people view being a pilot, including many pilots.

I want to be a pilot when I grow up because it is a fun job and easy to do. That's why there are many pilots flying today. Pilots don't need much school, they just have to learn numbers so they can read instruments. I guess they should be able to read road maps so they won't get lost. Pilots should be brave so they won't be scared if it's foggy and they can't see, or if a wing or a motor falls off they should stay calm so they will know what to do. Pilots have to see through cloud and can't be afraid of thunder or lightning because they are closer to them than we are. The salary the pilots make is another thing I like. They make more money than they can spend. This